# What Can I Do Now?

Business and Finance

# Books in the
# *What Can I Do Now? Series*

Animal Careers
Animation
Art
Business and Finance
Computers
Education
Engineering, Second Edition
Environment, Second Edition
Fashion
Film
Health Care
Journalism, Second Edition
Law
Music
Nursing, Second Edition
Radio and Television, Second Edition
Safety and Security, Second Edition
Science
Sports, Second Edition
Travel and Tourism, Second Edition

# What Can I Do Now?

## Business and Finance

Ferguson Publishing
*An imprint of Infobase Publishing*

**What Can I Do Now? Business and Finance**

Copyright © 2010 by Infobase Publishing

Ferguson
An imprint of Infobase Publishing
132 West 31st Street
New York NY 10001

**Library of Congress Cataloging-in-Publication Data**

What can I do now? Business and finance.
   p. cm. — (What can I do now?)
 Includes bibliographical references and index.
 ISBN-13: 978-0-8160-8081-6 (hardcover : alk. paper)
 ISBN-10: 0-8160-8081-X (hardcover : alk. paper) 1. Business—Vocational guidance—Juvenile literature. 2. Finance—Vocational guidance—Juvenile literature. I. Ferguson Publishing. II. Title: Business and finance.
 HF5381.2.W46 2010
 650.14—dc22
                            2009044394

Ferguson books are available at special discounts when purchased in bulk quantities for businesses, associations, institutions, or sales promotions. Please call our Special Sales Department in New York at (212) 967-8800 or (800) 322-8755.

You can find Ferguson on the World Wide Web at http://www.fergpubco.com

Text design by Kerry Casey
Composition by Mary Susan Ryan-Flynn
Cover printed by Sheridan Books, Ann Arbor, Mich.
Book printed and bound by Sheridan Books, Ann Arbor, Mich.
Date printed: May 2010
Printed in the United States of America

10 9 8 7 6 5 4 3 2 1

This book is printed on acid-free paper.

All links and Web addresses were checked and verified to be correct at the time of publication. Because of the dynamic nature of the Web, some addresses and links may have changed since publication and may no longer be valid.

# Contents

Introduction                                                    1

Section 1: What Do I Need to Know
                   About Business and Finance?          5

Section 2: Careers                                             23
   Accountants and Auditors                    24
   Administrative Support Workers               37
   Business Managers                            50
   Business Teachers                            63
   Economists                                   75
   Entrepreneurs                                85
   Financial Analysts                           94
   Financial Planners                          105
   Human Resources Workers                     116
   Management Analysts and Consultants         127

Section 3: Do It Yourself                                     139

Section 4: What Can I Do Right Now?                           149
   Get Involved                                150
   Read a Book                                 181
   Surf the Web                                195
   Ask for Money                               200
   Look to the Pros                            211

Index                                                        223

# Introduction

There are many people just like you who want to pursue a career in business or finance—whether at a Fortune 500 company or a small business, on the floor of the stock exchange, in a classroom, or in another setting. You may see a business- or finance-related career in your future and wonder how you can start exploring right away, while still in high school. There are countless areas of the business or finance industries you can work in—areas to which you can match your skills and talents. All you need to begin is a general interest in the field. Although most business and finance careers require a combination of formal training and experience, there is absolutely no reason to wait until you get out of high school to get serious about a career. That doesn't mean you have to make a firm, undying commitment right now. Indeed, one of the biggest fears most people face at some point (sometimes more than once) is choosing the right career. Frankly, many people don't choose at all. They take a job because they need one, and all of a sudden 10 years have gone by and they wonder why they're stuck doing something they hate—like being a human resources worker rather than being an accountant. Don't be one of those people! You have the opportunity right now, while you're still in high school and still relatively unen-cumbered with major adult responsibilities, to explore, to experience, to try out a work path, or several paths if you're one of those overachieving types. Wouldn't you rather find out sooner than later that you're not cut out to be a vice president of a large company after all, and that you'd actually prefer to be a high school business teacher or a small business owner?

There are many ways to explore business and finance careers. What we've tried to do in this book is give you an idea of some of your options. Section 1, What Do I Need to Know about Business and Finance?, will give you an overview of these fields (a little history, where they're at today, and promises of the future) as well as a breakdown of how they are organized and a glimpse of some of their many career options.

The Careers section includes 10 chapters, each describing in detail one or more career options: accountant and auditor, administrative support worker, business manager, business teacher, economist, entrepreneur, financial analyst, financial planner, human resources worker, and management analyst and consultant. These chapters rely heavily on first-hand accounts from real people on the job. They'll tell you what skills you need, what personal qualities you need to have, and what the ups and downs of the jobs are. You'll also find out about educational requirements—including specific high school and college classes—advancement possibilities, related jobs, salary ranges, and the employment outlook.

In keeping with the secondary theme of this book (the primary theme, for those of you who still don't get it, is "You can do something now"), Section 3, Do It Yourself, urges you to take charge and learn about business- and finance-related careers on your own and start your own programs and activities where none exist—school, community, or the nation. Why not?

The real meat of the book is in Section 4, What Can I Do Right Now? This is where you get busy and *do something*. The chapter "Get Involved" will clue you in on the obvious volunteer and intern positions, the not-so-obvious summer camps and summer college study, and other opportunities.

"Read a Book" is an annotated bibliography of books (some new, some old) and periodicals. If you're even remotely considering a career in business or finance, reading a few books and checking out a few magazines or professional journals is the easiest thing you can do. Don't stop with our list. Ask your librarian to point you to more materials. Keep reading!

While we think the best way to explore business- and finance-related careers is to jump right in and start exploring, there are plenty of other ways to get into the business and finance mind-set. "Surf the Web" offers you a short annotated list of Web sites where you can explore everything from job listings (start getting an idea of what employers are looking for now), to educational requirements, to on-the-job accounts and blogs from business professionals.

"Ask for Money" is a sampling of scholarships for people who are interested in pursuing business and finance careers. You need to be familiar with these because you're going to need money for school. You have to actively pursue scholarships; no one is going to come up to you one day and present you with a check because you're such a wonderful student. Applying for scholarships is work, and it takes effort. And it must be done right and often as much as a year in advance of when you need the money.

"Look to the Pros," the final chapter, lists professional organizations you can turn to for more information about accredited schools, education requirements, career descriptions, salary information, union membership, job listings, scholarships, and more. Once you become a college student in a business- or finance-related field, you'll be able to join many of these organizations. Time after time, professionals say that membership and active participation in a professional organization is one of the best ways to network (make valuable contacts) and gain recognition in your field.

High school can be a lot of fun. There are dances and football games; maybe you're in band or play a sport. Great! Maybe you hate school and are just biding your time until you graduate. That's too bad. Whoever you are, take a minute and try to imagine your life five years from now. Ten years from now. Where will you be? What will you be doing? Whether you realize it or not, how you choose to spend your time now—studying, playing, watching TV, working at a fast food restaurant, hanging out, whatever—will have an impact on your future. Take a look at how you're spending your time now and ask yourself, "Where is this getting me?" If you can't come up with an answer, it's probably "nowhere." The choice is yours. No one is going to take you by the hand and lead you in the "right" direction. It's up to you. It's your life. You can do something about it right now!

# SECTION 1

## What Do I Need to Know About Business and Finance?

When you think of business and finance careers, you probably think of Fortune 500 CEOs or small business owners. While these are exciting and rewarding professions, it might surprise you to learn that there are countless other careers available for those who are interested in business and finance. Did you know that cultural advisers are needed to teach people the cultural and business customs of other countries; that executive secretaries are needed to help top managers prepare important documents and manage other secretaries; that financial planners are needed to help people save for retirement, college, or other goals; that human resources professionals are needed to help workers understand benefits and hire just the right person for a job; that business teachers are needed to educate students about business, finance, and many other topics; and that business reporters are needed to provide coverage and analysis of industry developments on radio, television, and the Internet? And these examples really haven't even scratched the surface of the variety of jobs available to someone who is interested in these fields. There are jobs for people with every educational background—from master's and bachelor's degrees (business managers and accountants), to those with some college training (cost estimators), to those with just a high school diploma (secretaries, receptionists, and customer service representatives). Business and finance professionals work in a variety of settings, including offices, factories, stadiums, classrooms, hospitals, banks, television and radio broadcasting stations, home-based settings, and many others. There are also opportunities for aspiring entrepreneurs who want to open their own business or purchase a popular franchise. In short, the sky is the limit for people who are interested in careers in business and finance.

## GENERAL INFORMATION

People have conducted business for as long as civilization has existed. As long as people have been exchanging goods and services for payment of some sort, business transactions have been a part of life. Business was, in fact, one of the factors that led to America's independence, when the early settlers, who wanted to develop their own businesses and industries, rebelled against England's economic constraints.

Early businesses typically took one of two forms: private ownership or partnership. In a privately owned company, the person who established the business was solely responsible for the services provided, the employment of any workers, and the profits or losses of the business. Most of these early sole proprietorships evolved from a trade or skill the owner possessed. For example, a person skilled in preparing meat for sale might open a butcher shop, while a person skilled at sewing would open a tailor's shop.

Partnerships were businesses owned jointly by two or more individuals. In these business ventures, the partners usually pooled their resources to open and run a business, sharing in the profits and risks. In some cases, partners might equally split the financial cost of starting a business. In other cases, one partner might provide the funding, or capital, to start the business while another partner provided the idea, the managerial skills, the labor, or other less-tangible assets. Partnerships were especially common in family businesses, with two siblings often starting a business together. Often, the younger family members were trained on the job to follow their parents into the business when they were old enough to take over.

Corporations, today's common form of business, were developed in the early Middle Ages as a legal alternative to private businesses or partnerships. What made corporations significantly different from sole proprietorships or partnerships was that a corporation was considered its own entity in the business world independent of its controlling members. The first corporations were religious orders, universities, and town governments.

A very important change in the legal structure of businesses took place in England in the 15th century. New limited liability laws were passed, mandating that no individual could be held financially responsible for the debts incurred by a corporation. If a corporation ran into financial trouble, the courts could not pursue the personal earnings of any one member or members of the corporation. The only money that the corporation founders could lose was the money they used to start and run the company.

Between 1600 and the mid-1700s, some corporations took on the added responsibility of maintaining law in territories where they held a monopoly. The East India Company, a British firm in India, and the Hudson's Bay Company in North America were two such firms that regulated what eventually developed into British colonies. In their applications for incorporation, these companies had to state their goals for the advancement of public welfare.

The American concept of business changed dramatically with the American Revolution, however. The newly independent American colonists rejected the idea of business as a government regulator. Even so, most of the new corporations chartered in the early 1800s were involved in public service of some kind, such as construction of water routes, banking, and insurance. Eventually this changed, and commerce and manufacturing firms became the predominant applicants for charter in the United States.

With the burgeoning of the industrial revolution in the late 18th century, businesses became more mechanized and more specialized. Earlier companies had typically involved just a few people who together executed all the tasks necessary to manufacture a product or provide a service. As machinery made it possible for businesses to produce more materials faster, businesses expanded in size and scope. More workers were hired to keep up with the increased pace, and as a result, more management personnel were hired to oversee the workers and handle the financial aspects of the company. As they grew, companies began to structure themselves in different ways. Departments were formed to handle very specific aspects of the business: financial, marketing, personnel, etc. This departmentalization of business responsibilities became a significant feature of the modern corporation.

A new way of structuring a business emerged in the late 19th century, when the Singer Corporation first allowed individuals to sell its sewing machines in particular regions. Soon afterward, General Motors started selling cars in the same manner, as did Coca-Cola with its soft drinks. This method of doing business is called franchising.

Fast-food restaurants soon got into the franchising business. Dairy Queen, one of the oldest fast-food franchises, opened in 1940 and began selling franchises in 1944. During the 1950s, franchising became very prevalent. Among the most well-known franchisers to emerge at that time were McDonald's, Dunkin' Donuts, and AAMCO Transmission. McDonald's was one of the first franchisers to establish guidelines for what the stores could look like, what products could be sold, and what types of promotions could be run. In this way, the corporation was able to maintain strict control over the quality of the product line, guaranteeing consistency across the country and building brand recognition and loyalty.

Originally, most franchises were offshoots of goods-producing companies, like Singer sewing machines. Eventually, however, franchising spread into many other kinds of industries. Today, the trend is toward service-industry franchises, such as real estate offices, law

offices, insurance agencies, and cleaning services.

Today, the business world is more diverse than ever. In addition to the more traditional ways of structuring companies, factors such as technological improvements (especially computers and the Internet), loosening of trade restrictions, and changing demands on the part of employees have created new ways of doing business. One of the most important trends in today's business is that of doing business remotely, via the Internet. This type of business, called e-commerce, means that businesses can advertise their goods and services, take orders, and receive payments electronically. Businesses conducting e-commerce often can reach a far broader range of clients and customers than they would otherwise, at far less marketing and advertising cost.

Many companies have built e-commerce Web sites and are conducting business online in addition to their more traditional methods of doing business. For example, many manufacturers and merchandisers who have traditionally displayed their goods in actual stores or customer showrooms now also maintain Web sites through which customers can order and pay for items. Some companies have even taken e-commerce one step further and have done away with the actual, physical store altogether. These companies, sometimes called virtual companies, operate only via the Internet. These companies save enormous amounts of money by not having to maintain and staff a store.

Technological advances, along with changing employee expectations, have contributed to another trend in today's business world—working at home. There are basically two subtrends in the movement toward working at home: home-based businesses and telecommuting. Home-based businesses are, essentially, very small organizations that conduct all their business from the owner's home. Many home-based businesses are one- or two-person operations, although some have more employees. They may be goods-producers or service businesses. Property managers, lawyers, public relations and marketing professionals, cleaning services, graphic designers, artists, sign makers, photographers, and many other businesspeople have opted to run their businesses from home. By taking advantage of modern communications technology, these home-based businesses can market their goods across the country and even internationally by building a Web site, taking orders, and shipping their goods to the appropriate destinations.

Telecommuting, another at-home working trend, involves a company's employees working off-site, in their own homes, rather than at the company's offices. According to the U.S. Department of Labor, 13.7 million people worked away from the office at least once a week in 2004.

A final important trend is the increasingly global nature of business, as numerous firms take advantage of loosened trade restrictions to expand their operations into overseas markets. Many U.S. firms, for example, have targeted new and emerging markets by expanding into Latin America, India, Russia, China, and other countries. Commonly, a U.S. firm maintains its headquarters in the United States and has satellite offices or branches in various other countries. Corporations that operate in more than one country at a time are called multinational corporations, and they are becoming increasingly common.

## STRUCTURE OF THE INDUSTRY

All businesses can be defined as organizations that provide customers with the goods and services they want. Most businesses attempt to make a profit, that is, to make more money than it takes to run the business. Some businesses, however, attempt only to make enough money to cover their operating expenses. These businesses, which are often social service agencies, hospitals, foundations, or advocacy groups, are called nonprofits or not-for-profits.

There are three main types of businesses in the U.S. economy: manufacturers, merchandisers, and service providers. Manufacturers produce products of all kinds. From skateboards to limousines, from paper plates to soda, from shoelaces to designer suits, virtually everything around you comes from a manufacturer of some sort. Many manufacturers make only small parts, rather than complete, finished products. These manufacturers, often called suppliers, provide their parts to larger manufacturing firms, which use them to construct finished products. For example, an automobile manufacturer purchases the parts needed to make a car from a number of other manufacturers, who specialize in making those parts.

Merchandisers are businesses that help move products through a channel of distribution to the consumer or end user. There are two types of merchandisers: retailers and wholesalers. Wholesalers purchase goods from manufacturers and then sell them to buyers, who then resell them to consumers. Retailers are the businesses that actually sell the goods directly to the consumer. Grocery stores, office supply stores, and mall stores are all examples of retailers.

The third main type of business is the service provider. Service providers are businesses that do not sell an actual product but rather perform a service for a fee. Common examples of service providers are banks, restaurants, dry cleaners, hotels, and hairstylists.

Many U.S. businesses are defined as small businesses, businesses with fewer than 500 employees. According to statistics from the U.S. Small Business Administration, there are approximately 24 million small businesses in the United States. These businesses employ 50.1 percent of the private workforce and pay more than 50 percent of the total U.S. private payroll. Small businesses are usually started by an individual or group of individuals with an idea for a product or a talent or expertise in a certain area. Typically, these entrepreneurs fund a new business partly with their own savings. They may also get a small business loan from a financial institution, such as a

bank or a venture capital group. Venture capital groups are investment groups that invest in new or growing businesses that show promise.

Many of these small businesses are privately owned, which means that an individual or a small group of individuals own and operate the entire company, and are solely responsible for making its decisions. Other companies, especially larger ones, are publicly owned. Publicly owned companies are owned not by one or a few individuals, but by hundreds or thousands of individuals called shareholders. Each shareholder in a public company owns a part, or share, of that company. The amount of the company each shareholder owns is determined by how many shares of the company's stock he or she owns. Each shareholder gets to cast votes on certain company decisions in proportion to how many shares of stock he or she owns. Publicly held companies are governed by an elected board of directors, who have the power to hire or fire the top-level management of the company. The board of directors has the responsibility of overseeing the company's operations and its performance in the marketplace.

Frequently, small privately owned companies become publicly owned companies. For this to happen, the company's owners decide to sell off part of their ownership to interested buyers in an initial public offering, or IPO. In an IPO, buyers purchase shares of the company's stock. Shares of publicly held companies are bought and sold on the stock market. The increase or decrease in price of a

# Lingo to Learn

**annual meeting** A corporation's yearly management meeting, usually held after the end of its fiscal year. Members of the board of directors are usually elected during this meeting.

**assets** The holdings of a business, including land, buildings, inventory, machinery or equipment, investments, cash, and money owed (accounts receivable).

**capital investment** Money that a business invests in itself for growth purposes. Capital investments can include new buildings, vehicles, equipment, etc.

**consumer goods** Products, like food and clothing, that satisfy human needs and wants.

**debt-to-worth ratio** A company's total liabilities divided by its net worth.

**electronic commerce** Business that is conducted electronically via the Internet. Also known as e-commerce.

**entrepreneur** A person who organizes, manages, and assumes the risk of a business venture with the expectation of gaining a profit.

**ethics** A system or morals; the code of rules about how we treat others.

**financial planning** The process of meeting life goals through properly managing one's finances.

**fiscal** Referring to money matters.

**free-market economy** An economy, like the United States', in which wages and prices are primarily determined by competition instead of by the government.

**glass ceiling** A situation in which workers cannot advance to higher levels due to discrimination.

**incorporate** To form or become a corporation.

**labor market** Availability and demand for employees for a specific geographic area.

**liabilities** Whatever a business owes, including accounts payable, mortgages or other loans, and taxes.

**liquidate** To sell out completely.

**mutual funds** A group of financial assets (such as stocks) that are managed by a portfolio manager.

**net worth** The total book value of a business, minus the value of its liabilities.

**operating expenses** All the costs associated with running a business, including payroll, equipment, and materials.

**primary market** The initial target market for a product.

*(continued on next page)*

> *(continued from previous page)*
>
> **profit and loss statement**  Financial report that summarizes the revenues and expenses and shows the net profit or loss in a specified accounting period (also called an income statement).
>
> **secondary offering**  An offering by a company's shareholders to sell their stock to the public. In a secondary offering, the proceeds go to the shareholders, not the company.
>
> **stock**  A representation of financial ownership in a company. An individual who purchases a stock or stocks is called a shareholder or a stockholder. The value of a stock can rise or fall based on a company's performance or other factors.

company's shares of stock is very important to a company's value.

Although this is primarily a look at how business as a whole is structured, it is important to realize that there are certain structures in place within each individual business as well. There are a wide variety of corporate structures, but almost every successful company's structure contains four main components: production, marketing, finance, and human resources.

Production includes the conceptualizing, designing, and creation of products and services. Depending upon the size of the company and the type of product or service it produces, production subcategories might include a research and development department, which develops and tests new products; and a quality control department, which monitors products or services for consistency and quality. Production also includes the actual workers and equipment used to produce the product. For example, the factories and factory workers who make airplanes are a part of production.

The second of the four components is marketing. Marketing is the process of distributing and promoting the company's product to the right people at the right time. For example, a company's marketing department might determine which magazine advertisements or television commercial time slots would best reach a particular product's target consumer group. Marketing departments may develop marketing campaigns designed to catch consumers' attention and interest, like Dairy Management's "Got Milk?" and Nike's "Just Do It" campaigns. A company's marketing department is supported by advertising, public relations, and sales personnel.

The finance department of a company handles the management of money. Financial decisions, such as when to acquire new property, when to borrow capital, and when to raise or lower prices, are typically the responsibility of top-level management. In privately owned companies, the owners often oversee the finances. In larger, publicly held companies, a highly trained finance professional or staff may handle financial decisions.

Human resources management is the branch of a company that deals with employees. Recruiting, hiring, training, evaluating, disciplining, administering benefits packages, and firing employees are all activities that fall into this category. Many smaller companies do not have a specific department to handle human resources. Almost all larger companies do, however.

## CAREERS

The following paragraphs detail the wide variety of career options for people who are interested in business and finance. Careers are organized into the following general occupational groups: Managerial and Professional Positions, Support Workers, and Other Career Paths.

### Managerial and Professional Positions

*The chairman*, followed by the *president* and the *chief executive officer (or CEO)*, are the heads of companies. These officers are responsible for the management of the corporation and the staff. They usually achieve these positions by either working up through the ranks of their company or by transferring over from another company that does similar work. It is extremely rare that someone would head a business in one field if his or her employment history had not been in the same field.

Below the president and CEO is the *COO*, or *chief operating officer*, who is responsible for managing the general operation of a company. The CEO handles the long-term planning, and the COO handles the daily planning. He or she may be responsible for increasing or decreasing the number of people to be hired, determining the holiday and vaca-

> ## The World's Largest Companies by Revenue, 2009
>
> 1. Royal Dutch Shell (Netherlands)
> 2. Exxon Mobil (United States)
> 3. Wal-Mart Stores (United States)
> 4. BP (Great Britain)
> 5. Chevron (United States)
> 6. Total (France)
> 7. ConocoPhillips (United States)
> 8. ING Group (Netherlands)
> 9. Sinopec (China)
> 10. Toyota Motor (Japan)
> 11. Japan Post Holdings (Japan)
> 12. General Electric (United States)
> 13. China National Petroleum (China)
> 14. Volkswagen (Germany)
> 15. State Grid (China)
> 16. Dexia Group (Belgium)
> 17. ENI (Italy)
> 18. General Motors (United States)
> 19. Ford Motor (United States)
> 20. Allianz (Germany)
>
> Source: *Fortune*

tion schedule, establishing operations guidelines for the company, and managing any employee disputes on behalf of the company. The COO also usually has a history of employment in the industry in which he or she holds the office.

*Chief financial officers* direct the financial planning for their organizations. They are responsible for all financial management tasks, such as budgeting, capital expenditure planning, cash flow, and various financial reviews and reports.

*Chief information officers* are responsible for every aspect of their company's information technology. They use their knowledge of technology and business to determine how information technology can best be used to meet company goals. These managers, who are also known as *information systems directors,* sometimes take a role in implementing a company's Web site.

*Facility managers, district managers,* and *regional managers* all are responsible for maintaining the daily routine of their particular end of the business operation. *Store managers* handle the aspects of sales that directly affect the customers. *Plant managers* handle the operations of a production house, factory, or plant. District managers oversee the people who work directly with customers or work on making a product, usually for a territory that the district manager can visit on a regular, and sometimes daily, basis. The regional manager handles the management of several districts, and usually is responsible for expanding and maintaining facilities throughout the area of his or her supervision.

*Personnel managers* and *employment managers* are responsible for the overall functioning of the personnel department and may be involved with hiring, employee orientation, insurance reports, wage surveys, record keeping, grievances, budgets, and analyzing statistical data and reports. *Industrial relations directors* formulate the policies to be carried out by the various department managers.

*Advertising managers* formulate policies and administer their company's advertising operations. They are responsible for coordinating the work of researchers, copywriters, artists, telemarketers, space buyers, time buyers, and other specialists. One type of advertising manager is the *account manager,* who represents the company to its clients.

*Marketing managers* work with their staff and other professionals to determine how advertisements should look, where they should be placed (television, radio, print, etc.), and when the advertising should begin. Managers must keep staff focused on a target audience when working on the promotion of a particular product or service.

*Sales managers* develop and oversee sales programs. They coordinate distribution by establishing sales territories, quotas, and goals. Sales managers also direct staffing, training, and performance evaluations. If a company operates its own sales dealerships, sale managers advise dealers and distributors about sales and advertising techniques. They assess customer needs by reviewing market analyses, and help determine price schedules, discount rates, and sales campaigns. Sales managers may get actively involved in the production of the company's products to ensure that only the most desirable products stay on the sales line. An *export manager* directs foreign sales and service outlets of an organization.

*Public relations managers* plan and direct the development and communications of information designed to keep the public informed of their organization's programs, accomplishments, or point of view.

*Internet store managers and entrepreneurs* use the technology of the Internet to sell products or services. They may research the marketability of a product or service, decide on what product or service to sell, organize their business, and set up their storefront on the Web. *Internet entrepreneurs* operate their own businesses.

*Office administrators* direct and coordinate the work activities of employees within an office. They supervise office clerks and other workers in their tasks and plan department activities with other supervisory personnel. Administrators often define job duties and develop training programs for new workers. They evaluate the progress of their clerks and work with upper management officials to ensure that the office staff meets productivity and quality goals. Office administrators often meet with office personnel to discuss job-related issues or problems, and they are responsible for maintaining a positive office environment.

*Accountants* compile, analyze, verify, and prepare financial records, including profit and loss statements, balance sheets, cost studies, and tax reports. *Tax accountants* prepare federal, state, and local tax returns for their company. They advise management concerning the effects of business transactions on taxes, and may devise and install tax record systems. If necessary, tax accountants may represent their employers before governmental taxing bodies. *Auditors* are specialized accountants who examine and verify financial records to ensure that they are accurate, complete, and in compliance with federal laws. *Internal auditors* examine and analyze the establishment's accounting records and prepare reports concerning its financial status and operating procedures. They report to management on the scope of their audits and may make recommendations on how to improve operations and change the company's financial position.

*Advertising workers* perform the various creative and business activities needed to take an advertisement from the research stage, to creative concept, through production, and finally to its intended audience.

*Buyers* purchase merchandise or commodities for resale. *Wholesale buyers* purchase merchandise directly from manufacturers and resell it to retail firms, commercial establishments, and other institutions. *Retail buyers* purchase goods from wholesalers (and occasionally from manufacturers) for resale to the general public. In either case, buyers must understand their customers' needs and be able to purchase goods at an appropriate price and in sufficient quantity. Sometimes a buyer is referred to by the type of merchandise purchased—for example, jewelry buyer or toy buyer.

Highly trained *computer specialists* are playing a larger and larger role in businesses. For example, *computer database administrators* plan, develop, and administer database management policies to facilitate effective and efficient handling of business information. They create data processing systems designed to collect, analyze, store, and transmit computer information. *Systems analysts* plan, schedule, and coordinate the activities that are required to process data on computer systems. *Computer programmers* write and code the instructions that control the work of a computer. *Internet consultants* use their technological and computer skills to help people or businesses access and utilize the Internet. Their work may include implementing or refining a networking system, creating a Web site, establishing an online ordering or product support system, or training employees to maintain and update their newly established Web site. *Internet transaction specialists* are in charge of designing, developing, or implementing Internet transaction software or systems. This software or system is the technology that allows a customer to buy a pair of shoes online, for example, by giving his or her credit card number. Internet transaction specialists at the most advanced professional level are often called *information architects,* and they oversee the design of the whole transaction system. They decide what direction a system should take and what technology should be used. *Software developers* work under the guidance of architects to turn these designs into reality. Less experienced programmers may also contribute by working on smaller parts of the program that the developer or architect assigns them.

*Contract administrators* examine estimates of production costs, performance requirements, and delivery schedules to ensure completeness and accuracy. They prepare bids and other exhibits that may be required.

*Contract specialists* negotiate, administer, extend, terminate, and renegotiate contracts with suppliers. They may approve or reject requests for deviations from contract specifications and delivery schedules, and may arbitrate claims or complaints occurring in performance of contracts.

*Cost estimators* try to project how much it will cost their companies to manufacture a product, build a structure, or acquire a service. They conduct studies and use data such as labor and material costs to estimate how much a project will cost, and to help determine whether the project should be undertaken at all.

*Cultural advisers,* also known as *bilingual consultants,* work with businesses and organizations to help them communicate effectively with others who are from different cultural and language backgrounds.

*Economists* compile and interpret statistical data regarding the production and distribution of goods and services. They work closely with management and marketing specialists.

*Financial analysts* analyze the financial situation of companies and recommend ways for these companies to manage, spend, and invest their money. They are sometimes called *investment analysts* or *security analysts.* Many financial analysts have backgrounds in accounting.

Financial planning is the process of establishing financial goals and creating ways to reach them. *Financial planners* examine the assets of their clients and suggest what steps they need to take in the future to meet their goals. They take a broad approach to financial advice, which distinguishes them from other professional advisors, such as insurance agents, stockbrokers, accountants, attorneys, and real estate agents, each of whom typically focuses on only one aspect of a person's finances.

The marketing department of a company is in charge of promoting its products. *Marketing specialists* conduct and gather market research and analysis and evaluate sales reports in order to figure out how to best target the customers who will buy their product.

*Personnel and labor-relations specialists* formulate employee policies and conduct programs relating to all phases of personnel activity, such as recruitment, selection, training, development, retention, promotion, compensation, benefits, labor relations, and occupational safety.

*Procurement services managers* also analyze market conditions to determine present and future availability of desired materials.

*Public relations specialists* develop and maintain programs that present a favorable public image for an individual or organization. They provide information to the target audience (generally, the public at large) about the client, its goals and accomplishments, and any further plans or projects that may be of public interest.

*Purchasing agents* determine the quantity and quality of the items to be purchased and negotiate costs, delivery dates, and sources of supply. They keep records pertaining to items purchased, costs, delivery, product performance, and inventories. Purchasing agents may work under procurement services managers, who coordinate all the activities

## Facts About Small Businesses, 2008

- There were more than 29.6 million small business in the United States.

- Small businesses made up 99.7 percent of all employers in the United States.

- Approximately 52 percent of small businesses were home based.

- Small businesses employed 40 percent of high-tech workers such as engineers, scientists, and computer professionals.

Source: Office of Advocacy, Small Business Administration

of personnel involved in purchasing and distributing materials.

*Statisticians* collect, analyze, and interpret numerical data to help business professionals determine the best way to produce results in their work.

## Support Workers

*Billing clerks* produce and process bills and collect payments from customers. They enter transactions in business ledgers or spreadsheets, write and send invoices, and verify purchase orders. They post items in accounts payable or receivable, calculate customer charges, and verify the company's rates for certain products and services. Billing clerks must make sure that all entries are accurate and up to date. At the end of the fiscal year, they may work with auditors to clarify billing procedures and answer questions about specific accounts.

*Bookkeeping and accounting clerks* record financial transactions. They compute, classify, record, and verify numerical data in order to develop and maintain accurate financial records.

*Collection workers*—sometimes known as *bill collectors, collection correspondents,* or *collection agents*—are employed to persuade people to pay their overdue bills. Some work for collection agencies (which are hired by the business to which the money is owed), while others work for department stores, hospitals, banks, public utilities, and other businesses. Collection workers contact delinquent debtors, inform them of the delinquency, and either secure payment or arrange a new payment schedule. If all else fails, they might be forced to repossess property or turn the account over to an attorney for legal proceedings.

*Customer service representatives,* sometimes called *customer care representatives,* work with customers of one or many companies, assist with customer problems, or answer questions. Customer service representatives work in many different industries to provide "front-line" customer service in a variety of businesses. *Computer support specialists* investigate and resolve problems in computer functioning. They listen to customer complaints, walk customers through possible solutions, and write technical reports based on their work.

The duties of *event planners* are varied, and may include establishing a site for an event; making travel, hotel, and food arrangements; and planning the program and overseeing the registration. The planner may be responsible for negotiating, planning, and coordinating a major worldwide convention, or the planner may be involved with a small, in-house meeting involving only a few people.

*Graphic designers* are practical artists whose creations are intended to express ideas, convey information, or draw attention to a product. They design a wide variety of materials, including advertisements, displays, packaging, signs, computer graphics and games, book and magazine covers and interiors, animated characters, and company logos to fit the needs and preferences of their various employers.

*Janitors* or *cleaners,* sometimes known as *custodians,* are responsible for the cleaning and maintenance of office buildings, schools, apartments, hospitals, manufacturing plants, and other structures. In addition to daily cleaning duties, they may be responsible for performing light repair work when needed and for making sure heating and cooling systems are in proper working order.

*Office clerks* perform a variety of clerical tasks that help an office run smoothly, including file maintenance, mail sorting, and record keeping. In large companies, office clerks might have specialized tasks such as inputting data into a computer, but in most cases, clerks are flexible and have many duties, including typing, answering telephones, responding to emails, taking messages, making photocopies, and preparing mailings. Office clerks usually work under close supervision, often with experienced clerks directing their activities.

*Receptionists*—so named because they receive visitors in places of business—have the important job of giving a business's clients and visitors a positive first impression. These front-line workers are the first communication sources who greet clients and visitors, answer their questions, and direct them to the people they wish to see. Receptionists also answer telephones, take and distribute messages for other employees, and make sure no one enters the office unescorted or unauthorized. Many receptionists also perform additional clerical duties.

*Secretaries* perform a wide range of jobs that vary greatly from business to business. However, most secretaries key in documents, manage records and information, answer telephones, send and respond to emails and faxes, handle correspondence, schedule appointments, make travel arrangements, and sort mail. The amount of time secretaries spend on these duties depends on the size and type of the office as well as on their own job training. There are several popular specialties in the field. *Executive secretaries* provide support for top executives. They perform fewer clerical duties and more information management. *Legal secretaries* prepare legal papers, including wills, mortgages, contracts, deeds, motions, complaints, and summonses for lawyers. *Medical secretaries* take medical histories of patients; make appointments; prepare

## Future Skills for Success

In 2007 the Center for Creative Leadership asked business leaders to name three skills that they felt future leaders would need to be successful. Here are their responses, ranked in order of importance.

1. Collaboration
2. Change leadership (the ability to manage companies in changing markets and in other demanding circumstances)
3. Building effective teams
3. Influence without authority
5. Driving innovation
6. Coaching
7. Building and mending relationships
7. Adaptability
9. Seeing things from different angles
10. Learning from others through questions
10. Resourcefulness
12. Leveraging differences
13. Global awareness
14. Decisiveness
14. Doing whatever it takes to get results
15. Straightforwardness/composure
16. Credibility
17. Ethical decision-making

and send bills to patients, as well as track and collect them; process insurance billing; maintain medical files; and pursue correspondence with patients, hospitals, and associations.

*Typists and word processors* use typewriters, personal computers, and other office machines to convert handwritten, recorded, or otherwise unfinished material into clean, readable, typewritten copies. Typists create reports, letters, forms, tables, charts, and other materials for all kinds of businesses and services.

*Webmasters* design, implement, and maintain Internet Web sites for corporations, educational institutions, not-for-profit organizations, government agencies, or other institutions. Webmasters should have working knowledge of network configurations, interface, graphic design, software development, business, writing, marketing, and project management.

## Other Career Paths

*Business reporters* specialize in writing about the business world—from emerging companies and business leaders, to new products, to industry trends, to many other topics. They write for newspapers, magazines, book publishers, and Web sites. *Business broadcasters* gather, analyze, and report information about business topics for television and radio broadcasts.

*Business teachers* instruct students about business principles and theories. They may teach specialties such as accounting, economics, business communications, business management, business mathematics, e-commerce, finance, human resources, international business, labor relations and personnel management, and marketing.

*Executive recruiters* are hired by businesses to locate, research, and interview candidates for hard-to-fill employment positions, mainly on the junior to senior management level. Such recruiters work for executive search firms and are paid by clients on a commission basis, or flat fee.

*Labor union business agents* manage the daily business matters of labor unions and act as liaisons between the union and management during contract negotiations. They manage business affairs for the labor unions that employ them, and inform the media of labor union happenings. Labor union business agents are also responsible for informing employers of workers' concerns.

## EMPLOYMENT OPPORTUNITIES

Workers in the fields of business are employed at companies large and small. Opportunities are available throughout the United States and the world. Industries fall into either service-producing sectors (which include merchandisers) or goods-producing sectors. According to the 2007

North American Industry Classification System, service-producing sectors include Accommodation and Food Services; Administrative and Support and Waste Management and Remediation Services; Arts, Entertainment, and Recreation; Educational Services; Finance and Insurance; Health Care and Social Assistance; Information; Management of Companies and Enterprises; Other Services (except Public Administration); Professional, Scientific, and Technical Services; Public Administration; Real Estate and Rental and Leasing; Retail Trade; Transportation and Warehousing; Utilities; and Wholesale Trade. Goods-producing sectors include Agriculture, Forestry, Fishing, and Hunting; Construction; Manufacturing; and Mining, Quarrying, and Oil and Gas Extraction.

## INDUSTRY OUTLOOK

Because it is such a broad category, it is difficult to project growth for business as a whole. It is entirely possible, and even common, for one industry to suffer slow growth or decline while another industry thrives. There are certain trends, however, that affect business as a whole.

Almost all businesses are affected by changes in the economy. When the economy is thriving, consumers have more money to spend, which means that they buy more products and services. When the economy suffers a downturn, however, virtually all businesses suffer along with it as consumers cut back on spending. During economically unsound periods, many companies lay off or terminate employees in order to stay afloat.

Another trend that will affect many, if not most, businesses is that of increased technology use. As every industry becomes more automated, workers who have technological skills become ever more important, and technology-related industries will continue to be an area of rapid expansion. It is becoming increasingly difficult for workers in almost every position to survive in the modern business world without basic computer literacy. In addition, as computers continue to cut down on human work, some jobs may be eliminated or combined to reduce costs. Offshoring of U.S.-based jobs to countries that pay workers less for their labor will also reduce the number of workers in certain industries.

Technology will continue to influence the way business is done in other ways as well. The Internet will continue to experience strong growth as a buying-and-selling medium. Telecommuting and entrepreneurial home-based businesses, too, are expected to continue to increase due to technological advances and the ease of communication between computers.

Recent years have seen some changes in the corporate structure, which may continue. In the last decade, many companies have cut positions in an effort to reduce costs and enhance organizational efficiency. Called downsizing, this trend has the largest effect on middle-management workers, but also creates increased workloads for remaining employees who must take on the duties and responsibilities that were previously handled by the downsized workers.

Opportunities in business and finance are, to some degree, tied to the economy.

# SECTION 2

## Careers

# Accountants and Auditors

## SUMMARY

**Definition**
Accountants compile, analyze, verify, and prepare financial records, including profit and loss statements, balance sheets, cost studies, and tax reports. Auditors examine and verify financial records to ensure that they are accurate, complete, and in compliance with federal laws.

**Alternative Job Titles**
Finance professionals

**Salary Range**
$28,862 to $59,430 to $102,380+

**Educational Requirements**
Bachelor's degree; advanced degrees required for top positions

**Certification or Licensing**
Recommended

**Employment Outlook**
Faster than the average

**High School Subjects**
Business
Economics
Mathematics

**Personal Interests**
Business
Economics

"High school students should be aware that internal auditing is a great place to start a career," says Glenn Sumners, director of the Center for Internal Auditing at Louisiana State University. "You are exposed to so many aspects of a business and develop a 'big picture' of the organization very quickly. Internal auditing can be a rewarding career path or a launching pad to a management position."

## WHAT DOES AN ACCOUNTANT OR AUDITOR DO?

The four major areas of accounting and auditing are public, management, government accounting, and internal auditing.

*Public accountants* work independently on a fee basis or as members of an accounting firm, and they perform a variety of tasks for businesses or individuals. These may include auditing accounts and records, preparing and certifying financial statements, conducting financial investigations and furnishing testimony in legal matters, and assisting in formulating budget policies and procedures. Public accountants are also known as *external auditors*.

*Management accountants,* sometimes called *industrial, corporate, or private accountants,* oversee financial records of the firms at which they are employed.

Some of their main duties include budgeting, cost management, performance evaluation, and asset management. Some may hold the position of *financial analyst* at their companies.

*Government accountants* work on the financial records of government agencies or, when necessary, they audit the records of private companies. In the federal government, many accountants are employed as bank examiners, Internal Revenue Service agents, and investigators, as well as in regular accounting positions.

*Internal auditors* are professionals with an in-depth understanding of their organization's business, culture, systems, and processes. Internal auditors provide assurance that internal controls in place are adequate to mitigate their organization's risks, that governance processes are effective and efficient, and that organizational goals and objectives are met. They may ensure that financial records are accurate, complete, and in compliance with federal laws and review real-time computer data or items in original entry books such as purchase orders, tax returns, billing statements, and other important documents. Internal auditors may also suggest ways to improve productivity and profits, review procedures and controls, appraise the efficiency and effectiveness of operations, and make sure their companies comply with corporate policies and government regulations.

Within these fields, accountants and auditors can specialize in a variety of areas.

*General accountants* supervise, install, and devise general accounting, budget, and cost systems. They maintain records, balance books, and prepare and analyze statements on all financial aspects of business. Administrative officers use this information to make sound business decisions.

*Budget accountants* review expenditures of departments within a firm to make sure expenses allotted are not exceeded. They also aid in drafting budgets and may devise and install budget control systems.

*Cost accountants* determine unit costs of products or services by analyzing records and depreciation data. They classify and record all operating costs so that management can control expenditures.

*Property accountants* keep records of equipment, buildings, and other property owned or leased by a company. They prepare mortgage schedules and payments as well as appreciation or depreciation statements, which are used for income tax purposes.

*Environmental accountants* help utilities, manufacturers, and chemical companies set up preventive systems to ensure environmental compliance and provide assistance in the event that legal issues arise.

*Systems accountants* design and set up special accounting systems for organizations whose needs cannot be handled by standardized procedures. This may involve installing automated or computerized accounting processes and includes instructing personnel in the new methods.

*Forensic accountants* and *auditors* use accounting principles and theories to support or oppose claims being made in litigation.

*Tax accountants* prepare federal, state, or local tax returns of an individual, business, or corporation according to prescribed rates, laws, and regulations. They also may conduct research on the effects of taxes on firm operations and recommend changes to reduce taxes. This is one of the most intricate fields of accounting, and many accountants therefore specialize in one particular phase such as corporate, individual income, or property tax.

*Assurance accountants* help improve the quality of information for clients in assurance services areas such as electronic commerce, risk assessment, and elder care. This information may be financial or nonfinancial in nature.

*Tax auditors* review financial records and other information provided by taxpayers to determine the appropriate tax liability. *State and federal tax auditors* usually work in government offices, but they may perform a field audit in a taxpayer's home or office.

*Revenue agents* are employed by the federal government to examine selected income tax returns and, when necessary, conduct field audits and investigations to verify the information reported and adjust the tax liability accordingly.

*Chief bank examiners* enforce good banking practices throughout a state. They schedule bank examinations to ensure that financial institutions comply with state laws and, in certain cases, they take steps to protect a bank's solvency and the interests of its depositors and shareholders.

Accounting is known as a desk job, and a 40-hour workweek can be expected in public and private accounting. Although computer work is replacing paperwork, the job can be routine and monotonous at times, and concentration and attention to detail are critical. Public accountants experience considerable pressure during the tax period, which runs from November to April, and they may have to work long hours. There is potential for stress aside from tax season, as accountants can be responsible for managing multi-million-dollar finances with no margin for error. Self-employed accountants and those working for a small firm can expect to work longer hours; 40 percent work more than 50 hours per week, compared to 20 percent of public and private accountants.

In smaller firms, most of the public accountant's work is performed in the client's office. A considerable amount of travel is often necessary to service a wide variety of businesses. In a larger firm, however, an accountant may have very little client contact, spending more time interacting with the accounting team.

## WHAT IS IT LIKE TO BE AN ACCOUNTANT OR AUDITOR?

Tasheé Singleton is an accountant at Columbus State University's Foundation Properties, Inc. in Columbus, Georgia. "Foundation Properties Inc.," she explains, "is a real estate foundation that purchases properties for the university, which is strategic for future develop-

# Good Advice for Accountants

Ben Mulling, an accountant and the chief financial officer of Tente Casters Inc. in Hebron, Kentucky, offers the following advice to young people who want to become accountants:

Strive to find the work you enjoy doing. Before committing time and money to development in this career, spend time at the workplace of local accountants to get a feel for what they do from day to day. However, it is crucial to spend time with different types of accountants in different business sectors, including tax accountants, auditors, managerial accountants, and financial analysts, among others.

Many students assume that an accountant is an accountant and that there is no variety. On the contrary, accountants are sort of like doctors in the medical field. A doctor is a doctor, but that doctor could specialize in many different types of medicine. Accounting is very similar in that aspect. There are many different types of accountants, and their job even varies by industry. Be sure to explore all of your options in the field before committing to a particular direction. I would also recommend working in different fields and business sectors after school as well to get a better feeling of where to direct your career.

ment based on the university's goals and objectives." Tasheé has worked in the field for more than five years. "I became an accountant because I have a desire to teach but I wanted to teach in an unconventional manner," she says. "There are so many individuals and businesses that do not know how to manage their finances. So, I decided that I would become an accountant and have the opportunity to educate individuals and businesses. I also desire to change the face of accounting because there was such a stigma about being an accountant. Many people believe accountants literally walk around with green visors and pocket protectors. Additionally, if a poll were taken, a high percentage of people would think the only thing you can be when you are an accountant is to become a certified

public accountant and do taxes. I have a desire to do neither."

Tasheé says that her typical workday is scheduled from 8:00 A.M. to 5:00 P.M., but more often than not she works from 7:00 A.M. to 6:00 P.M. She begins a typical day by checking voice mail and emails. "Then I check my to-do list to see if I completed the project from the prior day in full," she says. "If not, I begin [working] on it. My typical responsibilities are ensuring the general ledger stands with the utmost integrity. I review receipts, cash disbursement transactions, manage five bank accounts (one being a British account in British pounds), maintain and update the fixed assets schedule and filing system, supervise an accounting assistant, manage cash flow and nine bond issues, prepare and complete the balance sheet and income statement reconciliations monthly, maintain related party transactions, oversee related party and external client invoicing, pursue collections if necessary, interact with property managers (internal and external), enter and support journal entries into the general ledger, work closely with the controller and executive director on projects, and prepare for and interact with auditors. I also serve on the university's Customer Service Advisory Committee. If there is time left in the day, I pull my reconciliation out to begin reviewing discrepancies from the previous month and find supporting documentation to complete the necessary adjusting entries."

## DO I HAVE WHAT IT TAKES TO BE AN ACCOUNTANT OR AUDITOR?

Successful accountants and auditors must have strong mathematical, analytical, and problem-solving skills. They need to be able to think logically and to interpret facts and figures accurately. Effective oral and written communication skills are also essential in working with both clients and management. Other important skills are attentiveness to detail, patience, and industriousness. Business acumen and the ability to generate clientele are crucial to those who work in service-oriented businesses, as are honesty, dedication, and a respect for the work of others.

Glenn Sumners, director of the Center for Internal Auditing at Louisiana State University, says that the most important skills for internal auditors are "integrity, oral communication, teamwork, analysis, and work ethic. Internal auditors typically work in teams and spend a significant amount of time interviewing and communicating with their customers. The ability to analyze a process or a piece of information and its impact on the organization is critical. Obviously, integrity is the foundation skill that allows auditors to fulfill their responsibility to the organization."

## HOW DO I BECOME AN ACCOUNTANT OR AUDITOR?

### Education

#### High School

If you are interested in an accounting or auditing career, you must be very proficient in arithmetic and basic algebra. Familiarity with computers and their applications is equally important. Course work in business, English, and speech will also be beneficial.

Danielle Damlouji, an internal auditor who recently graduated from Louisiana State University's E. J. Ourso College of Business, offers the following advice to high school students: "Focus on classes that are business oriented whenever possible. Being involved in different clubs and organizations will help you develop crucial leadership and communication skills."

#### Postsecondary Training

Postsecondary training in accounting or auditing may be obtained in a wide vari-

# Key Skills for Accountants

Tasheé Singleton details the most important personal and professional qualities for accountants:

I believe the most important qualities for accountants are competence, confidentiality, integrity, and credibility. These qualities are part of IMA's Statement of Professional Practice. However, these same qualities are [instrumental] to maintain true relationships and stand as a leader.

If an accountant proves competency in his or her work, this will also exemplify confidence. Accountants need to pursue continuing education in all formats—school, seminars, reading industry magazines, etc. What was taught today is obsolete tomorrow.

If an accountant can be trusted with sensitive information, the company has confidence in its strategy.

If an accountant has integrity, the accountant knows when to say "no" to something that does not seem right. If the accountant is not sure if the decision is right, he or she will know to ask questions and continue to push the issue until resolution is found. Sometimes, this does mean changing jobs or departments. With integrity, people have to remember that we have to live with ourselves after the deed is complete. No one wants to live with a black cloud over his or her head for the rest of his or her life.

If an accountant is creditable, people know the judgment call is objective and fair.

Acting in competence, confidentiality, integrity, and credibility daily establishes trust among peers, management, clients, and the community. Although, I used "the accountant" in all of the scenarios, it can easily be replaced with "a person" and be used as a personal quality. Additional qualities I'd like to mention are patience, the ability to listen, and personality.

Throughout my five years [in the field], I have learned how to maintain patience. If I had not, my employee-employer relationship could have been strained. I learned to listen to what was actually being said and not take decisions made or not made as personal attacks but as a business call that was best at that moment. Lastly, having a personality that allows people to speak with you about a situation helps stimulate ideas, which can help propel a business into a new, more positive direction.

ety of institutions such as private business schools, junior colleges, universities, and correspondence schools. A bachelor's degree with a major in accounting or auditing, or a related field such as economics, is highly recommended by professional associations for those entering the field and is required by all states before taking the licensing exam. It is possible, however, to become a successful accountant or auditor by completing a program at any of the aforementioned institutions. A four-year college curriculum usually includes about two years of liberal arts courses, a year of general business subjects, and 24 semester hours of accounting or auditing work. Better positions, particularly in public accounting, require a bachelor's degree with a major in accounting. Large public accounting firms often prefer people with a master's degree in accounting. For beginning positions in accounting, the federal government requires four years of college (including 24 semester hours in accounting or auditing) or an equivalent combination of education and experience.

Danielle says that successful internal auditing students "have a desire to learn about all different types of businesses and processes, curiosity, and the ability to ask the right questions."

## Certification or Licensing

A large percentage of all accountants and auditors are certified. Certified public accountants (CPAs) must pass a qualifying examination and hold a certificate issued by the state in which they wish to practice. In most states, a college degree is required for admission to the CPA examinations; a few states allow candidates to substitute years of public accounting experience for the college degree requirement. Currently 42 states and the District of Columbia require CPA candidates to have 150 hours of education, which is an additional 30 hours beyond the standard bachelor's degree. Four additional states plan to enact the 150-hour requirement in the future. These criteria can be met by combining an undergraduate accounting program with graduate study or participating in an integrated five-year professional accounting program. You can obtain information from a state board of accountancy or check out the Web site of the American Institute of Certified Public

Accountants (AICPA) to read about new regulations and review last year's exam.

The Uniform CPA Examination administered by the AICPA is used by all states. Nearly all states require at least two years of public accounting experience or its equivalent before a CPA certificate can be earned.

The AICPA offers additional credentialing programs (involving a test and additional requirements) for members with valid CPA certificates. These designations include accredited in business valuation, certified information technology professional (CITP), and personal financial specialist. These credentials indicate that a CPA has developed skills in nontraditional areas in which accountants are starting to play larger roles.

Some accountants seek out other credentials. Those who have earned a bachelor's degree, pass a four-part examination, agree to meet continuing education requirements, and have at least two years of experience in management accounting may become a certified management accountant (CMA) through the Institute of Management Accountants.

The Accreditation Council for Accountancy and Taxation confers the following designations: accredited business accountant or accredited business advisor, accredited tax preparer, accredited tax adviser, and elder care specialist.

To become a certified internal auditor, college graduates with two years of experience in internal auditing must pass a four-part examination given by The Institute of Internal Auditors (IIA). The IIA also offers the following specialty certifications: certified financial services auditor, certified in control self assessment, and certified government auditing professional. Visit the IIA's Web site for more information.

The designation certified information systems auditor is conferred by the ISACA to candidates who pass an examination and who have five years of experience auditing electronic data processing systems.

Other organizations confer specialized auditing designations. For example, the Association of Certified Fraud Examiners offers the certified fraud examiner designation.

Ben Mulling, an accountant and the chief financial officer of Tente Casters Inc. in Hebron, Kentucky, has several certifications. "My first certification was the CPA, followed by the CITP. The last certification that I received was my CMA. Of course, everyone likes to see the CPA designation behind your name, so I think that will open many doors for accountants, much more than if you did not have the certification. Once you walk through that door, you must perform. I feel in the manufacturing industry that the CMA will allow you to excel more than the CPA. In my opinion, it provides much more useful information for a managerial accountant. However, both certifications are crucial if an accountant wishes to rise to management ranks."

### Internships and Volunteerships

You may be required to participate in an internship as part of your college curriculum. This hands-on work experience at a company employing accountants or auditors will give you a chance to work closely with these professionals, observe possible employment settings, and make valuable networking contacts. Internships are usually arranged by the school, especially when the internship is a requirement for the degree. They are usually nonpaying, but do count toward credit hours.

The American Institute of Certified Public Accountants offers an excellent Web site (http://www.startheregoplaces. com) to help you learn more about the field. It features information on recommended high school courses, important personal skills for accountants, postsecondary training programs, scholarships, internships, and careers options in the field.

If you think a career as an accountant or auditor might be for you, try working in a retail business, either part time or during the summer. Working at the cash register or even pricing products as a stockperson is good introductory experience. You should also consider working as a treasurer for a student organization requiring financial planning and money management. It may be possible to gain some experience by volunteering with local groups such as religious organizations and small businesses.

## WHO WILL HIRE ME?

More than 1.1 million people work as accountants and auditors. Accountants and auditors are employed throughout private industry and government. About 21 percent work for accounting, tax preparation, bookkeeping, and payroll services firms. Approximately 10 percent are self-employed.

Junior public accountants usually start in jobs with routine duties such as counting cash, verifying calculations, and other detailed numerical work. In private accounting, beginners are likely to start as cost accountants and junior internal auditors. They may also enter in clerical positions as cost clerks, ledger clerks, and timekeepers or as trainees in technical or junior executive positions. In the federal government, most beginners are hired as trainees at the GS-5 level after passing the civil service exam.

Some state CPA societies arrange internships for accounting majors, and some offer scholarships and loan programs.

You might also visit the Career Planning & Development section (http://www.aicpa.org/YoungCPANetwork/Planning_Developing.htm) of the AICPA's Web site. It has detailed information on accounting careers, hiring trends, job search strategies, resumes and cover letters, and job interviews.

"My first job was heaven sent," says Tasheé Singleton. "I graduated with my BBA-Accounting in December 2003. In February 2004, a newly created position at the university was posted—accountant I for Foundation Properties Inc. Of course being a recent grad, I was always on the prowl for a job that would become my career—an accounting job that is. I stumbled upon this job vacancy by reviewing the university's Web site. I believe my boss at the time also mentioned it to me. He knew I desired to have a job in the accounting field. (I was working as a customer service tech I at the Muscogee County Tax Commissioner's Office in Columbus, Georgia). Later, I learned my exposure to property issues and being a Columbus State University graduate were the distinctions that won me the job."

## WHERE CAN I GO FROM HERE?

Talented accountants and auditors can advance quickly. Junior public accountants usually advance to senior positions within several years and to managerial positions soon after. Those successful in dealing with top-level management may eventually become supervisors, managers, and partners in larger firms or go into independent practice. However, only 2 to 3 percent of new hires advance to audit manager, tax manager, or partner.

Private accountants in firms may become audit managers, tax managers, cost accounting managers, or controllers, depending on their specialty. Some become controllers, treasurers, or corporation presidents. Others on the finance side may rise to become managers of financial planning and analysis or treasurers.

Federal government trainees are usually promoted within a year or two. Advancement to controller and to higher administrative positions is ultimately possible.

Although advancement may be rapid for skilled accountants, especially in public accounting, those with inadequate

# Student Profile: Rachel Bond

Rachel Bond is a senior at Louisiana State University's E. J. Ourso College of Business. She is majoring in accounting, with a concentration in internal audit. She discussed her education and career plans with the editors of *What Can I Do Now? Business and Finance*.

Q. **What has been one thing that has surprised you in the course of studying internal audit?**

A. Many people think of the term "audit" and only think of accounting and financial statements, and although the term "bird's eye view" and "big picture" are used loosely throughout the profession—I think it's the best way to sum it up. Internal audit has kept me on my toes since the first day of class. Due to such broad exposure, I have gained a better understanding of how a business operates and familiarized myself with different industries. I have learned more about business from one semester of internal audit than I have collectively learned throughout all of my business classes.

Q. **What are the most important skills for successful internal auditing students?**

A. Each semester more than 200 students come in to our internal audit program and at the end 30 to 40 percent of those people might realize that they are not cut out for it. The main skills emphasized in the classroom for success in internal audit include leadership, flexibility, detail-oriented, analytical skills, professional skepticism, interpersonal communication, and teamwork. Although many

students may be proficient in each of these skills, many students have just begun the journey to improve and perfect each of these skills. Most important is the concept of integrity—doing the right things for the right reasons and having the ability to defend what you believe is right. I think the best formula for success in internal audit is having the potential skill set with a mix of passion and ambition.

Q. **What advice would you give to high school students who want to become internal auditors?**

A. There are many people out there who have not even heard of internal audit, but for the people who have heard of it—they might not fully understand the value and opportunity within the field of study. The first question I kept asking when I started learning about internal audit was, "How have I never been informed of this great career path before?" Internal audit is a gateway to building key leadership for our future. Many high school students are unaware [of opportunities in] the business world, seeing as though [business] is not heavily emphasized and integrated into the core requirements of high school education. High schools should offer more business clubs, classes, and activities to start getting students informed and involved about the business culture and ethics. Business makes the economy go round. Regardless of a student's chosen career path, business will always

*(continued on next page)*

(continued from previous page)

be a necessity. I cannot think of a better environment to learn about business than internal audit. Perhaps the foundational concepts of internal audit can help the future generation achieve innovation and success.

**Q.  What are your career goals? What do you want to do after you graduate?**

**A.**  Currently, I have one year left as an undergraduate. I am sitting for the CIA (certified internal audit) exam right now. I plan to attend graduate school too, for either a master's degree or MBA. I plan to sit for the CPA (certified public accountant) exam after completing my 150 hours, the CISA (certified information systems audit), and eventually become a CFE (certified fraud examiner). Building a foundation in business, with proficiency and integrated skills in subject areas such as audit, accounting, information technology, and fraud, are the key to being a value-added internal auditor. Internal audit has already opened so many doors for me, each with endless amounts of opportunity that I believe will lead to an enriching and satisfying career.

academic or professional training are often assigned to routine jobs and find it difficult to obtain promotions. All accountants find it necessary to continue their study of accounting and related areas in their spare time. Even those who have already obtained college degrees, gained experience, and earned a CPA certificate may spend many hours studying to keep up with new industry developments. Thousands of practicing accountants enroll in formal courses offered by universities and professional associations to specialize in certain areas of accounting, broaden or update their professional skills, and become eligible for advancement and promotion.

## WHAT ARE THE SALARY RANGES?

The National Association of Colleges and Employers reports that average starting salaries for accountants with a bachelor's degree were $47,421 a year in 2007. General accountants at large companies with up to one year of experience earned between $36,750 and $44,750, according to a 2008 survey by Robert Half International. Entry-level internal auditors can earn as much as $55,000 annually, and mid-level internal auditors may earn up to $100,000, depending on factors such as their education level, experience, professional credential/designation, and the size or location of the company or firm, if working for an accounting firm or service provider.

Accountants and auditors had median annual earnings of $59,430 in 2008, according to the U.S. Department of Labor. Salaries ranges from less than $36,720 to $102,380 or more. In the federal government, the average starting salary for junior accountants and auditors was $28,862 in 2007. Some entry-level positions paid slightly more if the candidate had an advanced degree or superior academic performance. Accountants working for the federal government in supervisory and management positions had average salaries of $78,665 a year in 2007; auditors averaged $83,322. Although government accountants and auditors earn less than those in other areas, they do receive more benefits.

Accountants in large firms and with large corporations receive typical benefits including paid vacation and sick days, insurance, and savings and pension plans. Employees in smaller companies generally receive fewer fringe benefits.

## WHAT IS THE JOB OUTLOOK?

Employment of accountants and auditors is expected to grow faster than the average for all occupations through 2016, according to the U.S. Department of Labor. This is due to business growth, changing tax and finance laws, and increased scrutiny of financial practices across all businesses. There have been several notable scandals in the accounting industry in recent years, and this accounts for much of the increased scrutiny and changing legislation in this industry.

As firms specialize their services, accountants will need to follow suit. Firms will seek out accountants with experience in marketing and proficiency in computer systems to build management consulting practices. As trade increases, so will the demand for CPAs with international specialties and foreign language skills. CPAs with an engineering degree would be well equipped to specialize in environmental accounting. Other accounting specialties that will enjoy good prospects include assurance, cost, and forensic accounting.

The number of CPAs dropped off a bit after most states embraced the 150-hour standard for CPA education. However, numbers are once again starting to rise as students realize the many opportunities this industry holds, especially in the wake of recent accounting scandals. CPAs with valid licenses should experience favorable job prospects for the foreseeable future. Pursuing advanced degrees and certifications will also greatly increase one's chances of finding employment.

Accounting jobs are more secure than most during economic downswings. Despite fluctuations in the nation's economy, there will always be a need to manage financial information, especially as the number, size, and complexity of business transactions increases. However, competition for jobs will remain, certification requirements will become more rigorous, and accountants and auditors with the highest degrees will be the most competitive.

Veronica Johnson, manager of academic relations at The Institute of Internal Auditors, sees steady growth for internal auditors. "Although the hiring trends are not what they were during the mid-2000s," she says, "the employment outlook is still positive—especially when compared to the job availability of some other career fields. It is hoped that after the spectacular failures of many large corporations during the late-2000s, internal audit will be recognized for its value in assurance and consulting in the areas of risk management and effective governance, which may lead to further enhanced employment outlook." Veronica sees the field of internal audit becoming even stronger in the next five years, especially in the United States. "With government's focus on stimulating and ensuring a strong economy," she explains, "there will be a concerted effort to make companies and government agencies transparent and accountable. Internal auditing is positioned well to assist with oversight, project assessment, risk assessment, recommending improvements, and consulting activities. With the baby boomers leaving the job market for retirement, young people with the right skill sets will be sought after like never before."

"The internal audit job market has been generally very good for the last 25 years," says Glenn Sumners. "The major change in internal auditing will be a greater emphasis on governance, risks, and controls. The primary change in the skill sets will be the increased integration of technology. In order to add value, internal auditors will need to have good business knowledge as well as internal audit skills. The increased complexity of business and the rapid change in technology will impact the skills needed by future internal auditors."

# Administrative Support Workers

## SUMMARY

### Definition
Administrative support workers provide assistance to business managers and other professionals. Responsibilities range from receiving visitors and answering telephones to filing, typing, conducting research, and performing other clerical duties.

### Alternative Job Titles
Administrative assistants
Administrative clerks
Administrative professionals
Education secretaries
Executive administrative assistants
Executive assistants
Executive secretaries
File clerks
Information clerks
Legal secretaries
Office clerks
Personal secretaries
Receptionists
Secretaries
Secretaries
Technical secretaries

### Salary Range
$16,830 to $24,550 to $35,510+ (receptionists)
$18,440 to $29,050 to $62,290+ (secretaries)
$16,030 to $25,320 to $39,880+ (office clerks)

### Educational Requirements
High school diploma

### Certification or Licensing
None available (receptionists)
Voluntary (secretaries, office clerks)

### Employment Outlook
Faster than the average (receptionists)
About as fast as the average (secretaries, office clerks)

### High School Subjects
Business
Computer science
English

### Personal Interests
Business
Computers

"I am confident that the role I play in my organization is extremely valuable in that it is essentially the glue that bonds the administrative team to the leadership team," says Stephen Lutz, an executive assistant. "I thoroughly enjoy being an administrative professional. It is a very rewarding career choice."

## WHAT DOES AN ADMINISTRATIVE SUPPORT WORKER DO?

There are three main types of administrative support workers: receptionists, secretaries, and office clerks. The following paragraphs provide more information about these specialties.

*Receptionists*—so named because they receive visitors in places of business—have the important job of giving a business's clients and visitors a positive first impression. They greet customers, clients, patients, and salespeople, take their names, and determine the nature of their business and the person they wish to see. The receptionist then pages the requested person, directs the visitor to that person's office or location, or makes an appointment for a later visit. Receptionists often keep records of all visits by writing down the visitor's name, purpose of visit, person visited, and date and time.

Most receptionists answer the telephone at their place of employment; many operate switchboards or paging systems. These workers usually take and distribute messages for other employees and may receive and distribute mail. Receptionists may perform a variety of other clerical duties, including keying in and filing correspondence and other paperwork, proofreading, preparing travel vouchers, and preparing outgoing mail. In some businesses, receptionists are responsible for monitoring the attendance of other employees. In businesses where employees are frequently out of the office on assignments, receptionists may keep track of their whereabouts to ensure they receive important phone calls and messages. Many receptionists use computers and word processors to perform clerical duties.

Receptionists are partially responsible for maintaining office security, especially in large firms. They may require all visitors to sign in and out and carry visitors' passes during their stay. Since visitors may not enter most offices unescorted, receptionists usually accept and sign for packages and other deliveries.

Receptionists are frequently responsible for answering inquiries from the public about a business's nature and operations. To answer these questions efficiently and in a manner that conveys a favorable impression, a receptionist must be as knowledgeable as possible about the business's products, services, policies, and practices and familiar with the names and responsibilities of all other employees. They must be careful, however, not to divulge classified information such as business procedures or employee activities that a competing company might be able to use. This part of a receptionist's job is so important that some businesses call their receptionists *information clerks.*

*Secretaries* perform a variety of administrative and clerical duties. The goal of all their activities is to assist their employers in the execution of their work and to help their companies conduct business in an efficient and professional manner. Secretaries' work includes processing and transmitting information to the office staff and to other organizations. They operate office machines and arrange for their repair or servicing. These machines include computers, typewriters, dictating machines, photocopiers, switchboards, and fax machines. Secretaries also order office supplies and perform regular duties such as answering phones, sorting mail, managing files, taking dictation, and composing and keying in letters.

In many offices, secretaries make appointments for company executives and keep track of the office schedule. They make travel arrangements for the professional staff or for clients, and occasionally are asked to travel with staff members on business trips. Other secretaries might manage the office while their supervisors are away on vacation or business trips.

Secretaries take minutes at meetings, write up reports, and compose and type letters. They often will find their responsibilities growing as they learn the business. Some are responsible for finding speakers for conferences, planning receptions, and arranging public relations programs. Some write copy for brochures or articles before making the arrangements to have them printed, or they might use desktop publishing software to create the documents themselves. They greet clients and guide them to the proper offices, and they often supervise and train other staff members and newer secretaries, especially on how to use computer software programs.

Some secretaries perform very specialized work. *Legal secretaries* prepare legal papers including wills, mortgages, contracts, deeds, motions, complaints, and summonses. They work under the direct supervision of an attorney or paralegal. They assist with legal research by reviewing legal journals and organizing briefs for their employers. They must learn an entire specialized vocabulary that is used in legal papers and documents.

*Medical secretaries* take medical histories of patients; make appointments; prepare and send bills to patients, as well as track them and collect payments; process insurance billing; maintain medical files; and pursue correspondence with patients, hospitals, and associations.

They assist physicians or medical scientists with articles, reports, speeches, and conference proceedings. Some medical secretaries are responsible for ordering medical supplies. They, too, need to learn an entire specialized vocabulary of medical terms and be familiar with laboratory or hospital procedures.

*Technical secretaries* work for engineers and scientists preparing reports and papers that often include graphics and mathematical equations that are difficult to format on paper. The secretaries maintain a technical library and help with scientific papers by gathering and editing materials.

*Executive secretaries* provide support for top executives. They perform fewer clerical duties and more information management, according to the *Occupational Outlook Handbook*. Their duties include managing clerical staff; assessing memos, reports, and other documents in order to determine their importance for distribution; preparing meeting agendas; and conducting research and preparing reports.

*Social secretaries,* often called *personal secretaries,* arrange all of the social activities of their employers. They handle private as well as business social affairs, and may plan parties, send out invitations, or write speeches for their employers. Social secretaries are often hired by celebrities or high-level executives who have busy social calendars to maintain.

*Education secretaries* work in elementary or secondary schools or on college campuses. They take care of all clerical duties at the school. Their responsibilities may include preparing bulletins and reports for teachers, parents, or students, keeping track of budgets for school supplies or student activities, and maintaining the school's calendar of events. Depending on the position, they may work for school administrators, principals, or groups of teachers or professors. Other education secretaries work in administration offices, state education departments, or service departments.

*Office clerks* usually perform a variety of tasks as part of their overall job responsibility. They may type or file bills, statements, and business correspondence. They may stuff envelopes, answer telephones, respond to emails, and sort mail. Office clerks also enter data into computer databases, run errands, and operate office equipment such as photocopiers, fax machines, and switchboards. In the course of an average day, an office clerk usually performs a combination of these and other clerical tasks, spending an hour or so on one task and then moving on to another as directed by an office manager or other supervisor.

An office clerk may work with other office personnel, such as a bookkeeper or accountant, to maintain a company's financial records. The clerk may type and mail invoices and sort payments as they come in, keep payroll records, or take inventories. With more experience, the clerk may be asked to update customer files to reflect receipt of payments and verify records for accuracy.

Office clerks often deliver messages from one office worker to another, an especially important responsibility in larger companies. Clerks may relay questions and answers from one department head to another. Similarly, clerks may relay messages from people outside the company or employees who are outside of the office to those working in house. Office clerks may also work with other personnel on individual projects, such as preparing a yearly budget or making sure a mass mailing gets out on time.

*Administrative clerks* assist in the efficient operation of an office by compiling business records; providing information to sales personnel and customers; and preparing and sending out bills, policies, invoices, and other business correspondence. Administrative clerks may also keep financial records and prepare the payroll.

*File clerks* review and classify letters, documents, articles, and other information and then file this material so it can be quickly retrieved at a later time. They contribute to the smooth distribution of information at a company.

Most administrative support professionals work in pleasant offices with modern equipment. Office conditions vary widely, however. Most office workers work 35 to 40 hours a week. Very few administrative support professionals work on the weekends on a regular basis, although some may be asked to work overtime if a particular project demands it. The work is not physically strenuous or hazardous, although deadline pressure is a factor (for secretaries and office clerks) and sitting for long periods of time can be uncomfortable. Many hours spent in front of a computer can lead to eyestrain or repetitive-motion problems for secretaries and office clerks.

## WHAT IS IT LIKE TO BE AN ADMINISTRATIVE SUPPORT WORKER?

Jennifer Stoff is an executive administrative assistant and fleet manager who has worked in the secretarial/administrative field for the last 21 years. She is also the corresponding secretary for the Ohio Division of the International Association of Administrative Professionals. "Working in the administrative field is something I have always wanted to do," she says. "As a child, I was wide-eyed with curiosity as I watched my mother's fingers fly over the keys of her typewriter. That's all it took and I was hooked! I wanted to be just like my mother so I could type just as fast as or faster than she could."

Jennifer's scheduled work hours are from 8:00 A.M. to 5:00 P.M.; however, she says that she often works till at least 6:00 P.M. to complete tasks. "During certain times of the year when we have special projects, I will work many long days; however, I don't receive any overtime as I am on salary. I wear many interchangeable

## Keys Skills for Administrative Support Workers

Jennifer Stoff details the most important skills for administrative professionals:

The administrative profession has advanced over the last several years and continues to evolve at a rapid pace, requiring greater responsibility as well as adaptability.

You need to have strong technical skills in Microsoft Office applications and keep up with the current releases. Having some Web site software knowledge is also a plus with some companies. It is also critical to have experience conducting Internet research.

Soft skills are essential as we deal with varying types of personalities, so you need to know how to interact with these different individuals and maintain good rapport. Companies may choose to hire someone who has stronger soft skills than technical because they know that they can always teach the technical side. Another major factor that executives

look for is the ability to be entrusted with confidential information. So, I guess you could say that it is an extension of your soft skills pertaining to your dependability to the company and respective executive or department.

Many executives will present you with a rough idea of what they would like to convey to either a customer or to their employees, which means it is up to the administrative professional to be able to compose correspondence in the language and tone of that executive.

An administrative professional also needs experience with project management as we are being entrusted with more complex assignments.

You should have the desire to want to continue growing and adapting within your position as well as with the company's direction. Having the mind-set that the administrative profession is not just a job, but a career, plays a big part in the ability to have the drive to succeed.

hats throughout the day. I love it because my days are never the same and it works well for me because I by no means like to be bored. Sometimes I compare it to the character Gumby, being pulled in many directions.

"I provide diversified executive administrative support to the senior vice president (SVP) of our business unit as well as occasional support for his other SVP direct reports," Jennifer continues. "In addition, my other responsibilities on the executive administrative assistant side of my job include interacting with vice presidents and their controllers at 22 divisions throughout the U.S. (additional interaction with external builders, vendors, and other customers) as well as some executives in Canada; minute-taking at weekly SVP meetings; completing event and business meeting planning; email and calendar management for my executive with a second computer monitor on my desk; travel management for executives and other office staff including airline, hotel, and car rental without the utilization of a travel agent (until this past week, where we have just launched an online system connected to a travel agency); collecting and consolidating information for various weekly reports for distribution to senior management; creating presentations as requested for meetings and reporting purposes; maintaining and reconciling credit card account purchases and related expense reports monthly; fielding calls for my executive to ensure proper handling; and sorting mail according to type and priority while answering/composing correspondence for executives as requested."

As if all these tasks weren't enough, Jennifer also has fleet management responsibilities for a $25 million fleet in 22 divisions throughout the United States. "In this capacity," she explains, "I order vehicles to specifications as well as any additional upfitting needs, track manufacturing progress and applicable rebates, and order graphic decals for vehicles; manage the fuel card program for the fleet of 1,000+ vehicles; facilitate integration of the fleet from new acquisitions to incorporate into the company's processes; field regular questions or issues from divisions as well as run applicable reports related to their respective fleet; utilize online fleet management software systems from two separate fleet management companies; facilitate disposition of vehicles that have completed their leases; and communicate with fleet management companies, manufacturer, decal supplier, and upfit company to ensure that all processes are streamlined effectively and efficiently as well as assist in negotiations."

When asked to detail what she likes least about her job, Jennifer cites, "The little things, such as filing and having to make coffee and get lunches on occasion. What I like most are the challenges that I am presented with every day and the autonomy and trust to work through many situations."

Stephen Lutz is an executive assistant at Keswick Multi-Care Center, a provider of senior care in the Baltimore, Maryland, area. He has worked in the administrative professional arena for 13 years. He is also the president of a local chapter of the International Association of Administrative Professionals. "I decided to become an executive assistant because I eventually want to be a director or manager and, for a person to lead, he/she must first learn how to serve," Stephen says. "My hours are 9:00 A.M. to 5:00 P.M. The first thing I do when I arrive at work is ask the front desk security personnel if anything

## A Valuable Experience

Jennifer Stoff details the co-operative education experience that she participated in during high school:

During my junior and senior year at Fairmont High School in Kettering, Ohio, I participated in a co-op program entitled COE (Cooperative Office Education). I took a longer class in the morning with our COE instructor. During my senior year, our high school installed computers in our classroom. This was about the time that computers were beginning to have more prominence with WordPerfect and Lotus 123 applications, etc. We would practice our typing skills, striving to reduce errors, both on our typewriter and computer. We would also practice our 10-key punch on the calculators. We were taught some business practices to prepare us for the office environment. What I remember most was how intrigued I was with the computer. I would try to get all of my class work completed as quickly as possible so that I could spend the rest of my time working on the tutorials in WordPerfect (when they still had those included in the software) and it was fun! I remember learning so much about the program that I actually taught my instructor a few things that he had not yet learned at night school. Because of this, I felt like I could achieve great things in my field, learning along the way. That left an indelible mark with me.

In the other part of the COE program, during my senior year, we would attend school the first half of the day, and then we would go to work in an office the second half of the day. We had to go and interview with businesses that were accepting co-op students. I remember how hard I prepared for my interview. I'll never forget the English teacher who worked with me over the course of a few days and provided me with constructive criticism to show me what I was doing wrong in our mock interviews and how I could improve. She was wonderful! Because of her help, I truly believe this is why I got the job. She not only provided me with the correct methods of interviewing, but she instilled a spark of confidence in me each time we practiced.

After high school, I continued to work for the company I started with as a co-op. Over the next eight and one-half years I worked in a total of four different positions, with the last position being upgraded into another level, before I decided to change companies. To give you an idea of my progression, during my senior year I worked part time as an assistant to an administrative secretary. After my graduation, I began working full time as receptionist at the front desk in our building. After six months, I was promoted to clerk typist. After nine months I was promoted to take the administrative secretary position that I assisted as a co-op. A year and one-half later I was promoted to executive secretary. While in this position, consultants came in and evaluated the positions in the entire company. As a result, my position and title was upgraded to administrative support V.

is going on that administration should be aware of. The next thing I usually do is receive a call from the chief executive officer (CEO), and she usually asks for a morning update on anything that is going on in the building that she should be aware of. Next, I pull up Microsoft Outlook and look at the schedules for myself and the CEO and chief financial officer (CFO), and I look at the list of tasks to see if there is anything that is flagged that I need to address right away. From that point forward, I am usually involved with attending meetings, fielding questions from the leadership team, and working on tasks associated with my position as well as committees that I chair or serve on, including the employee activity committee, nursing home week committee, and United Way committee, among others.

"The most rewarding thing that has happened to me as an administrative professional," he continues, "is that I have been exposed to many CEOs and CFOs and have witnessed first-hand the various types of leadership styles and, most importantly, I have been a witness to which strategies work and which ones don't work. This will become extremely valuable as I climb the ladder."

## DO I HAVE WHAT IT TAKES TO BE AN ADMINISTRATIVE SUPPORT WORKER?

To be a good receptionist, you must be well groomed, have a pleasant voice, and be able to express yourself clearly. Because you may sometimes deal with demanding people, a smooth, patient disposition and good judgment are important. All recep-

tionists need to be courteous and tactful. A good memory for faces and names also proves very valuable.

Key qualities for all administrative support workers include an even temperament, strong communication skills, the ability to follow instructions, organizational ability, initiative, and the ability to work well with others. You should find systematic and detailed work appealing. Other personal qualifications include dependability, trustworthiness, and a neat personal appearance.

Stephen Lutz says that successful administrative professionals should "possess confidence without arrogance; be able to determine 'the right thing to do' in various workplace situations; be highly collaborative; be effective communicators as well as good listeners; be polished in terms of appearance and presentation skills; ensure that their spelling and grammar are always correct/appropriate; have a sense of humor; and be able to multitask without becoming overwhelmed or visibly disorganized."

## HOW DO I BECOME AN ADMINISTRATIVE SUPPORT WORKER?

### Education

#### High School

You will need at least a high school diploma to enter this field. To prepare for a career as an administrative support worker, take business, English, and speech classes. Keyboarding and computer science courses will also be helpful. "I took typing classes in high school," says

Stephen Lutz, "which enabled me to pass typing tests that landed me positions in this field. I have since earned my associate's of applied science and bachelor's of science degrees. You should also take computer science courses, as computers are used in nearly all offices.

## Postsecondary Training

Community colleges and vocational schools often offer business education courses that provide training for administrative support workers. Receptionists who want to advance at their companies should take courses in basic bookkeeping and principles of accounting. Secretaries and clerks need good office skills that include rapid and accurate keyboarding skills and good spelling and grammar. Some positions require typing a minimum number of words per minute, as well as shorthand ability. Knowledge of word processing, spreadsheet, and database management is important, and many employers require it. Many employers provide some on-the-job training as most administrative support work is typically entry level.

Professional associations also provide continuing education classes, workshops, and seminars that help administrative support professionals hone their skills and become candidates for advancement. Jennifer Stoff credits her membership in the International Association of Administrative Professionals (IAAP) with improving her professional skills and her relationship with her boss. "In the last six years of working for my executive, a remarkable transformation has occurred with regard to how he views me in my position," she says. "I credit my professional success in my career due to my membership and active involvement in the IAAP. Over the years, the IAAP and its Wings Chapter in Dayton, Ohio, have provided me with new skill sets and increased confidence in my abilities to allow me to take on new challenges and responsibilities as a career-minded administrative professional. My executive did not take me seriously when I began working for him, and particularly my involvement in IAAP. But because of my dedication and hunger to learn more in my field, and through my continuous involvement and growth in IAAP, his mind-set changed. He could see the transformation in my willingness and ability to take on new challenges. He now views IAAP as an asset to my professional growth and supports me in ways I never thought would have been possible. I didn't see the potential of earning the respect that I now have from my executive. Achieving that respect has been the most rewarding experience in my career thus far."

## Certification or Licensing

There is no certification available for receptionists.

The International Association of Administrative Professionals offers the following certification designations for administrative professionals: certified professional secretary and certified administrative professional. Secretaries with limited experience can become an accredited legal secretary by obtaining certification from the NALS . . . the association for legal professionals. Those with at least three years of experience in the legal field can be certified as a professional legal secretary from this same

## The Office of the Future

The staffing agency OfficeTeam recently released a research study that asked executives to opine about the future of the workplace in the next 10 to 15 years. Here are a few of its findings:

- 42 percent of executives believed that employees will work longer hours. Nine percent of respondents predicted that their employees would work fewer hours.

- 87 percent of executives believed that the number of workers who telecommute will increase. Workers will increasingly be able to do their jobs off-site with the help of miniature wireless devices, WiFi, WiMax, virtual environments, Web-based conferencing services, and mobile technology.

- 86 percent of executives predicted that workers would be required to be more in touch with the office while on vacation.

Source: Office of the Future: 2020, OfficeTeam

organization. Legal Secretaries International offers the certified legal secretary specialist designation in the following categories: business law, civil litigation, criminal law, intellectual property, probate, and real estate.

### Internships and Volunteerships

If you attend a college program, you will most likely be required to participate in an internship, which will introduce you to the basic skills required by administrative support professionals. Work-study programs will also provide you with an opportunity to work in a business setting to get a sense of the work performed by administrative support workers. Part-time or summer jobs as receptionists, secretaries, file clerks, and office clerks are often available in various offices. These jobs are the best indicators of future satisfaction in the administrative support field. You may find a part-time job if you are computer literate. Co-operative education programs arranged through schools and "temping" through an agency also are valuable ways to acquire experience. While in high school, Jennifer participated in a co-operative office education program that she credits with helping her land a job and develop her skills. See the sidebar on page 43 to learn more about Jennifer's co-op experience. In general, any job, internship, or volunteer opportunity that teaches basic office skills is helpful.

## WHO WILL HIRE ME?

According to the U.S. Department of Labor, nearly 1.1 million people are employed as receptionists; nearly 4.1 million people work as secretaries; and 2.9 million people are employed as office clerks. Administrative support professionals work in almost every type of industry.

While you are in high school, you may be able to learn of openings with local businesses through your school counselors or newspaper want ads. Local state employment offices frequently have information about positions for administrative support workers. You should also contact area businesses for which you would like to work; many available positions are not advertised in the paper because they are filled so quickly. Temporary-work agencies are a valuable resource for finding jobs, too, some of which may lead to permanent employment. Friends and relatives may also know of job openings.

## WHERE CAN I GO FROM HERE?

Advancement opportunities are limited for receptionists, especially in small offices. The more clerical skills and education workers have, the greater their chances for promotion to such better-paying jobs as secretary, administrative assistant, or bookkeeper. College or business school training can help receptionists advance to higher-level positions. Many companies provide training for their receptionists and other employees, helping workers gain skills for job advancement.

Secretaries often begin by assisting executive secretaries and work their way up by learning the way their business operates. Initial promotions from a secretarial position are usually to jobs such as secretarial supervisor, office manager, or administrative assistant. Depending on other personal qualifications, college courses in business, accounting, or marketing can help the ambitious secretary enter middle and upper management. Training in computer skills can also lead to advancement. Secretaries who become proficient in word processing, for instance, can get jobs as instructors or as sales representatives for software manufacturers. Many legal secretaries, with additional training and schooling, become paralegals. Secretaries in the medical field can advance into the fields of radiological and surgical records or medical transcription.

Office clerks usually begin their employment performing more routine tasks such as delivering messages and sorting and filing mail. With experience, they may advance to more complicated assignments and assume a greater responsibility for the entire project to be completed. Those who demonstrate the desire and ability may move to other clerical positions, such as secretary or receptionist. Clerks with good leadership skills may become group managers or supervisors. To be promoted to a professional occupation such as accountant, a college degree or other specialized training is usually necessary. The high turnover rate that exists among office clerks increases promotional opportunities. The number and kind of opportunities, however, usually depend on the place of employment and the ability, education, and experience of the employee.

## WHAT ARE THE SALARY RANGES?

Earnings for administrative support workers vary widely with the education and experience of the worker and type, size, and geographic location of the business.

In 2008 the median salary for receptionists was $24,550, according to the U.S. Department of Labor (DoL). The lowest paid 10 percent of these workers made less than $16,830 annually, while the highest paid 10 percent earned more than $35,510 per year.

Secretaries (except legal, medical, and executive) earned an average of $29,050 annually in 2008, according to the DoL. Salaries for these workers ranged from less than $18,440 to a high of more than $43,240. The DoL reports the following salaries ranges for secretaries by specialty: executive, $27,030 to $62,070; legal, $25,580 to $62,290; and medical, $20,870 to $42,660. Secretaries, especially those working in the legal profession, earn considerably more if certified.

According to the DoL, the median salary for full-time office clerks was $25,320 in 2008. The lowest paid 10 percent earned less than $16,030, while the highest paid group earned more than $39,880.

Administrative support workers are usually eligible for paid holidays and vacations, sick leave, medical and life insurance coverage, and a retirement plan of some kind.

## WHAT IS THE JOB OUTLOOK?

Employment for receptionists is expected to grow faster than the average for all careers through 2016, according to the *Occupational Outlook Handbook.* Growth in jobs for receptionists is expected to be greater than for other clerical positions because automation will have little effect on the receptionist's largely interpersonal duties and because of an anticipated growth in the number of businesses providing services. In addition, more and more businesses know how a receptionist can convey a positive public image. Opportunities should be especially good in physician's offices, law firms, temporary help agencies, and management and technical consulting firms.

The U.S. Department of Labor predicts that employment for secretaries who specialize in the medical field or who work as executive secretaries will grow faster than the average for all careers through 2016.

Employment for legal secretaries and general secretaries is expected to grow about as fast as the average through 2016. Computers, fax machines, email, copy machines, and scanners are some technological advancements that have greatly improved the work productivity of secretaries. Company downsizing and restructuring, in some cases, have redistributed traditional secretarial duties to other employees. There has been a growing trend in assigning one secretary to assist two or more managers, adding to this field's decline. Though more professionals are using personal computers for their correspondence, some administrative duties will still need to be handled by secretaries. The personal aspects of the job and responsibilities such as making travel arrangements, scheduling conferences, and transmitting staff instructions have not changed.

Many employers currently complain of a shortage of capable secretaries. Those with skills and experience will have the best chances for employment. Specialized secretaries should attain certification in their field to stay competitive. Industries such as professional, scientific, and technical services; health care and social services; and administrative and support services will create the most new job opportunities.

Although employment of clerks is expected to grow only about as fast as the average through 2016, there will still be many jobs available due to the large size of this field and a high turnover rate. With the increased use of data processing equipment and other types of automated office machinery, more and more employers are hiring people proficient in a variety of office tasks. According to OfficeTeam, the following industries show the strongest demand for qualified administrative staff: technology, financial services, construction, and manufacturing.

Opportunities will be best for workers with excellent computer skills, familiarity with machinery, strong communication skills, and the ability to perform many tasks at once. Temporary and part-time work opportunities should also increase, especially during busy business periods.

# Business Managers

## SUMMARY

**Definition**
Business managers plan, organize, direct, and coordinate the operations of companies. They may manage a specific department within a company, a geographical territory of a company's operations, or an entire company.

**Alternative Job Titles**
Business executives

**Salary Range**
$68,680 to $120,000 to $185,750+

**Educational Requirements**
Bachelor's degree

**Certification or Licensing**
Voluntary

**Employment Outlook**
Little or no change

**High School Subjects**
Business
Computer science
Economics

**Personal Interests**
Business
Business management
Economics
Selling/making a deal
Travel

"The most rewarding part of my job is having the ability to make other people's lives better," says Ben Mulling, chief financial officer (CFO) of Tente Casters Inc. "As a CFO, I get to make decisions that affect other's lives. High-level analysis and strategy development allows us to make knowledgeable decisions for the direction of the company. This in turn allows the company to be more efficient and profitable, which flows down to the employees and their attitude toward the organization. Employees are harder working and happier when they know that management cares for them and the direction of the company, and that management knows how to properly do their job. They put a lot of confidence in us to steer the ship in the right direction, and that is the ultimate compliment."

## WHAT DOES A BUSINESS MANAGER DO?

Managers work in every industry, including banking, education, food, clothing, technology, manufacturing, health care, and business services. All types of businesses have managers to develop policies and administer the firm's operations. Managers may oversee the operations of an entire company, a geographical territory of a company's operations, or a specific department, such as sales and marketing or human resources.

*Business managers* direct a company's or a department's daily activities within the context of the organization's overall plan. They implement organizational goals and policies. This may involve analyzing the department's budgetary requirements, developing sales or promotional materials, and hiring, training, and supervising staff. Business managers are often responsible for long-range planning for their company or department. This involves setting goals for the organization and developing a workable plan for meeting those goals.

A manager responsible for a single department might work to coordinate his or her department's activities with other departments. A manager responsible for an entire company or organization might work with the managers of various departments or locations to oversee and coordinate the activities of all departments. If the business is privately owned, the owner may be the manager. In a large corporation, however, there will be a management structure above the business manager.

The hierarchy of managers includes top executives, such as the *president,* who establishes an organization's goals and policies along with others, such as the chief executive officer, chief financial officer, chief information officer, executive vice president, and the board of directors. Top executives plan business objectives and develop policies to coordinate operations between divisions and departments and establish procedures for attaining objectives. Activity reports and financial statements are reviewed to determine

## To Be a Successful Business Manager, You Should...

- have good communication and interpersonal skills
- be able to think effectively on your feet
- have leadership abilities and be able to inspire others to follow you
- be able to solve problems
- be highly organized
- be decisive
- be willing to continue to learn throughout your career

progress and revise operations as needed. The president also directs and formulates funding for new and existing programs within the organization. Public relations plays a big part in the lives of executives as they deal with executives and leaders from other countries or organizations, and with customers, employees, and various special interest groups.

Some companies have an *executive vice president,* who directs and coordinates the activities of one or more departments, depending on the size of the organization. In very large organizations, the duties of executive vice presidents may be highly specialized. For example, they may oversee the activities of business managers of marketing, sales promotion, purchasing, finance, personnel training, industrial relations, administrative services, data processing, property management, transportation, or legal services. In smaller organizations, an executive vice president might be responsible for a number of these departments. Executive vice presidents also assist the chief executive officer in formulating and administering the organization's policies and developing its long-range goals. Executive vice presidents may serve as members of management committees on special studies.

Companies may also have a *chief financial officer* (CFO). In small firms, the CFO is usually responsible for all financial management tasks, such as budgeting, capital expenditure planning, cash flow, and various financial reviews and reports. In larger companies, the CFO may oversee financial management departments, to help other managers develop financial and economic policy and oversee the implementation of these policies.

*Chief information officers,* or CIOs, are responsible for all aspects of their company's information technology. They use their knowledge of technology and business to determine how information technology can best be used to meet company goals. This may include researching, purchasing, and overseeing the set up and use of technology systems, such as Intranet, Internet, and computer networks. These managers sometimes take a role in implementing a company's Web site.

In companies that have several different locations, managers may be assigned to oversee specific geographic areas. For example, a large retailer with facilities all across the nation is likely to have a number of managers in charge of various territories. There might be a Midwest manager, a Southwest manager, a Southeast manager, a Northeast manager, and a Northwest manager. These managers are often called *regional* or *area managers.* Some companies break their management territories up into even smaller sections, such as a single state or a part of a state. Managers overseeing these smaller segments are often called *district managers,* and typically report directly to an area or regional manager.

In today's business world, many companies that first began as brick-and-mortar businesses now have a presence on the Internet. Additionally, many new companies, known as dot-coms, are found only on the Internet. At both types of companies, *Internet executives* are the professionals who devise ways to meet their companies' objectives—making sales, providing services, streamlining the purchasing process, or developing a customer base, for example—as they relate to the Internet. *Management information systems directors* oversee computer and information systems for an entire company. They often report to the chief information officer. They may manage an organization's employee help desk, recommend hardware and software upgrades, and ensure the security and availability of information technology services. *Chief technology officers* evaluate and recommend new technologies that will help their organization reduce costs and increase revenue. They often report to the chief information officer. *Internet store managers and entrepreneurs* sell products or services on the

# Business Professional Profile: Len Deneault

Len Deneault is a quality expert, college educator, and a past examiner for the national Malcolm Baldrige Award, an award given by the federal government to businesses that are judged to be outstanding in seven areas: customer and market focus; leadership; measurement, analysis, and knowledge management; process management; strategic planning; results; and workforce focus. He is also the executive director of MassExcellence, a state Baldrige program. Len discussed his career and The Malcolm Baldrige Quality Program and related programs with the editors of *What Can I Do Now? Business and Finance.*

**Q. Why did you decide to pursue a career in business?**

**A.** I instantly realized I was behind the times when my five-year-old son would tell my wife and me all that he knew about using the computer at his nursery school. I had no idea what he was talking about. He was excited, but I felt like I was losing pace with the world. I wanted to stay current and learn about these new things. In addition, I was striving for a leadership position, so I saw that a business curriculum and career provided everything I wanted. I was about 30 years old and a police officer at the time. All my education and work experience was geared for that role. Time for a change.

**Q. Can you tell us a little about your professional background and interests?**

**A.** Leaving law enforcement, I was hired at a local high-tech company. During the next 12 years, I finished a bache-

lor's degree in business, an MBA, and a master's degree in quality. Prior to starting the MBA, I interviewed with Dr. Michael Quigley, the dean of the graduate school at Rivier College and he recommended their quality in leadership program. He was an associate of Dr. W. Edwards Deming, the guru of quality who, after World War II, turned the Japanese economy around—bringing it from war-torn destruction to the global player it is today. A couple of these classes really had an impact on me. I continued my education at Anna Maria College with a MS that focused on the quality tools, including the International Organization for Standardization (ISO) and the Baldrige Program. Both of these interested me—the tools were a good fit to the quality in leadership concepts.

During the master's program, I met an examiner for the Malcolm Baldrige National Quality Program. The Baldrige Criteria is a business framework used by world-class companies seeking performance excellence. He recommended I look into participating in its state program, which I did, and continued for the next 10 years. I became an examiner, then training faculty member, and chaired the board of state examiners for several years. I was also accepted for seven separate terms as a national Baldrige examiner.

My work with the state and national Baldrige programs was actually in addition to my regular job, which was department manager for the quality,

*(continued on next page)*

*(continued from previous page)*

purchasing, transportation, and facilities departments in a large nonprofit agency. Using the Baldrige Criteria as our guide for our departments, my staff and I saved more than a half-million dollars within just a few years from reducing waste in our systems—without loss of services. I am proud of two other key accomplishments, one is that none of my employees ever left or retired during my tenure there. They were very valuable [employees] and were treated as such. Second, while working for the CFO, I promised him that I would ultimately work myself out of my position—and I did. When it was time to move on, my position was no longer needed. And I know for the next few years they didn't hire a replacement. I moved on by starting my own business called The NorthEast Center for Excellence, a consulting consortium, with a specialty in Baldrige-based consulting. I had always done this for free, but now it was time to make a go of it.

Although I still do consulting, I was recently hired as the executive director for MassExcellence, a state Baldrige program. Now I work with companies that want to use the Baldrige Criteria, and want the assessment and training to get feedback to improve their companies. It's a blast to work with people who actually want to improve their companies, and are real and genuinely committed to doing the best for their employees, including keeping them employed.

For several years now, I've added the role of adjunct professor for several schools, including Rivier College in Nashua, New Hampshire, and

Bentley University in Waltham, Massachusetts, both at which I am still active. I teach courses in graduate and undergraduate programs such as General Business, Strategic Planning, Project Management, and of course, Quality, Baldrige-related courses, and Operations Management. It's a lot of work, but I learn a lot as well. It really engages you when you see the light bulbs come on!

**Q. Can you tell us a little about the NorthEast Center for Excellence, MassExcellence, and the Malcolm Baldrige Quality Program?**

**A.** The Malcolm Baldrige Quality Program (http://www.quality.nist.gov/Founda tion.htm and http://www.nist.gov/ public_affairs/factsheet/baldfaqs. htm) is a private-public partnership between the Department of Commerce, National Institute of Standards and Technology, and The Foundation for the Malcolm Baldrige National Quality Award, which was created to provide the private sector a means of accomplishing award program objectives. Congress established the award program in 1987 to recognize U.S. organizations for their achievements in quality and performance and to raise awareness about the importance of quality and performance excellence as a competitive edge. The award is given by the president of the United States to businesses— manufacturing and service, small and large—and to education, health care, and nonprofit organizations that apply and are judged to be outstanding in seven areas: customer and market focus; leadership; measurement, analysis, and knowledge management; process management; strategic planning;

results; and workforce focus. Being a member of the board of examiners is a volunteer position, and you are essentially doing a service to your country.

MassExcellence (http://www.mas sexcellence.com) is the statewide Baldrige-based education and award program modeled on the national Baldrige Program. We are not a government entity; we are a 501(c)(3) private nonprofit. There are several key differences between us. We try to utilize all interested business professionals to participate as examiners. We call it "Professional Development through the Examiner Experience." It has been compared to a mini-accelerated MBA program. The Baldrige Program has selective examiner acceptance criteria and many who apply are not accepted to the board of examiners.

Another key difference is that Mass-Excellence guarantees a site visit to all applicants—the national Baldrige program doesn't. We are here to help "work the bugs" out for companies for far less expense than the national program. Every applicant, regardless of award level, gets a feedback report.

A third difference is that we aren't just about the award. We often become key partners after the award process to help continue to educate and guide in the significance of the Baldrige Core Values and Criteria as key to their attaining and maintaining long-term success, economic sustainability, and competitive advantage.

Our program has very high standards. Like myself, all of our faculty and coaches are past or present senior/alumni national Baldrige examiners or judges. We have more Baldrige expertise connected with our program than in all of New England combined.

All our award examiner teams are assigned one of our coaches—which also enhances the quality of our team feedback. We are the experts. I co-authored the first nonprofit national examiner case study used to train examiners nationally and for the state programs.

The NorthEast Center for Excellence (http://www.necenter.org) is my five-year-old Baldrige consulting company. Simply put, I specialize in guiding companies in all things Baldrige—strategy, leadership, process management, human resource development, knowledge transfer, and so on. I have several Baldrige-trained colleagues I call on for any additional assistance. I also write or review applications for state and national Baldrige Award programs, do individual assessments, create or interpret feedback reports, and assist in setting any action plans to address priorities.

Q. **What is one of the most interesting or rewarding things that has happened to you while working in the field?**

A. I would have to say that having participated in national Baldrige site visits to world-class organizations is the ultimate. The view from the mountaintop is wonderful and these companies are about as close as you can get. Senior leaders in these companies are genuinely interested in their people and their success. You want to work for someone like that. It's infectious. They are true leaders, and you can see why people follow them anywhere without hesitation. It's a big difference from those self-appointed "leaders"

*(continued on next page)*

*(continued from previous page)*

we won't even follow across the street. People want to come to work—they feel valued and that they are making a difference. They each have a personal connection to the business. It is an honor and very rewarding to provide feedback to these top-notch organizations.

**Q. What are the most important personal and professional qualities for business professionals?**

**A.**

- Be a continuous learner. Experiencing different things will expand your horizons unbelievably, and make you a far more valuable and knowledgeable employee.

- Be cooperative, not competitive. It's not about you. If it's not a win-win, then let them win. It's a way to build those genuine, honest, and trusting relationships.

- Be flexible. It might be your competitive advantage. If you find yourself working in the company from hell, learn from it while you are there. You'll get a lot of insight from working in a "case study of what not to do."

- Become a leader. Sitting back and watching gets you nowhere, like those people who holler at the TV. There is a lot of complaining, but no one does anything, and nothing ever changes. Don't be afraid to speak up, and when you do so, bring your facts and your offer to become part of the process. Start things and finish them, all the while building influence and relationships. Be a role model for others.

---

Internet. They may research the marketability of a product or service, decide on what product or service to sell, organize their business, and set up their storefront on the Web. Internet entrepreneurs run their own businesses. *Internet store managers* are employed by Internet entrepreneurs and stores.

Business managers usually work in comfortable offices near the departments they direct, although managers may have to work in cubicles. Top executives may have spacious, lavish offices and may enjoy such privileges as the use of company cars, executive dining rooms, country club memberships, and liberal expense accounts.

Managers often travel between local, regional, and national offices. Top executives may travel to meet with executives in other corporations, both within the United States and abroad. Meetings and conferences sponsored by industries and associations occur regularly and provide invaluable opportunities to meet with peers and keep up with the latest developments. In large corporations, job transfers between the parent company and its local offices or subsidiaries are common.

Business managers often work long hours under intense pressure to meet, for example, production and marketing goals. Some executives spend up to 80 hours working each week. These long hours limit time available for family and leisure activities.

## WHAT IS IT LIKE TO BE A BUSINESS MANAGER?

Ben Mulling is an accountant and the chief financial officer (CFO) of Tente Casters Inc. in Hebron, Kentucky. He was hired as the controller at Tente in 2006 and promoted to CFO in January 2008. "Tente Casters is a global manufacturer of casters," Ben explains. "Our parent company is based in Germany. The company was started in 1923, and is now located in more than 20 different countries. Tente US was started in 1979, and we specialize in casters for the medical industry, including hospital beds and other medical carts and containers. Our European sisters offer a much broader spectrum of caster types, including heavy duty and industrial as well as medical."

Ben says that he spends the first hour or so of his day on his company's business intelligence dashboard reviewing the operational results of the prior day from cash flow activities, production, sales, and orders. "I then usually follow up with supervisors if any problems or concerns arise from my analysis. Following that I usually begin going through my in-box and sign any processed checks, manual journal entries, credit hold releases, or other documents (including customer/vendor agreements)." Ben usually spends about an hour with the president of his company each day discussing financial/sales developments, strategy directions, and forecast scenarios. "We stay in close contact," he says, "and I try to keep him informed regarding all the business developments and possible scenarios that we could face in the upcoming months. I usually have a meeting or two through-out the day as well. The remaining parts of my day are spent working on various projects and analysis. Constant analysis is the key to keeping up with the direction of the business and having multiple scenarios on hand should some of these various scenarios play out.

"In addition to the accounting department," Ben continues, "I am also in charge of the human resources and information technology departments. So I spend time each day working on various issues with each of these managers. In addition to making sure these departments run smoothly, I am ultimately in charge of the financial well-being of the company. This includes a wide array of items, including various financial analyses and working with the president and other key management team members on the strategy development of the organization. A typical workweek for me involves around 50 hours or so."

## DO I HAVE WHAT IT TAKES TO BE A BUSINESS MANAGER?

There are a number of personal characteristics that help one be a successful business manager, depending upon the specific responsibilities of the position. A manager who oversees other employees should have good communication and interpersonal skills. The ability to delegate work is another important personality trait of a good manager. The ability to think on your feet is often key in business management. A certain degree of organization is important, since managers often manage several different things simultaneously. Other traits considered important for top executives are intelligence, decisiveness, intuition, creativity, honesty, loyalty, and a sense of responsibility. Finally, the successful manager should be flexible and interested in staying abreast of new developments in his or her industry.

"The most important personal quality for a business manager is having the ability not only to lead others, but for those people to want to follow you," says Ben Mulling. "Many managers today call themselves leaders, but if nobody is following you, are you really a leader? This also flows into professional qualities as well. You must be respected by your peers and subordinates. Respected, not feared. Many managers get those two confused. Respect is usually initially given as a result of position, knowledge, and/or skill (work history and education). It is kept by being a leader who people want to follow."

# HOW DO I BECOME A BUSINESS MANAGER?

## Education

### High School

Business managers have a wide variety of responsibilities and skill sets; as a result, they have a wide range of educational backgrounds. Many have a bachelor's degree in liberal arts or business administration. Others have degrees in accounting or science or engineering. If you are interested in becoming a business manager, you should start preparing in high school by taking college preparatory classes. Your best bet academically is to get a well-rounded education. Because communication is important, take as many English and speech classes as possible. Courses in business, mathematics, and computer science are also excellent choices to help you prepare for careers in business management. Finally, take a foreign language. As U.S. businesses continue to expand their operations across the globe, workers who are fluent in one or more foreign languages will have excellent employment prospects.

## Postsecondary Training

Business managers often have a college degree in a subject that pertains to the department they direct or the organization they administer; for example, accounting or economics for a business manager of finance, computer science for a business manager of data processing, engineering or science for a director of research and development. As computers continue to help businesses do more with less, many managers are expected to have experience with the information technology that applies to their field.

Many business managers have graduate and professional degrees. Many managers in administrative, marketing, financial, and manufacturing activities have a master's degree in business administration. Managers in highly technical manufacturing and research activities often have a master's degree or doctorate in a technical or scientific discipline. A law degree is mandatory for business managers of corporate legal departments, and hospital managers generally have a master's degree in health services administration or business administration. In some industries, such as retail trade or the food and beverage industry, competent individuals without a college degree may become business managers.

## Certification or Licensing

Some business managers with backgrounds in accounting earn various certifications. For example, those who have earned a bachelor's degree, pass a four-part examination, agree to meet continuing education requirements, and have at least two years of experience in management accounting may become a certified management accountant through the Institute of Management Accounting. Contact the institute for more information. Ben Mulling has several certifications, including the certified public accountant, certified information technology professional, and certified management accountant designations.

## Internships and Volunteerships

Many business schools require that their students participate in an internship. Internships provide students with hands-on work experience, the opportunity to network, and the chance to explore career options and employment settings. Schools are usually instrumental in locating internships, but placing cold calls or writing query letters to companies you have already carefully researched can also be an effective way of locating a quality internship. Internships required by the school are usually non-paying; students are often compensated in the form of credit toward semester hours.

---

## Best Undergraduate Business Schools, 2009

1. University of Virginia (McIntire School of Commerce, http://www.commerce.virginia.edu/index_flash.html)
2. University of Notre Dame (Mendoza College of Business, http://www.nd.edu/~cba/011221)
3. University of Pennsylvania (The Wharton School, http://www.wharton.upenn.edu)
4. University of Michigan (Ross School of Business, http://www.bus.umich.edu)
5. Brigham Young University (Marriott School, http://marriottschool.byu.edu)
6. University of California—Berkeley (Haas School of Business, http://www.haas.berkeley.edu)
7. Massachusetts Institute of Technology (Sloan School of Management, http://mitsloan.mit.edu)
8. Cornell University (http://www.cornell.edu)
9. Emory University (Goizueta Business School, http://www.goizueta.emory.edu/degree)
10. University of Texas—Austin (McCombs School of Business, http://www.mccombs.utexas.edu)

To create the list, *BusinessWeek* used a "methodology that included nine measures of student satisfaction, post-graduation outcomes, and academic quality." Visit http://www.businessweek.com/ss/09/02/0226_best_undergrad_bschools/index.htm for more information.

Source: BusinessWeek

If you are unable to land an internship, a volunteer opportunity is one of your next best options. As a high school or college student, there are countless businesses near you that might need help conducting research, filing documents, composing basic memos or reports, and completing a variety of other clerical tasks. While you won't be able to get experience managing employees, you will get the opportunity to interact with managers and see how businesses operate.

## WHO WILL HIRE ME?

There are approximately two million general and operations managers and executives employed in the United States. They work in every industry. However, approximately 75 percent work in service industries.

Virtually every business in the United States has some form of managerial positions. Obviously, the larger the company is, the more managerial positions it is likely to have. Another factor is the geographical territory covered by the business. It is safe to say that companies doing business in larger geographical territories are likely to have more managerial positions than those with smaller territories.

Generally you will need a college degree, although many retail stores, grocery stores, and restaurants hire promising applicants who have only a high school diploma. Job seekers usually apply directly to the manager of such places. Your college career services office is often the best place to start looking for these positions. A number of listings can also be found in newspaper help wanted ads or online.

Many organizations have management trainee programs that college graduates can enter. Such programs are advertised at college career fairs or through college job placement services. Often, however, these management trainee positions in business and government are filled by employees who are already working for the organization and who demonstrate management potential.

## WHERE CAN I GO FROM HERE?

Most business management and top executive positions are filled by experienced lower-level managers and executives who display valuable managerial traits, such as leadership, self-confidence, creativity, motivation, decisiveness, and flexibility. At smaller firms, advancement to higher positions may come slowly, while promotions may occur more quickly at larger firms.

Advancement may be accelerated by participating in different kinds of educational programs available for managers. These are often paid for by the organization. Company training programs broaden knowledge of company policy and operations. Training programs sponsored by industry and trade associations and continuing education courses in colleges and universities can familiarize managers with the latest developments in management techniques. In recent years, large numbers of middle managers have been laid off as companies streamlined operations. Competition for jobs is keen, and business managers committed to improving their knowledge of the field and of related disciplines—especially computer information systems—will have the best opportunities for advancement.

Business managers may advance to executive or administrative vice president. Vice presidents may advance to peak corporate positions—president or chief executive officer. Presidents and chief executive officers, upon retirement, may become members of the board of directors of one or more firms. Sometimes business managers establish their own firms.

## WHAT ARE THE SALARY RANGES?

Salaries for business managers vary substantially, depending upon the level of responsibility, length of service, and type, size, and location of the organization. Top managers in large firms can earn much more than their counterparts in small firms. Also, business managers who work in large metropolitan areas, such as New York City, earn higher salaries than those who are employed in smaller cities.

General and operations managers had a median yearly income of $91,570 in 2008, according to the U.S. Department of Labor. To show the range of earnings for general and operations managers, however, the department notes that those in the computer and peripheral equipment manufacturing industry had an annual mean of $150,710; those in management, scientific, and technical consulting ser-

vices, $142,310; and those employed in local government, $87,720.

Chief executives earned a mean salary of $158,560 annually in 2008, according to the U.S. Department of Labor. Ten percent of chief executives earned less than $68,680. And again, salaries varied by industry. For example, the mean yearly salary for those involved in the management of companies and enterprises was $185,750, while those employed by depository credit intermediation companies earned a mean of $163,050. The business publication *The NonProfit Times,* which conducts periodic salary surveys, reports the average earnings for CEOs and executive directors at nonprofit social services and welfare organizations were approximately $100,118 in 2006. Some executives, however, earn hundreds of thousands of dollars more than this annually.

Benefit and compensation packages for business managers and executives are usually excellent, and may even include such things as bonuses, stock awards, company-paid insurance premiums, use of company cars, paid country club memberships, expense accounts, and generous retirement benefits.

## WHAT IS THE JOB OUTLOOK?

Overall, employment of business managers and executives is expected to experience little or no grow through 2016, according to the U.S. Department of Labor. Many job openings will be the result of managers being promoted to better positions, retiring, or leaving their positions to start their own businesses. Even so, the compensation and prestige of these positions make them highly sought-after, and competition to fill openings will be intense.

Projected employment growth varies by industry. For example, employment in the professional, scientific, and technical services industry should increase faster than the average, while employment in some manufacturing industries is expected to decline. Job opportunities in administrative and support services are expected to grow about as fast as the average.

The outlook for business managers is closely tied to the overall economy. When the economy is strong, businesses expand both in terms of their output and the number of people they employ, which creates a need for more managers. In economic downturns, businesses often lay off employees and cut back on production, which reduces the need for managers.

Business managers who have knowledge of one or more foreign languages (such as Spanish or Mandarin) and experience in marketing, international economics, and information systems will have the best employment opportunities.

# Business Teachers

## SUMMARY

### Definition
Business teachers instruct students about business principles and theories. They may teach specialties such as accounting, business management, economics, business communications, business mathematics, electronic commerce, international business, finance, labor relations and personnel management, marketing, and human resources.

### Alternative Job Titles
Business educators

### Salary Range
$34,020 to $50,000 to $80,970+ (middle and secondary school teachers)
$32,880 to $68,000 to $133,930+ (college professors)

### Educational Requirements
Bachelor's degree (middle and secondary school teachers)
Master's degree; doctorate required for top positions (college professors)

### Certification or Licensing
Required by all states (middle and secondary school teachers)
None available (college professors)

### Employment Outlook
About as fast as the average (middle school teachers)
More slowly than the average (secondary school teachers)
Much faster than the average (college professors)

### High School Subjects
Business
English
Speech

### Personal Interests
Business
Economics
Reading/books
Teaching

"The best part of teaching is the students," says Mary Flesberg, a high school business teacher. "It is wonderful to watch them grow into adulthood from grades nine through 12. Their entire lives lie before them and they are literally planning their futures. Since there are so many opportunities for different courses in the area of business I teach eight courses and there are some students that I have seven or eight times [during the course of their high school careers]. What is most rewarding is when former students come back to let me know what is happening in their lives and when they thank me for preparing them for their careers."

## To Be a Successful Business Teacher, You Should...

- be patient
- be self-disciplined
- be a good listener
- have confidence
- have excellent communication skills
- have leadership abilities
- have comprehensive knowledge of your business specialty
- have some experience in the business world
- enjoy interacting with and teaching students
- be willing to spend many hours preparing for class and grading tests and assignments
- be willing to continue to learn throughout your career

## WHAT DOES A BUSINESS TEACHER DO?

Middle and high school business teachers begin their day early in the morning. Before class, they respond to mail, email, or telephone messages; organize their teaching material; and meet with students who have questions about material taught in recent classes. They might also meet with fellow faculty or department heads to discuss course work, testing, or other issues.

Once in class, business teachers use a variety of teaching methods to convey information to their students. They spend a great deal of time lecturing, but they also facilitate student discussion and develop projects and activities to interest the students in the subject. They show films and DVDs, use computers and the Internet, and bring in guest speakers. They assign essays, presentations, and other projects. Each individual subject calls upon particular approaches, and may involve computer labs, role-playing exercises, and field trips.

Outside of the classroom, middle and high school business teachers prepare lectures, lesson plans, and exams. They evaluate student work and calculate grades. In the process of planning their class, business teachers read textbooks and workbooks to determine reading assignments; photocopy notes, articles, and other handouts; and develop grading policies. They also continue to study alternative and traditional teaching methods to hone their skills. They prepare students for special events and conferences and submit student work to competitions. Some business teachers also have the opportunity for extracurricular work as athletic coaches or business club advisors.

College business professors teach at junior colleges or at four-year colleges and universities. At four-year institutions, most faculty members are assistant professors, associate professors, or full professors. These three types of professorships differ in regards to status, job responsibilities, and salary.

College business professors' most important responsibility is to teach students. Their role within a college department will determine the level of courses they teach and the number of courses per semester. Most professors work with students at all levels, from college freshmen to graduate students. They may head several classes a semester or only a few a year. Some of their classes will have large enrollment, while graduate seminars may consist of only 12 or fewer students.

Though college business professors may spend fewer than 16 hours a week in the actual classroom, they spend many hours preparing lectures and lesson plans, grading papers and exams, and preparing grade reports. They also schedule office hours during the week to be available to students outside of the lecture hall, and they meet with students individually throughout the semester. In the classroom, professors lecture, lead discussions, administer exams, and assign textbook reading and other research.

In addition to teaching, most business professors conduct research and write publications. Professors publish their research findings in various scholarly journals. They also write books based on their research or on their own knowledge and experience in the field. Publishing a significant amount of work has been the traditional standard by which assistant professors prove themselves worthy of becoming permanent, tenured faculty.

Most teachers are contracted to work 10 months out of the year, with a two-month vacation during the summer. During their summer break, many continue their education to renew or upgrade their teaching licenses and earn higher salaries. Teachers in schools that operate year-round work eight-week sessions with one-week breaks in between and a five-week vacation in the winter.

Business teachers work in generally pleasant conditions, although some older schools may have poor heating or electrical systems. The work can seem confining, requiring them to remain in the classroom throughout most of the day.

Middle and high school hours are generally 7:00 or 8:00 A.M. to 3:00 P.M., but business teachers work more than 40 hours a week teaching, preparing for classes, grading papers, and directing extracurricular activities. Similarly, most college business teachers work more than 40 hours each week. Although they may teach only two or three classes a semester, they spend many hours preparing for lectures, examining student work, and conducting research.

## WHAT IS IT LIKE TO BE A BUSINESS TEACHER?

Mary Flesberg is a business teacher at Moorhead High School in Moorhead, Minnesota. She is also the president of Minnesota Business Educators (http://www.mbei-online.org), a professional organization that is comprised of secondary and postsecondary business education teachers and any person working in or interested in business education. She has worked at Moorhead High School her entire career, which began in 1982. "I always wanted to be a teacher," Mary says, "and I especially enjoy the field of business because it changes all the time.

## Mean Annual Earnings for College Business Teachers by Industry Sector, 2008

Colleges, universities, and professional schools: $83,370

Junior colleges: $65,030

Business schools and computer and management training: $57,820

Technical and trade schools: $54,720

Source: U.S. Department of Labor

Because of the ever-changing nature of all areas of business it takes more work and constant preparation than other subject areas—but the good news is that it never gets boring. I can turn on any news network and within five minutes get news for any of my classes such as law, management, entrepreneurship, finance, and technology."

Mary begins a typical workday around 7:00 A.M. by attending a planning meeting at her school. "Most school meetings are scheduled before school to keep the after-school hours free for those who coach," she explains. "Then I check my mail and email. Students arrive and classes begin. Our school is on the block schedule so we run 90-minute classes with 10 minutes of passing time between. With the block schedule I will teach three classes each day and have the fourth as prepara-

tion time. I use my preparation time to get ready for the days ahead. After school students come in to do make-up work and get help. Many days I attend meetings in the community. It is important to be a member of many community organizations in order to keep the connection between school and community strong."

Mary says that she uses the hours from 3:30 P.M. to between 6:00 and 8:00 P.M. for preparation, research, curriculum changes, grading and recording grades, running copies, writing tests, working with department budgets, orders, writing reference letters for students, etc. "As you can see," she says, "it is a total myth that teachers only work from 8:30 to 3:30. Business teachers have to be willing to work as long as they need to in order to be current and knowledgeable. The next day arrives quickly and it is imperative that I leave school the night before ready for the next day."

Dorothy Morin has worked in the field of education since 1992 in various roles. Before working in education, she had a career in the real estate industry. Dorothy has worked as a teacher at Nashua High School North in Nashua, New Hampshire, for nearly 10 years. Prior to teaching at Nashua High School, she was an associate professor of business at Nashua Community College and prior to that she worked at Daniel Webster College in the Office of Continuing Studies. Dorothy is also the president of the New Hampshire Business Education Association. "I really enjoyed my real estate career, but I always felt the calling to teach," she recalls. "When my children were in high school, I decided that it was time to explore teaching. I was the traditional soccer, ski, dance lessons, music lessons mom and was spending a good deal of time at school with all of their activities. So, it just happened. A neighbor was the vice president of Empire State College, and he encouraged me to go to graduate school."

Dorothy's school is on block scheduling, which requires her to teach three 90-minute classes per day. "For the most part," she explains, "the classes are dual enrollment college courses with Southern New Hampshire University. I teach marketing and business management. The students pay a nominal fee to the university and receive college credit for the course. As part of the marketing course, the students are partnered with a company to 'work' on a marketing project. For the past two years, we worked with Life is good [a company that features positive messages on its products]. Through the kindness of companies like Life is good, students are exposed to real world experience."

Dorothy says that one of the most rewarding aspects of her job is that every day is interesting. "It never ceases to amaze me how creative and dedicated the students are with the businesses they create or the entrepreneurial products that they discover to bring to market," she says. "Quite often the students have actually started the businesses that they wrote the business plan for in high school. The true reward is to hear from former students who have graduated from college and remember exactly where they sat in the classroom, what they did presentations on, and how all the hard work that they did in high school really prepared them for their college experience."

## DO I HAVE WHAT IT TAKES TO BE A BUSINESS TEACHER?

To be a successful business teacher (or any other kind of teacher), you must be patient, self-disciplined, energetic, and

### The Benefits of Professional Association Membership

Dorothy Morin, president of the New Hampshire Business Education Association, provides an overview of her organization and details the importance of membership in a professional organization:

The New Hampshire Business Education Association was organized more than 80 years ago. We are a small state, but diverse in demographics. Our teachers and college professors are from all corners of the state. We have a yearly conference that brings our members together for a general membership meeting and workshops.

As technology and business change rapidly, it is important for our teachers to have the opportunity to be current through professional development. Through our Web site, newsletters, and yearly conference we strive to offer members the venue to share ideas, develop lesson plans, and hear from industry what the needs are in the workplace.

self-confident. You will also need to have excellent communication skills in order to convey your thoughts and ideas to your students. Strong people skills will be paramount, since you will need to deal with students, administrators, and other faculty members on a daily basis. Experience in the business world will help you demonstrate how class lessons apply to real-life business settings.

"Business teachers must be willing to put in many hours of extra time preparing and researching to always be on top of what is most current," says Mary Flesberg. "It is necessary to be credible! In terms of professional qualities, business teachers must have the ability to network. In many schools there may be only one business teacher so they must network with other business teachers to exchange ideas and concerns. They also need to connect to the business leaders in their community in order to have working relationships for advisory committees and for business mentorship opportunities for the students."

"Business teachers tend to take a 'hands-on' approach and train the students to think like business people," says Dorothy Morin. "The courses in the business program lend themselves well to this approach. So often, I remind the students that everyone goes to work. The skills and analytical training that the students acquire in the business classes transcend all disciplines. I feel that it is important that the teacher fills the role of facilitator for the students, thereby allowing the students to develop their own learning skills. This in turn promotes lifelong learning."

# HOW DO I BECOME A BUSINESS TEACHER?

## Education

### High School

To prepare for a career in business education, follow your school's college preparatory program and take advanced courses in business, mathematics, English, science, history, and government. Composition, journalism, and communications classes are also important for developing your writing and speaking skills.

### Postsecondary Training

Your college training will depend on the level at which you plan to teach. All 50 states and the District of Columbia require public elementary education teachers to have a bachelor's degree in either education or in the subject they teach. Prospective teachers must also complete an approved training program, which combine subject and educational classes with work experience in the classroom, called student teaching. "My first experience was teaching in a summer orchestra program for three years," recalls Mary Flesberg. "I also taught private piano lessons for seven years. Of course, I completed a 10-week student teaching requirement in college prior to graduation."

If you want to teach at the high school level, you should major in business or business education. Similar to prospective elementary teachers, you will need to student teach in an actual classroom environment. A typical bachelor's degree program in business education will include classes on marketing, business law, business accounting, consumer education and personal finance, business communication, and computer technology.

Mary graduated from Concordia College in Moorhead, Minnesota, with a bachelor's of arts degree in business education. She earned a master's of science degree in business education from Minnesota State University-Moorhead. "Since then," she says, "I have earned more than 60 credits—both in order to keep up to date and also to fill license renewal requirements. Teachers are required to complete 125 hours or more of continuing education credits in order to renew their licenses."

Like many business teachers, Dorothy Morin entered the teaching field after a career in the business world. "My training and learning was not in the traditional classroom," she says. "I returned to college and graduate school after a successful career in the real estate industry. I had attained most of my goals, learned marketing and management skills, and now I am able to use examples that have meaning to my students."

For prospective professors, you will need at least one advanced degree in business. The master's degree is considered the minimum standard, and graduate work beyond the master's is usually desirable. If you hope to advance in academic rank above instructor, most institutions require a doctorate. Your graduate school program will be similar to a life of teaching—in addition to attending seminars, you'll research, prepare articles for publication, and teach some undergraduate courses.

Business teachers at all levels must continue to learn throughout their careers via seminars, workshops, and conferences—many of which are offered as a benefit of membership in professional associations. "Membership in professional organizations is so important to one's success as a business teacher," says Mary. "It gives you the opportunity to network locally, regionally, statewide, and nationally. Organizations give your subject area strength, as there is strength in numbers. They are there to help work through issues that impact both students and your teaching. The resources that they provide are invaluable. [Membership in professional associations] will not only help build your resume, but also allow you to make lifelong connections."

## Certification or Licensing

Elementary and secondary business teachers who work in public schools must be licensed under regulations established by the state in which they are teaching. If moving, teachers have to comply with any other regulations in their new state to be able to teach, though many states have reciprocity agreements that make it easier for teachers to change locations.

Licensure examinations test prospective teachers for competency in basic subjects such as mathematics, reading, writing, teaching, and other subject matter proficiency. In addition, many states are moving toward a performance-based evaluation for licensing. In this case, after passing the teaching examination, prospective teachers are given provisional licenses. Only after proving themselves capable in the classroom are they eligible for a full license.

Another growing trend spurred by recent teacher shortages in elementary and high schools is alternative licensure arrangements. For those who have a bachelor's degree but lack formal education courses and training in the classroom, states can issue a provisional license. These workers immediately begin teaching under the supervision of a licensed educator for one to two years and take education classes outside of their working hours. Once they have completed the required coursework and gained experience in the classroom, they are granted a full license.

### Internships and Volunteerships

While in college, you will participate in an internship or teaching practicum that will help you to gain hands-on experience in the field. Dorothy Morin's graduate studies practicum involved participating in an internship at the Center for Distance Learning at Empire State College in Saratoga Springs, New York. "This was a wonderful experience. Thinking back now nearly 15 years, Empire State College was and still is the 'cutting edge' in education innovation. I really believe internships are a very important piece in the learning experience. I supervised an internship class for several years until it was cut from the school budget. Students learned so much from the experience and it really made a difference in their choice of major in college."

To explore a teaching career, look for leadership opportunities that involve working with children. You might find summer work as a counselor in a summer camp, as a leader of a scout troop, or as an assistant in a public park or community center. To get some firsthand teaching experience, volunteer for a peer-tutoring program. Many other teaching opportunities may exist in your community. If you plan to teach younger children, look for opportunities to coach youth athletic teams or help out in day care centers.

## WHO WILL HIRE ME?

Business teachers are employed at middle schools, high schools, community colleges, and colleges and universities. They may work at public and private institutions, vocational schools, and charter schools. Although rural areas maintain schools, more teaching positions are available in urban or suburban areas.

There are approximately 70,000 college business teachers employed in the United States, according to the U.S. Department of Labor. Employment opportunities vary based on area of study and education. With a doctorate, a number of publications, and a record of good teaching, college business professors should find opportunities in universities all across the country.

Middle and high school teachers can use their college career services offices and state departments of education to find job openings. Many local schools advertise teaching positions in newspapers or at their Web sites. Another option is to directly contact the administration in the schools in which you'd like to work. While looking for a full-time position, you can work as a substitute teacher. In more urban areas with many schools, you may be able to find full-time substitute work.

# Business Teacher Profile: Maria Matarazzo

Maria Matarazzo is the chair of the Division of Business Administration at Rivier College in Nashua, New Hampshire. She discussed her career with the editors of *What Can I Do Now? Business and Finance.*

**Q. How long have you worked in the field? Why did you decide to become a business teacher?**

**A.** I have worked in the field of business education since 1974. Prior to entering the education field, I had worked in industry for several years in the accounting field. My interest in teaching evolved as a result of two primary needs that I learned were inherent in my persona: one was the need to be of service to society and the other a need to be involved with lifelong learning.

I had always enjoyed school as a student and I wanted to be able to create an environment that would inspire learners. My first teaching experience occurred at the high school level where I was totally immersed in academics and cocurricular activities. After six years teaching at the high school level, I began my career in higher education. My experiences with students over the past 35 years have enriched my life in immeasurable ways. When one loves their work, the dimension of time is unbounded.

**Q. Please take us through a day in your work life. What are your typical responsibilities and hours?**

**A.** Professional business educators at the higher education level have the primary responsibility of teaching,

scholarship, and committee work. As chair of the Division of Business Administration, my responsibilities are primarily administrative. One very interesting aspect of business education is that no one day is typical of another.

Business education chairs are responsible for budgeting, hiring, faculty development, recruitment and retention of students, program and curriculum development, student advising, supervision of internships, creating articulation agreements, professional networking, and creating visibility for their college and programs. Each day is exciting and new.

In higher education, professors have a significant amount of autonomy over academic decisions and their work schedules. Most full-time faculty work nine months of the year from September through May. Administrators such as myself usually work a full 12 months.

**Q. Can you tell me about how your students gain real-world experience in the business world?**

**A.** A successful business program provides academic and real-world knowledge. At Rivier College, every business course is threaded with fundamental concepts of globalization, diversity, technology, and ethics regardless of content specialization. Moreover, every course engages the learner in applications-based, real-world learning. As noted earlier, professors have

*(continued on next page)*

*(continued from previous page)*

previous field experience and are able to deliver instruction in creative, meaningful modes of learning. Content comes to life when learners gain experience as they engage in analytical processes. The ability to navigate through change is a key element in sustained learning and career success. We employ a relevant, timely mechanism of strategic teaching to ensure that our students can thrive in today's volatile marketplace.

**Q. What are the most important personal and professional qualities for business teachers?**

**A.** Anyone considering the field of business education must have an advanced degree in business, usually an MBA or a master's degree in a specific specialty such as marketing, finance, economics, etc. Professors at four-year colleges are usually required to hold a doctorate degree in the field of business. Professional work experience is also a requirement for business educators as they must be able to teach real-world lessons. Business educators are mentors who network in their community and explore career and learning opportunities for the students they serve. A professional educator is ethical, empathetic, knowledgeable, and an active learner.

To be successful as a professor, one must have energy, passion, patience, and creativity. One's leadership style is an important element in achieving successful learning outcomes for students. Teaching is inherently, intrinsically rewarding. It requires a vast commitment of time and investment of one's lifestyle.

**Q. What is one of the most interesting or rewarding things that has happened to you while working as a business teacher?**

**A.** Over the 35 years of my career I have been honored with a number of prestigious awards. Several years ago I received the state of New Hampshire "Excellence in Education Award" which is fundamentally being named "business teacher of the year." I was overwhelmed with emotion when I achieved this honor. I have been recognized for my work on many occasions; however, the most rewarding experience is learning from past students about their successes. Students stay connected and keep me apprised of their career achievements. I find that being able to touch a life and to make a small contribution to a young person's life is the most rewarding experience of my career and my personal life.

**Q. What is one thing that young people may not know about business education and/or a career in business?**

**A.** Every workplace is a business. While this may seem obvious, many individuals underestimate the value of business education. Whether a workplace is a nonprofit organization, a sports-oriented entity, an artistic or creative enterprise, or even a religious institution, it must operate using business principles. A business degree is very portable and essentially invaluable in today's globalized society. Business is ethical, exciting, passionate, and socially responsible.

Prospective college professors should start the process of finding a teaching position while in graduate school. You will need to develop a curriculum vitae (a detailed, academic resume), work on your academic writing, assist with research, attend conferences, and gain teaching experience and recommendations. Because of the competition for tenure-track positions, you may have to work for a few years in temporary positions. Some professional associations maintain lists of teaching opportunities in their areas. They may also make lists of applicants available to college administrators looking to fill an available position. You might also consider subscribing to *The Chronicle of Higher Education* (http://chronicle.com). This publication features job listings for college faculty, including business teachers.

## WHERE CAN I GO FROM HERE?

As middle and high school teachers acquire experience or additional education, they can expect higher wages and more responsibilities. Teachers with leadership skills and an interest in administrative work may advance to serve as principals or supervisors, though the number of these positions is limited and competition is fierce. Another move may be into higher education, teaching business classes at a college or university. For most of these positions, additional education is required.

At the college level, the normal pattern of advancement is from instructor to assistant professor, to associate professor, to full professor. All four academic ranks are concerned primarily with teaching and research. College business faculty who have an interest in and a talent for administration may be advanced to chair the business department or become a dean of their college. A few become college or university presidents or other types of administrators.

Other common career transitions are into related fields. With additional preparation, teachers can become librarians, reading specialists, or counselors. Business teachers may also decide to advance by moving out of the education arena to work in the business sector. They might get involved in corporate training, marketing, entrepreneurship, or management.

## WHAT ARE THE SALARY RANGES?

There are no specific salary statistics available for middle and secondary school business teachers. The median salaries for all middle and secondary school teachers were $49,700 and $51,180, respectively, in 2008, according to the U.S. Department of Labor. Salaries ranged from less than $34,020 to $80,970 or more.

Earnings for college business professors vary depending on their academic department, the size of the school, the type of school (public, private, women's only), and by the level of position the professor holds. The median salary for college business professors was $68,000 in 2008, according to the U.S. Department of Labor. The lowest paid 10 percent earned less than $32,880, while the highest paid 10 percent earned $133,930 or more annually.

Benefits for business teachers depend on the employer; however, they usually include such items as health insurance, retirement or 401(k) plans, and paid vacation days.

## WHAT IS THE JOB OUTLOOK?

According to the *Occupational Outlook Handbook (OOH)*, employment opportunities for middle school teachers are expected to grow about as fast as the average for all occupations through 2016.

Employment for secondary school teachers is expected to grow more slowly than the average for all careers during this time span. The *OOH* predicts much faster than average employment growth for college and university professors through 2016. College enrollment is projected to grow due to an increased number of 18 to 24 year olds, an increased number of adults returning to college, and an increased number of foreign-born students. Job opportunities for college business professors will also be good. Retirement of current faculty members will also provide job openings. However, competition for full-time, tenure-track positions at four-year schools will be very strong.

# Economists

## SUMMARY

### Definition
Economists are concerned with how society uses scarce resources such as labor, raw materials, land, and machinery to produce goods and services for current consumption and future production. Economists study how economic systems address three basic questions: "What shall we produce?" "How shall we produce it?" and "For whom shall we produce it?" The economist then compiles, processes, and interprets the answers to these questions.

### Alternative Job Titles
Business analysts

### Salary Range
$35,752 to $83,590 to $149,110+

### Educational Requirements
Master's degree; some top positions require a doctorate

### Certification or Licensing
None available

### Employment Outlook
About as fast as the average

### High School Subjects
Business
Economics
Mathematics

### Personal Interests
Business
Computer science
Economics

"My greatest rewards working as an economist have involved instances where I have helped people," says Dr. Lynn Reaser, chief economist at Point Loma Nazarene University and the president of the National Association for Business Economics. "This has ranged from helping a unit of the bank develop forecasts for its particular product to helping a reporter understand a particular economic statistic. Having people approach me after a client presentation with the words: 'Thank you—you are the first economist I have ever understood,' also has been gratifying. The opportunity to meet various leading officials in Washington, D.C., appear on major national television networks, travel abroad to speak on the U.S. economy to foreign dignitaries, meet with U.S. business leaders, and exchange views with economists in various companies and other institutions [has] been interesting and exciting."

# WHAT DOES AN ECONOMIST DO?

*Economists* grapple with many issues relating to the supply and demand of goods and services and the means by which they are produced, traded, and consumed. While most economists either teach at the university level or perform research for government agencies, many work for individual for-profit or nonprofit organizations.

*Economics professors* teach basic macro- and microeconomics courses as well as courses on advanced topics such as economic history and labor economics. (Macroeconomics deals with the "big picture" of economics, and microeconomics deals with individual companies and persons.) They also perform research, write papers and books, and give lectures, contributing their knowledge to the advancement of the discipline.

In their education, economists usually specialize in a particular area of interest. While the specialties of university economists range across the entire discipline, other economists' expertise generally falls into one of several categories. *Financial economists,* also known as *monetary economists,* examine the relationships among money, credit, and purchasing power to develop monetary policy and forecast financial activity. *International economists* analyze foreign trade to bring about favorable trade balances and establish trade policies. *Labor economists,* also known as *demographic economists,* attempt to forecast labor trends and recommend labor policies for businesses

---

> ## To Be a Successful Economist, You Should...
>
> - be good at mathematics
> - be detail oriented
> - enjoy conducting research
> - have excellent communication skills
> - be able to explain your findings and theories to people from all different backgrounds
> - be willing to continue to learn throughout your career

---

and government entities. *Industrial economists,* also known as *organizational economists,* study the way businesses are internally organized and suggest ways to make maximum use of assets. *Environmental economists* study the relationships between economic issues and the allocation and management of natural resources. *Agricultural economists* study food production, development in rural areas, and the allocation of natural resources.

*Government economists* come from many economic disciplines. They study national economic trends and problems; their analyses often suggest possible changes in government policy to address such issues.

Economists generally work in offices or classrooms. They typically work 40 hours a week, although academic and business economists' schedules often can be less predictable. Economists in nonteaching positions often work alone writing reports, preparing statistical charts, and using computers, but they may also be part of a research team. Most economists work under deadline pressure and sometimes must work overtime. They may be required to travel regularly to collect data or to attend conferences or meetings.

## WHAT IS IT LIKE TO BE AN ECONOMIST?

Stuart Mackintosh is the executive director of The Group of Thirty (G30) in Washington, D.C. He has been working in international economics for 20 years and has headed The Group of Thirty (http://www.group30.org) since 2006. "The Group of Thirty," Stuart explains, "is a private, nonprofit, international body composed of very senior representatives from the private and public sectors and academia. The G30 aims to deepen understanding of international economic and financial issues, to explore the international repercussions of decisions taken in the public and private sectors, and to examine the choices available to market practitioners and policy makers. As executive director I oversee the G30 work program, the studies and meetings organized by this international think tank. Current areas of particular research attention include the structure of financial supervision, financial regulatory reform proposals for the United States, and methods of enhancing coopera-

tion and coordination between national supervisors and central banks. I manage all aspects of the G30's work program in the U.S. and internationally."

Stuart says that one of his most rewarding experiences as an economist has been "seeing a major series of G30 recommendations on financial reform from creation through to their becoming part of the U.S. government's economic and financial policy. Taking proposals from theory to action is always a challenge and most often difficult; when it works this is very rewarding."

Dr. Lisa House is a professor of agricultural economics at the University of Florida. "What I like the most about my career is working in a university where we get to study cutting-edge issues. My work is never boring, and I have good colleagues to work with. What I like least is that there is never enough time to do all the things I like!"

Dr. House says that a day in the life of an economics professor can be very interesting. "First," she explains, "I have the opportunity to interact with college students. I teach classes on subjects like Comparative World Agriculture, where we investigate agriculture and related policies from around the world; Survey Research Methods for Economists, where I teach others how to collect primary data; and Food and Agribusiness Marketing Management, where we discuss marketing strategies of agribusiness firms. I also interact with graduate students to help them conduct the research they need to receive their advanced degrees. My recent students have studied issues like trust in international food supply chains; the impact of bilateral trade negotiations on food product labeling; and consumer willingness to try new food products."

In addition to working with students, Dr. House conducts her own research with research partners from different fields. "Being part of a large university, especially a land-grant university that has a College of Agricultural and Life Sciences, I have the opportunity to work with many interesting people. I team with other professors from agricultural economics, agricultural communications and education, food science and human nutrition, animal science, and horticultural sciences to name a few. We research topics like consumer demand for food products, the impact of advertising on childhood obesity, and consumer knowledge of food safety and quality issues."

Dr. House also serves as the director of the Florida Agricultural Market Research Center at the university. "My research focuses on developing a deeper understanding of consumer behavior related to food consumption," she explains. "We use a combination of survey methods, such as focus groups, telephone surveys, and experimental auctions, to collect data from consumers. We then employ research methods from economics, such as econometric analysis, to interpret the data we collect. The Florida Agricultural Market Research Center is a part of the Food and Resource Economics Department in the University of Florida's Institute for Food and Agricultural Sciences. Founded in 1975, the center was established to provide timely, applied research on current and emerging marketing problems affecting Florida's agricultural and marine industries. A basic goal of the center is to provide marketing research and related information to producer organizations, trade associations, and governmental agencies concerned with improving and expanding markets for Florida's agricultural and marine producers.

"Since the center's inception, many formal, funded projects have been conducted at the request of agricultural commodity groups, food and agricultural industry associations, and governmental agencies. Consumer or trade studies have been conducted for the Florida Department of Citrus; the Florida Lime and Avocado Committees, the Florida Dairy Products Association; Florida Nursery, Growers, and Landscape Association; Dade County Farm Bureau; the Florida Department of Agriculture and Consumer Services; the Florida Department of Environmental Protection; and many others. Examples of center publications can be viewed at http://www.agmarketing.ifas.ufl.edu."

Candice Flor Hynek is an economist and senior research analyst at the Milken Institute (http://www.milkeninstitute.org), a nonprofit, nonpartisan, independent think tank located in Santa Monica, California. She has also served as the president of the Los Angeles Chapter of the National Association for Business Economics. "I have been doing economic research and analysis for nine years," she says. "I knew that a degree and training in economics was flexible. I can always go further and branch out with it, apply my

# Economist Profile: Diane Swonk

Diane Swonk is the chief economist and senior managing director of Mesirow Financial, a financial services firm in Chicago, Illinois. She is the author of *The Passionate Economist: Finding the Power and Humanity Behind the Numbers* (Hoboken, N.J.: Wiley, 2003) and the past president of the National Association for Business Economics. She sits on several advisory committees to the Federal Reserve Board and the Council of Economic Advisers for the White House, and is active in a variety of other organizations. Diane is a highly sought-after commentator on national and international news shows as well as in the print media. She discussed her career with the editors of *What Can I Do Now? Business and Finance.*

**Q. How long have you worked in the field? Why did you decide to become an economist?**

**A.** I have worked as an economist since I was 23. That makes it 24 years in the field. I decided to become an economist by accident. In college, all the other classes were closed and economics was my only option. From that first class on, it was the most intuitive class I had ever taken. It just made sense. It actually helped me understand the train wreck of an economy that I grew up in in Detroit. It made me realize that the pain and suffering I witnessed was preventable. I really thought I could make a difference not only in the field, but also for the broader policy debate. Recent times have challenged that view, but only heightened my resolve.

**Q. What are your main responsibilities at Mesirow Financial?**

**A.** I am a strategist, keeping clients (internal and external) focused on the bigger picture. I try to figure out where the economy might surprise us. I specialize in finding structural change. Most people ask the wrong questions of economics. For example, what will the Gross Domestic Product be next quarter? or What's going to happen at the next Federal Reserve Board of Governors meeting? I try to reframe the debate: How do the shifts that we are seeing affect the bigger long-term picture?

During the height of the financial crisis, I also acted as counselor, holding people's hands and reminding them that we would survive. I spent a lot of time talking clients and colleagues off "the cliff."

**Q. What are the most important personal and professional qualities for economists? Economists who provide media commentary?**

**A.** Intuition, passion, and patience. You either are or you are not an economist. Economics is the collective study of human behavior, and at its core, all the math in the world can't explain our collective decision making.

You also must stay connected to Main Street. Being real and relatable are very important if you want to be a communicator. I speak from my heart and avoid areas outside of my expertise like the plague.

*(continued on next page)*

*(continued from previous page)*

Q. **What advice would you give to young people who want to become economists?**

A. Don't do it unless you really love it. Your life's work takes passion and economists tend to have a long shelf life. Look at Alan Greenspan [who was nearly 80 years old when he retired as the chairman of the Federal Reserve Board of Governors]. The information age and structural change has meant you will change who you work for many times. As an economist, you need to not only be flexible but also constantly reinvent where you are valuable.

Q. **What is one of the most interesting or rewarding things that has happened to you while working as an economist?**

A. Having a say in the debate, whether it be in the boardroom of the Federal Reserve, the White House, Congress, or face to face with a client.

training to other analytical occupations, or even start my own business. What really drew me into the field was the belief that I can offer decision makers in business and government a clear understanding of economic issues through good analysis and recommendations. My work helps them form efficient, sound, and sustainable policies that have a positive impact on society. This is what keeps me motivated.

"The Milken Institute," Candice continues, "conducts research to address social and economic challenges. We also provide unique and innovative solutions to those challenges. I am a senior research analyst for the regional economics group. We conduct research on various regions or industries in a specific geographic location, in the United States as well as other countries." Candice's job involves data gathering, background research and analysis, and presenting findings through written reports. "I work on a variety of projects that include topics ranging from manufacturing and trade to state-level and country-level economic profiles," she explains. "I am fortunate to work with analysts and experts with different backgrounds in economics and public policy. This gives our group a unique and balanced perspective for our reports. A project can be small and finished in a week or big and last for several months. Working hours vary, from eight hours a day to sometimes 10 hours or so, depending if there is a deadline or a conference."

## DO I HAVE WHAT IT TAKES TO BE AN ECONOMIST?

Economists perform very detail-oriented work. They conduct extensive research and enjoy working in the abstract with theories. Their research must be precise and well documented. In addition, economists must be able to clearly explain their ideas to a range of people, including other economic experts, political leaders, and even students in a classroom.

"Being an economist requires strong analytical skills, computer skills, communication skills, patience, flexibility, and discipline," says Candice Flor Hynek. "A good economist is well informed about the latest news and upcoming trends. Today's successful economist is able to work independently, as well as with a team."

"For an economist, an important quality is being able to be objective," says Dr. House. "Often we deal with everyday issues, and it is important not to bring your personal bias into your work. We study data, and learn how to interpret it without only searching for what we want to find. Another important quality for an economist is to be a person that likes working with numbers. Some students come to us afraid of math because they have had some difficulty in the past. However, if you are going to be an economist, you are going to use math and statistics regularly, and I think it is important to enjoy your work."

# HOW DO I BECOME AN ECONOMIST?

## Education

### High School

If you wish to enter this career, you should pursue a strong college preparatory program in high school. Courses in other social sciences, economics, mathematics, and English are extremely important to a would-be economist, since analyzing, interpreting, and expressing one's informed opinions about many different kinds of data are the main tasks of someone employed in this field. Also, take computer classes so that you will be able to use this research tool in college and

later on. Finally, since you will be heading off to college and probably postgraduate studies, consider taking a foreign language to round out your educational background.

## Postsecondary Training

A bachelor's degree with a major in economics is the minimum requirement for an entry-level position such as research assistant. A master's degree, or even a Ph.D., is more commonly required for most economist positions.

Typically, an economics major takes at least 10 courses on various economic topics, plus two or more mathematics courses, such as statistics and calculus or algebra. The federal government requires candidates for entry-level economist positions to have a minimum of 21 semester hours of economics and three hours of statistics, accounting, or calculus. Graduate-level courses include such specialties as advanced economic theory, econometrics, international economics, and labor economics.

## Certification or Licensing

No certification or licensing is available for this profession.

## Internships and Volunteerships

College students and recent graduates can participate in internships with government agencies and businesses. After earning her bachelor's degree in business economics from California State University-Long Beach, Candice Flor Hynek worked as an intern at Salomon Smith Barney. "I made hundreds of cold calls a day for a couple of months," she recalls.

## Good Advice
● ● ● ● ● ● ●

Stuart Mackintosh offers the following advice to young people who want to become economists:

Focus on what you enjoy most of all. This will drive your decision making later on and help you determine if down the line studying one or another aspect of economics in university as an undergraduate or postgraduate suits you.

If you decide to study economics you should also grasp opportunities to study or live abroad, to widen your horizons and allow you to better understand the many perspectives in the field of economics, trade, and geopolitics—which all affect the actual real world impact of economics.

"It was not glamorous, but it gave me the training and ability to easily interact with all types of people, which turned out to be helpful in other positions."

It will be difficult to land a volunteer position at an economics-related employer, but you can gain general experience by joining high school economics or business clubs.

## WHO WILL HIRE ME?

Approximately 15,000 economists are employed in the United States. Many economists teach at colleges and universities. Others work as researchers at government agencies, such as the U.S. Department of Labor, or international organizations, such as the United Nations. Still others find employment at nonprofit or for-profit organizations, helping these organizations determine how to use their resources or grow in profitability. Most economics-related positions are concentrated in large cities, such as New York, Chicago, Los Angeles, and Washington, D.C., although academic positions are spread throughout the United States.

The bulletins of the various professional economic associations are good sources of job opportunities for beginning economists. Your school's career services office should also assist you in locating internships and in setting up interviews with potential employers.

## WHERE CAN I GO FROM HERE?

Economists advance depending on their training, experience, personal interests, and ambition. All specialized areas provide opportunities for promotion to jobs requiring more skill and competence. Such jobs involve more administrative, research, or advisory responsibilities. Consequently, promotions are governed to a great extent by job performance in the beginning fields of work. In university-level academic positions, publishing papers and books about one's research is necessary to become tenured.

## WHAT ARE THE SALARY RANGES?

Economists are among the highest-paid social scientists. The median salary for economists was $83,590 in 2008, according to the U.S. Department of Labor (DoL). The lowest paid 10 percent made less than $44,050, and the highest paid 10 percent earned more than $149,110.

Economists employed by the federal government earned mean annual salaries of $101,020 in 2008, according to the DoL. Starting salaries for federal government economists vary by degree attained. In 2007, economists with a bachelor's degree earned approximately $35,752; economists with a master's degree, $43,731; and those with a Ph.D., $52,912 or $63,417 depending on their level of experience.

College economics educators earned salaries that ranged from less than $43,720 to $144,140 or more in 2008, according to the DoL. Educators employed at colleges and universities had mean annual earnings of $92,630, while those employed at junior colleges earned $68,200 a year.

Benefits such as vacation and insurance are comparable to those of workers in other fields.

## WHAT IS THE JOB OUTLOOK?

The employment of economists is expected to grow about as fast as the average for all careers through 2016, according to the DoL. Most openings will occur as economists retire, transfer to other job fields, or leave the profession for other reasons. Economists employed by private industry—especially in management, scientific, and technical consulting services—will enjoy the best prospects. Employment for government economists is expected to grow more slowly than the average.

Stuart Mackintosh believes that the employment outlook for economists—especially those with Ph.D.'s—is quite good. "In addition to studying hard," he advises, "students must be sure to work, even at university, at building their network within the economics field. Join the local economics associations, attend public speeches and events in your area, introduce yourself, get

### Join an Association

Candice Flor Hynek details the importance of membership in the National Association for Business Economics, the largest professional association for business economists:

The National Association for Business Economics (NABE) has provided tremendous help and support to me in my career. I joined the NABE, initially with the local chapter where I attended the meetings regularly, became a board member, and eventually served as president. NABE gave me an opportunity to network with other economists and learn that there were different types of economists, hear different perspectives, and learn about other industries. It helps broaden my knowledge and keeps me up to date regarding the latest trends. It is a community and I feel passionate about it and its initiatives in advancing the field.

I would recommend membership to anyone who is interested in business economics. Both my former and current bosses are members, and I met one of them through my association with the group. NABE provides mentors for young professionals like me. The encouragement, support, and knowledge they share are priceless.

known by your fellows. After all it is often not just what you know but who you know that will be crucial to getting the best job or best opportunity; build your network constantly; this is a constant requirement that should always be observed."

In the academic arena, economists with master's and doctoral degrees will face strong competition for desirable teaching jobs. The demand for secondary school economics teachers is expected to grow.

Economics majors with only bachelor's degrees will experience the greatest difficulty landing a job, although their analytical skills can lead to positions in related fields such as management and sales. Those who meet state certification requirements may wish to become secondary school economics teachers.

The DoL reports that "demand for economic analysis should grow, but the increase in the number of economist jobs will be tempered as firms hire workers for more specialized jobs with specialized titles." Workers with educational backgrounds in economics will find jobs as financial analysts, market analysts, purchasing managers, public policy consultants, researchers, and research assistants.

# Entrepreneurs

## SUMMARY

**Definition**
Entrepreneurs own and operate their own businesses.

**Alternative Job Titles**
Business owners
Franchise owners

**Salary Range**
$0 to $30,000 to $100,000+

**Educational Requirements**
High school diploma; bachelor's degree and higher required for certain careers

**Certification or Licensing**
Required by certain franchisers (certification)
Required by certain states (licensing)

**Employment Outlook**
About as fast as the average

**High School Subjects**
Business
Mathematics

**Personal Interests**
Business
Business management
Selling/making a deal

"Starting my own business was one of the best career moves I ever made," says Todd Ramis, the owner of a small publishing company. "While I have never worked harder in my life, the rewards definitely outweigh the negatives, and I would recommend an entrepreneurial career for anyone who is self-motivated, doesn't mind taking risks, and has a desire to build and manage their own business."

## WHAT DOES AN ENTREPRENEUR DO?

Entrepreneurship covers a huge range of business endeavors from the homemaker who makes, packages, and sells her cookies from her home to the electronics manufacturer who employs more than 500 workers in five factories.

Many people who own small businesses start small, often part time, from a home office and expand as the demand grows. They perform all the functions normally found in any business, including those of president, manager, manufacturer or service provider, secretary, accountant, investor, benefits administrator, salesperson, marketing worker, and maintenance engineer.

Owners of home-based businesses might be involved in making and selling products, such as food items, jewelry, furniture, ceramics, or clothing. Or they might provide services, either performed in the home office or at other locations outside the home, such as writing and editing, telemarketing, home staging, housekeeping, computer service, pet sitting, or catering. Owners of these types of businesses can be quite successful for a long time, working completely on their own. They enjoy answering only to themselves and having control over every part of their work. They take all the responsibilities, suffer all the hardships, and reap all the rewards.

Some entrepreneurs may work as *consultants.* Consultants usually work independently out of their own homes or offices, although some work on a part- or full-time basis for consulting firms. Traditionally, consultants have provided professional expertise in such areas as marketing, public and media relations, business plan development, finances, productivity, automation, computer programming, and downsizing. Today, the field of consulting has expanded to include almost every possible aspect of modern life. You can find consultants who will charge you a fee to help you plan your wedding, design and build your home, coordinate your wardrobe, purchase the right car, manage your finances, find an affordable college for your children, and place your parents in the right nursing home. Small, start-up businesses, mid-sized companies, large corporations, and governmental agencies frequently contract with consultants who have a specific area of business expertise.

Successful home-based businesses often grow and expand, and the owner must decide how to handle the expansion. If the owner, for example, has started an art framing business out of love for the fine arts, he or she may decide to hire another person to handle business affairs, such as accounting, taxes, licenses, and bill payment. Another business owner may decide to purchase updated, more efficient equipment or technology, hire one or two staff, and rent office or studio space outside of the home to better serve a growing clientele. The larger a business becomes, the more complicated its structure also becomes. In addition to managing the business, the owner has to manage people, and instead of providing a service or manufacturing a product personally, the owner must find workers, train them, monitor their work, provide a safe and productive work environment, and pay salaries and benefits.

A small business doesn't necessarily have to start as a home-based business. An entrepreneur with a somewhat larger investment capacity can start a business, such as a small restaurant, a public relations firm, a travel agency, or a secondhand clothing store, for example. These types of small businesses require a detailed plan and enough money to purchase start-up equipment and materials, rent space, pay utilities, purchase insurance, fund advertising, and pay salaries and benefits for at least a year. The owner may get loans from a bank, the Small Business Administration, or a commercial finance company. In addition to the complicated financial arrangements, the plan for a small business includes such things as finding a market, establishing a presence in the community, creating a demand for the product or service, hiring capable staff, and monitoring quality control.

Another choice for entrepreneurs is to purchase a franchise, such as a Baskin-Robbins, a RadioShack, or a Mail Boxes Etc. The franchisor lends its trademark or trade name and a business system to franchisees, who pay a royalty and often an initial fee for the right to do business under the franchisor's name and system. Entrepreneurs who choose this option have the security and support of an established name, a ready market, and a business system already in place. Some of the most popular franchise industries include fast food, retail, service, automotive, restaurants, maintenance, building and construction, retail food, business services, and lodging. An estimated 1,500 franchise companies operate in the United States, doing business through more than 320,000 retail units. The average initial investment level for nearly eight out of 10 franchises, excluding real estate, is less than $250,000, and the average length of a franchise contract is 10 years, according to the International Franchise Association.

A person can become an entrepreneur by taking over an already existing business. A son or daughter may take over from a parent who is retiring, a long-time employee may purchase a business from a boss, or someone could purchase a business without having previous ties. As with a franchise, the location is already established and outfitted with equipment and materials. A business system is in place, and suppliers and clientele are established. Unlike a franchise, however, the new owner can change the business system or any other aspect of the business as desired. (An exception might be if the new owner keeps the same business name and the sales contract stipulates certain business practices based on the use of that name.)

## WHAT IS IT LIKE TO BE AN ENTREPRENEUR?

Sonat Birnecker is the co-owner (along with her husband Robert) of Koval, a boutique distillery in Chicago. (Visit http://www.koval-distillery.com to learn more about Sonat and the distillery.) "Koval began as my husband and I started to discuss what we really wanted out of life," Sonat recalls. "We were about to have a child and did not really enjoy where we were living. We thought that if we were

### To Be a Successful Entrepreneur, You Should...

- be self-motivated
- be organized
- be willing to take calculated risks
- have excellent communication skills
- be willing to work long hours, including nights and weekends
- enjoy learning new skills

going to make a change, it was time. We already had successful careers in Washington, D.C. I was a professor and Robert was the deputy press secretary for the Austrian Embassy, but we knew that these jobs would force us to commute, spend time apart, and ultimately require that we put our child in day care. We had worked hard to get where we were but we wanted something different out of life: to be in a city we love, close to family and friends, have the chance to work together on a daily basis, and be with our son all the time. Robert's grandfather is a distiller and brewer in Austria and Robert grew up with a great deal of knowledge of spirits and their production. We began to notice a revived interest in craft spirits in the United States and, given our unique family connection and insight, decided to make this our family business in Chicago. So we moved to where we wanted to be and opened our distillery using traditional European techniques to make high quality organic and kosher spirits."

Sonat says that she and her husband's responsibilities vary depending on the day. "Some days are devoted to production," she explains, "while other days involve marketing and public relations. The production of spirits, when made from scratch (as in our case), takes time; so we cannot go from rye flour to a bottle of our Rye Chicago in a day. If we are 'mashing,' i.e., getting the fermentation process going, we begin in the morning by boiling hot water and adding it to the rye flour so that we create a kind of rye soup. We then add enzymes and yeast and while the mash is cooling we clean

up and either start making another one or distill one of the mashes made a few days before that is ready for the still. The distillation process takes about three hours and needs to be monitored all the time. When finished, we have to clean up the spent mash and the still. All the while, whether mashing or distilling, we are taking turns playing with our one-year-old son. If there is a spare second, we make calls, answer emails, and label and fill bottles with finished product. I guess we never really have a typical day, since some days we will have to do an interview, race to fill a last-minute order for our distributor, work on our Web site, make shelf talkers or sell sheets, and even make calls to restaurants to see if our distributor could come by for a tasting. There is never a dull moment."

Two of the biggest challenges Sonat and her husband faced when starting the distillery were learning the laws relating to alcohol production in the United States and working through the large volume of paperwork that was involved in starting a distillery. "Alcohol production is highly controlled and there are numerous documents that need to be filed when applying for a license," she says. "Even after one obtains a license there are papers to be filed monthly with both the state and the federal government, not to mention logs to be filled out daily."

Sonat and Robert had to be very creative as they worked to get the various aspects of the distillery up and running. "We did not have the money to have the kind of automation many of the big distilleries have," she explains, "so we have had to do everything by hand. Trying to find ways to make the process a bit more streamlined has been a constant challenge. When we shipped for the first time, we found ourselves working 72 hours straight to get everything bottled and packaged in time. We already feel as if we have come a long way—we have not put in any all-nighters in months!"

Despite the challenges involved in building the business, Sonat says that the pros outweigh the negatives and that she has experienced many rewarding moments during the distillery's short history. "It has been a real joy to see how a family business really manages to bring together family and friends," she says. "It has been a lot of fun as well, and we are of course always thrilled to see our products being written up in magazines, on the shelves of liquor stores, or in bars and restaurants. Most of all we love working together in a city we adore with our son close by and, despite all the hard work, we are really glad we decided to risk it all to make the kind of life and lifestyle we hoped for a reality."

## DO I HAVE WHAT IT TAKES TO BE AN ENTREPRENEUR?

Entrepreneurs must have strong self-motivation and discipline in order to make their businesses successful. They should also be well organized, have excellent communication skills, and be willing to take calculated and educated risks as they build their businesses. Entrepreneurs should be willing to work long hours—including at nights and on week-

> ### Self-Assessment Tools for Entrepreneurs on the Web
>
> Would you be a successful entrepreneur? Visit the following Web sites to assess your readiness to start a business:
>
> **BizMove.com: The Entrepreneur Test**
> http://www.bizmove.com/other/quiz.htm
>
> **Mentors, Ventures & Plans: Self-Assessment**
> http://mvp.cfee.org/en/selfassessment.html
>
> **U.S. Small Business Administration: Assessment Tool**
> http://www.sba.gov/assessmenttool

ends—to achieve success. "A successful entrepreneur has to be comfortable wearing many hats," says Todd Ramis. "In my business, I am not just responsible for writing, editing, and laying out our books and newsletters. I must also have strong communication skills in order to deal with customers, suppliers, and printers and excellent organizational skills in order to keep track of customer orders and invoicing, manage warehouse inventory, and keep my staff and projects on schedule."

Sonat Birnecker says that successful entrepreneurs have "a belief in oneself, an ability to take risks, patience, determination, willingness to ask for help and to know where to get it, and the ability to be at peace with the fact that very little comes easily."

## HOW DO I BECOME AN ENTREPRENEUR?

### Education

#### High School

Business, math, economics, and accounting courses will be the most valuable to you in preparing a career as an entrepreneur. Before starting a business or buying a franchise, you'll have to do a lot of research, analyzing local demographics to determine whether a business is a sound investment. English classes will help you develop the research skills you'll need. In addition, you will need to hone your communication skills that will be essential in establishing relationships with customers and clients. Take computer classes since it is virtually impossible to work in today's business world without knowing how to use a computer or the Web. If you already know of a particular area that interests you—such as food service, fashion, or, fitness—take classes that will help you learn more about it. Such classes may include home economics, art, dance, or physical education.

### Postsecondary Training

Because there is such a variety of opportunities available, there is no single educational path for everyone to take on the road to becoming an entrepreneur. Some entrepreneurial careers require degrees; for example, to own an environmental consulting agency, a business that helps companies meet government environmental standards, you'll have to be an engineer or geologist (careers that, in most cases, require at least a bachelor's degree). In terms of franchising, there are also many companies willing to sell to someone wanting to break into a new business. Franchisers will often include special training as part of the initial franchise fee.

Experts in the field stress the importance of gaining work experience before starting out with your own business. Hone your sales, management, and people skills and take the time to learn about the industry that interests you. Even if you don't plan on getting a college degree, consider taking some college-level courses in subjects such as business and finance. One recent survey of franchisees found that more than 80 percent had attended college or had a college degree. This reflects the fact that many franchisees have worked for many years in other professions in order to have the money and security needed for starting new businesses.

A growing number of colleges and universities offer courses and programs in entrepreneurship. In fact, there are more than 600 colleges and universities that offer entrepreneurship courses, 400 more than in 1984. Additionally, more than 100 schools offer entrepreneurism as a degree program. A database of postsecondary entrepreneurial education programs can be found at http://www.entrepreneuru.org/eudb.

## Certification or Licensing

Some franchisers have their own certification process and require their franchisees to go through training. You may also want to receive the certified franchise executive designation offered by the Institute for Certified Franchise Executives, an organization affiliated with the International Franchise Association (IFA). This certification involves completing a certain number of courses in topics such as economics and franchise law, participating in events such as seminars or conventions, and work experience. Although certification is voluntary, it will show your level of education and commitment to the field as well as give you the opportunity to network with other franchise professionals.

You may also need to obtain a small business license to own a business or franchise unit in your state. Regulations vary depending on the state and the type of business, so it is important that you check with your state's licensing board for specifics before you start a business or invest in a franchise.

## Internships and Volunteerships

Many college entrepreneurship programs require students to complete an internship as a requirement of graduation. Participating in an internship will give you hands-on experience operating a business. You can also gain experience by volunteering with a company in your field of interest. For example, if you are interested in getting into publishing, you could volunteer with a local publishing company to get a feel for the demands and rewards of the profession.

## WHO WILL HIRE ME?

As an entrepreneur, you will be your own boss. It will be up to you to build your business, hire staff (if necessary), and market your products and services. Sonat Birnecker offer the following advice to aspiring entrepreneurs: "By all means go for it. Try to find a business for which you have a network of people behind you, whether family or friends, and do not cut corners or compromise on quality."

## Top Entrepreneurship Programs

*Entrepreneur* magazine rated the following colleges as offering the best entrepreneurial education programs in 2009:

1. Babson College (http://www3.babson.edu/eship)
2. University of Houston (http://www.bauer.uh.edu/wce)
3. University of Arizona (http://ugrad.eller.arizona.edu/academics/majors/entrepreneurship)
4. Baylor University (http://www.baylor.edu/business/entrepreneur)
5. Temple University (http://sbm.temple.edu/iei)
6. Drexel University (http://www.lebow.drexel.edu/Centers/Baiada)
7. University of Dayton (http://www.udayton.edu/business/management_and_marketing/aos_content/entrepreneurship.php)
8. DePaul University (http://www.ent.depaul.edu)
9. City University of New York—Baruch College (http://zicklin.baruch.cuny.edu/centers/field)
10. University of Southern California (http://www.marshall.usc.edu/greif)

For more information on the program rankings, visit http://www.entrepreneur.com/topcolleges.

Some entrepreneurs start their businesses after working as regular salaried employees in their chosen industry. That's how Todd Ramis entered the field. "I was working as an editor at a publishing company when an acquaintance I knew who published a newsletter decided to retire," he recalls. "He asked me if I wanted to purchase his newsletter, and I jumped at the chance. I had a built-in customer base that I could tap as I began to publish more newsletters and books."

There are a number of franchise directories available that list hundreds of franchise opportunities in diverse areas. While some franchisers sell units all across the country, others only do business in a few states. Some of the most successful franchises can guarantee a franchisee great revenue, but these franchise units can require hundreds of thousands of dollars in initial investment. Many franchisees own more than one franchise unit with a company; some even tie two different franchises together in a practice called "cross-branding." For example, a franchisee may own a pizza franchise, as well as an ice cream franchise housed in the same restaurant. Another combination owners find popular is having a convenience store that also houses a fast food outlet.

## WHERE CAN I GO FROM HERE?

Entrepreneurs advance by building profitable businesses that are well respected in their communities or industries. They may also advance by expanding the size of their business or receiving more prestigious contracts or expanding the types of services or products that they offer.

A new franchise unit usually takes a few years to turn profitable. Once the business has proven a success, franchisees may choose to invest in other franchise units with the same company. Franchise owners may also be able to afford to hire management and other staff to take on some of the many responsibilities of the business.

## WHAT ARE THE SALARY RANGES?

Earnings for entrepreneurs vary greatly depending on such factors as the type of business they own, the amount of money they were able to initially invest without taking a loan, the location of the business, and other factors. Some entrepreneurs may earn nothing in the first year of operating their businesses, while others may earn $30,000 to $50,000 or more. Entrepreneurs with successful businesses can earn more than $100,000 annually.

An IFA survey of 1,000 franchise owners found that the average yearly salary of this group was $91,630. Approximately 24 percent made more than $100,000 annually.

Since entrepreneurs operate their own businesses, they generally do not have paid sick days or holidays. In addition, they are typically responsible for providing their own insurance and retirement plans.

## WHAT IS THE JOB OUTLOOK?

Entrepreneurship is risky. Only 44 percent of new businesses with employees last at least four years, according to the U.S. Small Business Administration's Office of Advocacy. It takes considerable money, time, and effort to open a business and to keep it going long enough to start seeing profits. Success also depends on trends, customer demand, political climate, competition, the economy, and other unpredictable social factors.

Despite the risks, entrepreneurship will continue to be strong. It is part of the American identity—the United States is viewed worldwide as a land of opportunity. A Harris Interactive Survey found that 40 percent of people between the ages of eight and 21 have or would like to start their own business.

There are no educational, racial, or gender barriers to starting a new business, so there are opportunities for people of all backgrounds. According to The Kauffman Firm Survey, nearly 25 percent of new businesses in 2008 were owned by minorities. In 2008–09 the nation's 10.1 million women-owned businesses employed more than 13 million people and contributed $1.9 trillion to the economy, according to the Center for Women's Business Research.

The trend in home-based businesses is growing rapidly. The trend was started primarily by women who wanted to stay home to care for their children but either didn't want to give up their jobs or needed the income. Now more than half of the people working from home are men. Other factors that have contributed to the increase of at-home businesses include downsizing during hard economic times, the growth of the Internet and computer technology, and the growth of the service sector of the economy.

# Financial Analysts

## SUMMARY

**Definition**
Financial analysts analyze the financial situation of companies and recommend ways for these companies to manage, spend, and invest their money. Financial analysts also conduct similar research on companies that might become investment opportunities. They perform these duties for companies and individual investors.

**Alternative Job Titles**
Investment analysts
Security analysts

**Salary Range**
$43,440 to $73,150 to $141,070+

**Educational Requirements**
Bachelor's degree

**Certification or Licensing**
Recommended

**Employment Outlook**
Much faster than the average

**High School Subjects**
Business
Computer science
Mathematics

**Personal Interests**
Business
Economics

"Working as a financial analyst enables you to join with other professionals to improve the way the business operates," says Jessica Allen, a financial analyst for Rolls-Royce. "The finance role goes far beyond just working with numbers. There is a constant challenge to determine what is driving the figures, why that action is taking place, and propel positive change. Some of the key indicators of a company's strength are financial results. As a financial analyst, you will have a direct impact and a vital role in reporting those results."

## WHAT DOES A FINANCIAL ANALYST DO?

The specific types, direction, and scope of analyses performed by *financial analysts* are many and varied, depending on the industry, the employer or client, and the analyst's training and years of experience. Financial analysts study their employer's or client's financial status and make financial and investment recommendations. To arrive at these recommendations, financial analysts examine the employer's or client's financial history and objectives, income and expenditures, risk tolerance, and current investments. Once they understand the employer's or client's financial standing and investment goals, financial analysts scout out potential investment opportunities. They research other companies, perhaps in a single industry, in which their employer or client may want to invest. This in-depth research consists of investigating the business of each company, including history, past and potential earnings, and products. Based on their findings, financial analysts may recommend that their employer or client buy stock in these companies. If the employer or client already holds stock in a particular company, financial analysts' research may indicate that stocks should be held or sold, or that more should be purchased.

Financial analysts work for companies in any number of industries, including banking, transportation, health care, technology, telecommunications, and energy. While investment options and concerns differ among these, financial analysts still apply the same basic analytic tools in devising investment strategies. They try to learn everything they can about the industry they're working in. They study the markets and make industry comparisons. They also research past performances and future trends of bonds and other investments.

Financial analysts compile many types of reports on their employer or client and on investment opportunities, such as profit and loss statements and quarterly outlook statements. They help develop budgets, analyze and oversee cash flow, and perform cost-benefit analyses. They conduct risk analyses to determine what the employer or client can risk at a given time and/or in future. Another responsibility is to ensure that their employer or client meets any relevant tax or regulatory requirements. Financial analysts compile their work using various software programs, often developing financial models, such as charts or graphs, to display their data.

Companies that want to go public (sell company shares to individual investors for the first time) often ask financial analysts to make projections of future earnings as well as presentations for potential investors. Financial analysts also make sure that all paperwork is in order and compliant with Securities and Exchange Commission rules and regulations.

Entry-level financial analysts, usually working under direct supervision, mainly conduct research and compile statistical data. After a few years of experience, they become more involved in presenting reports. While a financial analyst generally offers recommendations, a senior financial analyst often has the authority to actually decide purchases or sales. Senior financial analysts implement a company's business plan. In larger companies, they also assist different departments in conducting their own financial analyses and business planning. Those in senior positions become supervisors as well, training junior financial analysts.

Many specialties fall under the job title of financial analyst. These specialties vary from employer to employer, and duties overlap between different types of analysts. In smaller firms a financial analyst may have extensive responsibility, while at larger firms a financial analyst may specialize in one of any number of areas. *Budget analysts*, often accountants or controllers, look at the operating costs of a company or its individual departments and prepare budget reports. *Credit analysts* examine credit records to determine the potential risk in extending credit or lending money. *Investment analysts*, also known as investment strategists, evaluate investment data so they can make suitable investment recommendations. Analysts are considered either buy-side analysts, who usually work for money management firms, or sell-side analysts, sometimes called *sales analysts* or *Wall Street analysts*, who usually work for brokerage firms. *Mergers and acquisitions analysts* conduct research and make recommendations relating to company mergers and acquisitions. *Money market analysts* assess financial data and investment opportunities, giving advice specifically in the area of money markets. *Ratings analysts* explore a company's financial situation to determine whether or not it will be able to repay debts. *Risk analysts* focus on evaluating the risks of investments. The intent is to identify and then minimize a company's risks and losses. *Security analysts* specialize in studying securities, such as stocks and bonds. *Tax analysts* prepare, file, and examine federal, state, and local tax payments and returns for their employer or client and perhaps also for local affiliates. They analyze tax issues and keep up with tax law changes. *Trea-*

## To Be a Successful Financial Analyst, You Should...

- have excellent research skills
- be a good communicator
- be highly organized
- have strong analytical skills
- be highly ethical
- have the ability to work as a member of a team
- be willing to travel, when necessary
- be able to work well under pressure
- have good interpersonal skills

*sury analysts* manage their company's or client's daily cash position, prepare cash journal entries, initiate wire transfers, and perform bank reconciliations.

*Financial planners*, also known as *personal financial advisers*, have many similar responsibilities (assessing finances, projecting income, recommending investments), but these are performed on behalf of individuals rather than companies.

Most financial analysts work in an office in a corporate setting. Frequently, they work alone (e.g., when talking on the phone to clients or conducting research). Some may have home offices. They spend considerable time working on a computer, conducting research and compiling data. Financial analysts often travel as part of their jobs. There are clients to meet, meetings and social functions to attend, and companies to research at their place of business. Because financial analysts spend much of their normal business hours talking or meeting with clients, they often conduct research after hours and generally work long days. It is not uncommon for financial analysts to clock well in excess of 50 hours per week.

## WHAT IS IT LIKE TO BE A FINANCIAL ANALYST?

Jessica Allen is a financial analyst for Rolls-Royce, an international company that provides power systems in the civil aerospace, defense aerospace, marine, and energy industries. She has worked in the field for two years. "My decision to pursue a career in business came gradually in college," Jessica recalls. "The foundation was built from years of working part-time jobs and developing a thought pattern that aligned to business decision making. As part of my university's core curriculum, certain business classes were required regardless of major. Taking these classes helped me to realize that business is where I belong.

"As a financial analyst," she continues, "I partner with the business to make sure the financial implications of decisions are understood. I provide reports and analysis on areas that are excelling, and areas that are open for opportunity. I develop budgets and forecasts of our financial position at various points in time. Month-end closing of results is a crucial element of the job, and it is during that week or certain budget/forecasting times when extra hours are necessary."

Jessica says that one of the challenges faced by financial analysts is that usually the analyst is not the one executing the day-to-day steps that are being examined. "Consequently," she says, "the analyst has the opportunity to develop influencing skills in order to get people on-board with actions that need to take place. One of the best things about being a financial analyst is that it gives you a unique perspective into the operations of the business. You have to understand the effects of business transactions in order to be able to analyze the financial results. This means that the analyst sees a broader view of the business as a whole compared to functions that might be more limited to their particular piece."

John Largent is the chief investment strategist at MEMBERS Trust Company in Tampa, Florida. He has worked in the field for 25 years. "When I was around 16," he recalls, "I worked on a cattle feedlot and my uncle taught me the cattle futures market. The story goes like this: While I was shoveling wet feed one day, my uncle 'Topper' drove by and asked, 'Is this what you want to do for the rest of your life?' I said, 'NO!,' so he proceeded to teach me the cattle futures market. He said, 'I know how much the cattle cost in this pen, how much the cattle will gain in weight over 120 days, and I know how much the feed costs, but what I don't know is what the price for cattle is going to be in 120 days when I want to sell. However, there is something called the cattle futures market in which I can sell a contract on cattle and almost guarantee a profit by locking in a sale price.' This was the tangible explanation that I needed to understand a method of investing and inspired me to enter the financial industry as a financial analyst."

A typical day for John lasts from 6:30 A.M. to 5:30 P.M. "I start out every day watching the market to develop my strategy for the day," he says. "I spend the majority of my day researching the markets, assisting clients, trading, and developing initiatives to grow our company. Basically, I manage people and their retirement money. I really enjoy my career and enjoy working longer than normal hours."

John says that the best part of his job is its variety. "I can be looking at international markets one hour, domestic markets the next, and then switch between the bond market and the stock market," he explains. "One minute I am helping a client and the next I am analyzing or developing a huge initiative for our firm. The economy and markets are always changing. I enjoy the challenge to stay up to date and try to figure out where it is all going. This is a job for the person who always wants to grow and learn. I like writing policies and procedures the least."

John says that one of the most interesting and rewarding things that has happened to him is being ranked number one by Forbes.com among national ETF managers in 2008. "On a personal note," he says, "one of the most rewarding things to me was when in these volatile markets, one of my clients recently asked me 'Why am I still retired and happy while my friends are going back to work?' It blew me away that I was a big part of helping them accomplish this dream."

Catherine Chan is a senior operations finance analyst at Boston Scientific Corporation. She has worked in the field since she graduated from college in 2004. "I have always been interested in corporate finance," she says. "My co-op opportunity with Johnson & Johnson in the summer of 2004 really helped me to decide this is the right field for me. I did consider getting into investment banking like every other young graduate. I have interviewed at many firms [on] Wall Street and interned at Goldman Sachs, but I decided that I would fit better in the world of corporate finance.

"My current position is senior financial analyst at operation finance," she continues. "Primarily, it is a consolidation role for all operation financial data. I perform monthly close duties and quarterly/annual forecasts for corporate operation function. I also work with controllers from 15 sites (manufacturing, distribution, and global supply chain) to provide financial reporting. During the busy time, my workday can last as long as 12 hours or more, but during downtime, my workday is 8:30 to 5:30 with a nice, relaxing lunch. It gets busy during monthly close (first week of the month), quarter forecasting (middle month of the quarter), and annual forecast (second half year, Q3–Q4). Quick turnaround and short time line are just part of the job."

## DO I HAVE WHAT IT TAKES TO BE A FINANCIAL ANALYST?

To be successful in this field, you will need to have strong research, organizational, and communication skills. Financial analysts conduct in-depth research, often looking for hard-to-find data. Organizational skills are important when it comes to compiling and presenting this data. Once you have explored a company's financial situation, you must communicate complicated ideas through presentations and/or written reports. You should be able to clearly communicate ideas, both verbally when making presentations and on paper when writing reports. "A financial analyst has to have an excellent base knowledge of both the finance and accounting fields of study," says Jessica Allen. "The finance and accounting skills will overlap and intertwine depending on the task at hand. However, the financial analyst needs more than just strong technical skills. A significant part of the job involves interacting with other people in the business and representing the finance voice for strategic decisions. Therefore, the financial analyst must work well with others, be confident in his or her position during difficult situations, be able to teach challenging concepts, and be a leader."

"Successful people in our field are extremely detail-oriented and very familiar with the common financial software tools (SAP, Hyperion) and Microsoft Office applications," says Catherine Chan. "They are excellent communicators, especially in roles like mine. They also have to be quick learners and flexible. They have to be very responsible with deadlines. Missing some deadlines can create a domino effect that would make many people unhappy. It is an all-around team sport."

This work requires strong analytic skills, so a knack for numbers and attention to detail are also helpful. An interest

---

## Mean Annual Earnings for Financial Analysts, 2008

Other financial investment activities: $111,500

Securities and commodity contracts intermediation and brokerage: $100,900

Management of companies and enterprises: $78,760

Depository credit intermediation: $74,640

Insurance carriers: $73,660

Source: U.S. Department of Labor

---

in solving problems will go a long way. It is important that a financial analyst be accurate and thorough in preparing financial statements.

You should enjoy reading and be able to retain what you read, since it is important to keep up with what's happening in the industry and take it into account when offering financial solutions to employers or clients. Since many financial analysts must travel at a moment's notice to conduct research or complete a deal, flexibility is another important characteristic.

You should have good interpersonal skills and enjoy interacting with others. Deals or important contacts can be made at social functions or business conferences. Financial analysts should be able to work well under pressure, as this line of work often demands long hours and entails strict deadlines. "Dependability and integrity are huge," says John Largent. "In my case, these clients' financial well-being is in my hands. They have to be able to depend on me to do my job and have integrity in the process. Time management is also important. The markets open at 9:30 A.M. EST and close at 4:00 P.M. EST whether I am ready or not."

"Analytical and quantitative skills are a must," says Barbara MacLeod, CFA, a professor of finance at Ohio Wesleyan University in Delaware, Ohio, and a former financial analyst. "Other important skills include communication (both oral and written), time management, decisiveness, willingness to take responsibility but not let one bad decision influence your mood or outlook, and ability to make decisions in an uncertain environment. A strong dose of common sense and a curiosity streak also help. Depending on the particular position, people and sales skills are also quite important."

# HOW DO I BECOME A FINANCIAL ANALYST?
## Education

### High School

Since financial analysts work with numbers and compile data, you should take as many math classes as are available. Accounting, business, economics, and computer classes will be helpful as well. A good grasp of computer spreadsheet programs such as Excel is vital. Take extra care as you research and write reports in any subject matter or in public speaking, and it will pay off later when you must con-

duct investment research and write and present investment recommendations.

### Postsecondary Training

Most employers require that financial analysts hold a bachelor's degree in accounting, business administration, economics, finance, or statistics. Other possible majors include communications, international business, and public administration. Some companies will hire you if you hold a bachelor's degree in another discipline as long as you can demonstrate mathematical ability. In college, take business, economics, and statistics courses. Since computer technology plays such a big role in a financial analyst's work, computer classes can be helpful as well. English composition classes can prepare you for the writing you will need to do when preparing reports. Some employers require a writing sample prior to an interview.

"My primary method of preparation for the finance field was through rigorous study for my financial management major in college," says Jessica Allen. "I also double minored in applied business technology and international business. I knew that these three areas of knowledge would complement each other well and help me to be better prepared to apply my finance skills in a global organization." Jessica also participated in a strategic planning competition for two years in college, serving as the "CFO" and "CEO," respectively. "This experience," she says, "helped me to understand the decisions that the executive team of a company must work through in order to make their company a success. The competition included developing both a business plan and an annual report, evaluating actual results to targets, and justifying our business decisions in a presentation to judges."

Financial analysts generally continue to take courses to keep up with the ongoing changes in the world of finance, including international trade, state and federal laws and regulations, and computer technology. Proficiency in certain databases, presentation graphics, spreadsheets, and other software is expected. Some employers require their employees to have a master's degree.

## Certification or Licensing

Financial analysts can earn the title chartered financial analyst (CFA). While certification is not required, it is recommended. The CFA program, which is administered by the CFA Institute, consists of three levels of examinations. These rigorous exams deal with such topics as economics, financial statement analysis, corporate finance, and portfolio management. The CFA Institute states that a candidate may need to spend at least 250 hours studying to prepare for each level. A candidate can take only one level per year, so a minimum of three years is required to become a CFA charterholder. If a candidate fails a level, it can be taken the next year. Candidates who do not successfully complete all three levels within seven years must reregister.

Before taking the exams, you must already have a bachelor's degree (or four years of professional experience). There is no required course of study. Prior to earning the CFA charter, you must have spent three years in a related field working in the investment decision-making process and you must first apply to become a member of the CFA Institute as well as a local society.

The CFA charter is recognized around the world as a standard in the finance industry. Many employers expect job seekers to be CFA charterholders.

Many financial analysts also choose to earn the certified financial planner (offered by the CFP Board) or chartered financial consultant (offered by The American College) designations.

John Largent says that certification is very important to career success. "It adds to your technical knowledge," he explains, "which allows the person to excel above many others without the designation. It comes with an ethical requirement that can positively influence the industry we serve. It adds credibility that you have mastered a rigorous set of objectives in a very competitive environment."

Many financial analysts have a background in accounting. Many analysts with such a background pursue the certified management accountant (CMA) designation from the Institute of Management Accountants. Applicants must have earned a bachelor's degree, pass a four-part examination, agree to meet continuing education requirements, and have at least two years of experience in management accounting. "Becoming a certified management accountant has been one of the most rewarding things I have experienced as a financial analyst," says Jessica Allen. "It took a lot of hard work, dedication, and a commitment to professional development. Embracing the challenge, I not only passed all four required tests my first time taking them, but I was able to complete them within four-and-a-half-months. In fact, I finished the examination requirement of the CMA designation before I met the two-year experience requirement. A professional certification such as the CMA sets me apart from others in the field and provides me with opportunities to network in the financial industry."

For certain upper-level positions, some firms require that you have a certified public accountant license.

## Internships and Volunteerships

College programs that require an internship usually either have an established internship program set up in partnership with local companies, or the program's placement department works with the student to locate a suitable internship that will fulfill the requirements. Required internships generally last between one and two semesters and offer no pay; instead, the experience counts for a stipulated number of credit hours, in accordance with the degree program's requirements. Many top firms offer summer internship programs. Check company Web sites for the particulars, such as assignments and qualifications. An internship can provide you with helpful contacts and increase your chances of landing a job when you finish college.

While in high school, you might volunteer to handle the bookkeeping for a school club or student government, or help balance the family checking account to become familiar with simple book-keeping practices.

John Largent participated in several experiential educational opportunities while in college. "First, I would visit a local brokerage company and hang out learning as much as I could," he recalls. "Then, I accepted an invitation to volunteer for a portfolio manager with a local banking group. I gained many valuable insights from that experience. For example, my first day on the job, I set up delivery of approximately $10 million in municipal bond swaps. Then, I was picked from a college class to be an intern on the floor of the New York Stock Exchange. This gave me both technical and real-world, ground-level experience in the market."

## WHO WILL HIRE ME?

Financial analysts work in the private and public sectors. Employers include banks, brokerage and securities firms, corporations, mutual and pension funds, individuals, government agencies, manufacturers, and financial management, insurance, investment, trust, and utility companies. Many financial analysts are self-employed.

According to the *Occupational Outlook Handbook*, more than 40 percent of financial analysts work for security and commodity brokers, banks and credit institutions, and insurance carriers. The rest work mainly for insurance carriers, computer and data processing services, and management and public relations firms.

Since financial analysts often work in Wall Street companies, many employers are found in New York City. They are

## Pros and Cons

Barbara MacLeod, a professor of finance and a former financial analyst, details what she liked most and least about working as a financial analyst:

What I most enjoyed was having the freedom to investigate almost anything that interested me in relation to a firm or industry, and then taking the data and striving for a better analysis so that my company would do better than others. It brought out my competitive streak through using my intelligence. Getting it right is so much fun! My least favorite thing, other than being wrong of course, was the mountains of information cascading in a never-ceasing flow. One has to be very adept at sifting through sources, and realizing that there is no possible way to be as thorough as one would like, and still have to make a decision that affects other people's lives through their investments.

also concentrated in other large cities but work in smaller cities as well. Approximately 221,000 financial analysts are employed in the United States.

Representatives from hiring companies (e.g., banks, brokerage firms, or investment companies) may visit college campuses to meet with students interested in pursuing careers as financial analysts. College career services offices will have details on such visits. Company Web sites may also offer campus recruiting schedules.

Gaining an entry-level position can be difficult. Some companies offer in-house training, but many don't. Beginning as a research assistant or as a temporary worker are two ways to break into the business. Read member profiles at association sites to see where members have worked as financial analysts. Explore those companies that look appealing. Catherine Chan was hired as temporary worker by Boston Scientific and within three months was hired full time.

Make contacts and network with other financial analysts. Your local CFA Institute society or chapter will probably hold regular meetings, affording ample networking opportunities. You can become a CFA Institute member whether or not you are a CFA charterholder, but charterholders enjoy full member benefits, such as access to job postings. (Complete details, including listings for local societies and chapters, can be found at the CFA Institute's Web site, http://www.cfainstitute.org.)

As an interview tool, the New York Society of Security Analysts suggests that you compile an investment recommendation for potential clients to give them an idea of the kind of research you're capable of and how you present your data.

You can search for job ads online. One resource is the Jobsinthemoney.com network (http://www.jobsinthemoney.com). If you know what companies you'd like to work for, visit their Web sites. Chances are you will find online job listings there.

## WHERE CAN I GO FROM HERE?

Financial analysts who accurately prepare their employer's or client's financial statements and who offer investment advice that results in profits will likely be rewarded for their efforts. Rewards come in the form of promotions and/or bonuses. Successful financial analysts may become senior financial analysts, sometimes in only three or four years. Some become portfolio or financial managers. Rather than simply making recommendations on their company's or client's investment policies, those who advance to a senior position have more decision-making responsibility.

Some financial analysts move on to jobs as investment bankers or advisors. Others become officers in various departments in their company. Positions include chief financial officer and vice president of finance. In time, some cultivate enough contacts to be able to start their own consulting firms.

## WHAT ARE THE SALARY RANGES?

Median annual earnings for financial analysts were $73,150 in 2008, according to the U.S. Department of Labor. Salaries ranged from less than $43,440 to $141,070 or more.

In addition to their salary, financial analysts may receive a bonus if their investment advice proves successful. With bonuses, skilled financial analysts can make much more than their base salary.

Benefits include paid vacation, health, disability, life insurance, and retirement or pension plans. Some employers also offer profit-sharing plans. Tuition reimbursement may also be available.

## WHAT IS THE JOB OUTLOOK?

The employment outlook for financial analysts is directly tied to the state of the economy and the stock market. When the economy is doing well, companies are more likely to make investments, resulting in a need for financial analysts. When the economy is doing poorly, companies are less likely to make investments, and there will be less need for financial analysts. The *Occupational Outlook Handbook (OOH),* anticipating an increase in business investments, predicts much faster than average employment growth in this field through 2016. The *OOH* also notes that international securities markets, the complexity of financial products, and business mergers and acquisitions demand that financial analysts sort through all the issues involved. Because of the close scrutiny analysts have been under, it might become more desirable for financial analysts to hold the CFA charter. Despite the prediction for strong growth, competition for positions as financial analysts will be very strong since many people are interested in entering this field. Applicants with strong college grades in finance, accounting, and economics courses and an MBA or certification will have the best job prospects.

Individual investing will also affect the need for financial analysts, in that the more people invest in mutual funds (often through 401(k) plans), the greater the need there will be for financial analysts to recommend financial products to the mutual fund companies.

# Financial Planners

## SUMMARY

### Definition
Financial planning is the process of establishing financial goals and creating ways to reach them. Financial planners examine the assets of their clients and suggest what steps they need to take in the future to meet their goals.

### Alternative Job Titles
Fiduciary advisers
Financial advisers
Investment advisers
Personal financial advisers

### Salary Range
$34,390 to $69,050 to $195,394+

### Educational Requirements
Bachelor's degree

### Certification or Licensing
Recommended (certification)
Required for certain positions (licensing)

### Employment Outlook
Much faster than the average

### High School Subjects
Business
Mathematics

### Personal Interests
Business
Economics
Helping people: personal service

"The most rewarding thing I have seen as a certified financial planner is when a plan I helped start many years before comes full circle," says Theodore Feight, president of Creative Financial Design. "I have many clients who I have worked with for 20, 30, or more years. I have helped them plan and seen those plans all the way to their end. I have seen people save for goals, retire, and die—accomplishing everything they wanted within their lifetimes. I have had clients die leaving a young family. Then seen the children of that client grow, go to col-

lege, marry, have children, and prepare their children for college. All because of the planning work we had done many years before.

"I have been told that many of my current clients do not have enough money for me to manage and that I should fire them," Theodore continues. "I can't do that; if they had set their plans in motion with me and have met their end of the planning, I want to be there in the end to see how their story ends. They are my friends, my clients, my life's work, and why God has put me where I am."

## WHAT DOES A FINANCIAL PLANNER DO?

*Financial planners* advise their clients on many aspects of finance. Although they seem to be jacks-of-all-trades, financial planners do not work alone; they meet with their clients' other advisers, such as attorneys, accountants, trust officers, and investment bankers. Financial planners fully research their clients' overall financial picture. After meeting with the clients and their other advisers, financial planners analyze the data they have received and generate a written report that includes their recommendations on how the clients can best achieve their goals. This report details the clients' financial objectives, current income, investments, risk tolerance, expenses, tax returns, insurance coverage, retirement programs, estate plans, and other important information.

Financial planning is an ongoing process. The plan must be monitored and reviewed periodically so that adjustments can be made, if necessary, to assure that it continues to meet individual needs.

The plan itself is a set of recommendations and strategies for clients to use or ignore, and financial planners should be ready to answer hard questions about the integrity of the plans they map out. After all, they are dealing with all of the money and investments that people have worked a lifetime accruing.

People need financial planners for different things. Some might want life insurance, college savings plans, or estate planning. Sometimes these needs are triggered by changes in people's lives, such as retirement, death of a spouse, disability, marriage, birth of children, or job changes. Financial planners spend the majority of their time on the following topics: investment planning, retirement planning, tax planning, estate planning, and risk management. All of these areas require different types of financial knowledge, and planners are generally expected to be extremely competent in the disciplines of asset management, employee benefits, estate planning, insurance, investments, and retirement, according to the Certified Financial Planner Board of Standards. A financial planner must also have good interpersonal skills, since establishing solid client-planner relationships is essential to the planner's success. It also helps to have good communication skills, since even the best financial plan, if presented poorly to a client, can be rejected.

The job of financial planners is driven by clients. The advice planners provide depends on their clients' particular needs, resources, and priorities. Many people think they cannot afford or do not need a comprehensive financial plan. Financial planners must have a certain amount of expertise in sales to build their client base.

Financial planners use various methods to develop their client lists, including telephone solicitation, giving seminars on financial planning to the general public or specific organizations, and networking with social contacts. Referrals from satisfied customers also help the business grow.

Although financial planners are trained in comprehensive financial planning, some specialize in one area, such as asset management, investments, or retirement planning. In most small or self-owned financial planning companies, they are generalists. However, in some large companies, planners might specialize in particular areas, including insurance, real estate, mutual funds, annuities, pensions, or business valuations.

Most financial planners work by themselves in offices or at home. Others work in offices with other financial planners. Established financial planners usually work the same hours as others in the business community. Those new to the field who are seeking customers probably work longer hours. Many planners accommodate customers by meeting with them in the evenings and on weekends. They might spend a lot of time out of the office meeting with current and prospective clients, attending civic functions, and participating in trade association meetings.

## WHAT IS IT LIKE TO BE A FINANCIAL PLANNER?

Todd Black is a certified financial planner and the owner of Dogwood Capital Management, Inc., a private wealth management firm in Cumming, Georgia. "I graduated from the University of Arizona in 1995 with a bachelor's degree in finance," he says. "At the time I didn't know what I wanted to be when I grew up. I went to work for Bank of America in its large corporate/middle-market lending unit in the hopes I would find something that really inspired me. Maybe I would go to work for one of our customers? Bank of America trained me to be a corporate credit analyst. My job was to analyze financial statements and write an analysis, which my superiors (who were the relationship managers of the account) would use in managing the banks' loan portfolio. We worked on syndicated and non-syndicated credit facilities ranging from $1 million to $1 billion. I like economics and financial analysis, but I love interacting with people. Financial planning was a marriage of my analytical training and my personality. When I switched from banking to financial planning in 1997, I was contemplating becoming a mutual fund manager. Financial planning was a much better fit for my temperament. I've been in financial planning since 1997 and I started my own company in 1999."

Todd says that the relationships he develops with his clients are one of his favorite aspects of his job. "I have [an atypical] financial planning business model," he explains. "I serve a small number of high net-worth families and I give advice on a wide range of issues (including nonfinancial ones)."

Todd begins his workweek each Monday by reviewing his clients' portfolios. "I review accounts and perform routine maintenance," he explains. For retired clients who are drawing a 'salary' from their portfolios, I make sure that the cash is available for their monthly draw and that the draw goes through according to our plan. The rest of my week is consumed with research and interacting with my clients via email, the telephone, or lunch meetings. Ninety-five percent of my client meetings are lunch meetings. I work about 30 to 50 hours per week. I read a tremendous amount of material, most of which pertains to managing client portfolios."

Todd says that his company has evolved significantly since 1999. "It looks nothing like I thought it would when we started the practice," he says, "but it is much better and more personally rewarding than I could have hoped it to be. My clients are my family and my friends and 90 percent of the calls I receive from them are social. There have been stressful times over the past decade, including a bear market and the [2008] market crash, but ultimately those difficult times have helped me to be a better wealth manager and a better servant for my clients. No career works

out exactly as you plan, be it in wealth management or any other industry, but that's all right. The world around us is changing at a rapid rate and we must have the flexibility and the perseverance to take advantage of the opportunities it presents us."

Carl Amos Johnson is a fiduciary adviser (fee-only) at Ames Planning Associates Inc. in Peterborough, New Hampshire. He says that there is no such thing as a typical day as a financial planner. "The work day can be eight to 14 hours long," he says. "Usually there are many emails to check in the morning, some phone calls to return, a few meetings with clients, and some research in between. Dramatic examples of the responsibilities of a fiduciary adviser can be to comfort a widow and organize [her] financial affairs. It can also involve some very serious math and analysis of legal documents. But ultimately, there is almost always a direct interaction with someone who needs your help and expertise. And when I am able to help, I am so gratified.

"My most rewarding tasks as a financial planner are threefold," he continues. "First, directly caring for and creating solutions for clients are the best elements to this profession. Secondly, I get to work with and develop a team of professionals whose mission is to empower those same clients. And lastly, the depth and breadth of wealth management keeps my interest every day as I work with [topics ranging from] technical investment issues, to personal relationships with families and business owners, to legal issues like estate planning."

## Choosing a Career Path

Carl Amos Johnson details how he became a fee-only financial planner:

I invested in my first mutual funds while I was still in high school and continued to read and learn more about the financial world while in college. I began doing some investment work just a couple years after college. It started out helping friends, then family, and then seriously contemplating a business career. I was an active duty naval officer for nine years. During that time I earned an MBA at Jacksonville University in Florida. I saw that not only was I interested in business, but I also grasped the business concepts quickly. However, just as quickly I realized that I wanted to work more personally, and in my mind, in a more impactful way, to help those that I cared about. I did not want to make, market, or lead a company that produced tangible things. Most businesses are about creating and selling a product. I wanted to be of service, to help people directly on an individual basis. So with my MBA experience, I went to the more specific world of investments and financial planning. I learned about the certified financial planner program and jumped on it.

It turned out not to be that easy, however. The academics and the concepts weren't the problem—I loved that part. The issue was the career path. The vast majority of professionals in the field of investment and financial planning were salespeople. Ultimately, they gave advice and were compromised because they had to sell a particular line of mutual funds, annuities, or something else like insurance. They were not really advisers working for the client. I was so disappointed. I did not want to be a salesman. A year or so later, while still serving in the navy, I learned about an independent advisory method called "fee-only." This was exactly what I wanted: to be a true fiduciary adviser with no conflicts.

## DO I HAVE WHAT IT TAKES TO BE A FINANCIAL PLANNER?

"Financial planners must exhibit the four C's: character, competency, chemistry, and communication," says Todd Black. "The most important quality of a successful financial planner is character. Financial planners are fiduciaries. This means they are morally, ethically, and legally required to put the interests of their clients ahead of their own interests. No amount of regulation or professional designations will mitigate a character deficit. Analytical competency (like the CFP license) must be married with good people skills (which means good personal chemistry and communication skills)."

"One has to truly love people in this business, not just numbers," says Carl Amos Johnson. "You must have a servant-leader heart to do this job well. That may be said of most professions, but when you are dealing with people and their money, the issues and communication inevitably are deeper and more complex than most expect."

Other factors that contribute to success as a financial planner include obtaining referrals from clients, keeping up with continuing education, developing in-demand specializations, and having a strong educational background.

# HOW DO I BECOME A FINANCIAL PLANNER?

## Education

### High School

If financial planning sounds interesting to you, take as many business classes as possible as well as mathematics. Communication courses, such as speech or drama, will help put you at ease when talking in front of a crowd, something financial planners must do occasionally. English courses will help you prepare the written reports planners present to their clients. Computer classes will help you learn how to use computers to conduct research and communicate with clients.

### Postsecondary Training

Earning a bachelor's degree starts financial planners on the right track, but it will help if your degree indicates a skill with numbers, be it in science or business. A business administration degree with a specialization in financial planning or a liberal arts degree with courses in accounting, business administration, economics, finance, marketing, human behavior, counseling, and public speaking is excellent preparation for this sort of job.

## Certification or Licensing

Education alone will not motivate clients to easily turn over their finances to you. Many financial professionals are licensed on the state and federal levels in financial planning specialties, such as stocks and insurance. The U.S. Securities and Exchange Commission and most states have licensing requirements for investment advisers, a category under which most financial planners also fall. However, most of the activities of planners are not regulated by the government. Therefore, to show credibility to clients, most financial planners choose to become certified as either a certified financial planner (CFP) or a chartered financial consultant (ChFC).

To receive the CFP mark of certification, offered by the CFP Board, candidates must meet what the board refers to as the four E's, which comprise the following:

Education: To be eligible to take the certification exam, candidates must meet education requirements in one of the following ways. The first option is to complete a CFP board-registered program in financial planning. The second is to hold a specific degree and professional credentials in one of several areas the board has approved of; these include certified public accountant, licensed attorney, chartered financial consultant, chartered life underwriter, chartered financial analyst, doctor of business administration, and Ph.D. in business or economics. Lastly, applicants may submit transcripts of their undergraduate or graduate education to the board for review. If the board feels the education requirements have been met, the candidate may sit for the exam. Additionally, applicants must have a bachelor's degree in any area of study or program to obtain CFP certification. They do not need to have earned this degree at the time they take the examination, but must show proof of completion of this degree in order to complete the final stage of certification.

Examination: Once candidates have completed the education requirements, they may take the certification exam, which tests knowledge on various key aspects of financial planning.

Experience: Either before or after passing the certification exam, candidates must have three years of work experience.

Ethics: After candidates have completed the education, examination, and experience requirements, they must voluntarily ascribe to the CFP Board's Code of Ethics and Professional Responsibility and Financial Planning Practice Standards to be allowed to use the CFP mark. This voluntary agreement empowers the board to take action if a CFP licensee violates the code. Such violations could lead to disciplinary action, including permanent revocation of the right to use the CFP mark.

The American College offers the ChFC designation. To receive this designation, candidates must complete certain course work stipulated by The American College, meet experience requirements, and agree to uphold The American College's Code of Ethics and Procedures.

To maintain the CFP and the ChFC designations, professionals will need to meet continuing education and other requirements as determined by the CFP Board and The American College.

Two other organizations offer certification to financial planning professionals. Fi360 offers the accredited investment fiduciary and accredited investment fiduciary analyst designations. The Investment Management Consultants Association offers the following designations: certified investment management analyst and char-

tered private wealth advisor. Contact these organizations for more information.

## Internships and Volunteerships

Your college's career services office will be able to suggest companies or financial planners that offer internships to college students. As an intern, you will receive hands-on experience working with financial planners and get a chance to explore the various aspects of the field. You will also make valuable contacts, which you might be able to use to help you land a job after you graduate. If you can't land an internship, try contacting a financial planner in your community to inquire about volunteer opportunities.

"If I were starting over as a young man, I would get a financial or financial planning degree," advises certified financial planner Theodore Feight. "During college I would offer to work free for a financial planner in my area, preferably a member of the National Association of Personal Financial Advisors (NAPFA). Then I would go to a major national convention put on by NAPFA or the Financial Planning Association. I would listen to the speakers and pick one I wanted to learn from. I would then offer to work for them for whatever I had to so they would teach me. I have seen this done and it worked very well."

## WHO WILL HIRE ME?

There are approximately 176,000 personal financial advisers employed in the United States. Financial planners work for financial planning firms across the country. Many of these firms are small, perhaps employing two to 15 people, and most are located in urban areas. A smaller, but growing,

## Financial Planner Profile: Theodore Feight

Theodore Feight is a certified financial planner and the president of Creative Financial Design, a financial planning firm that has offices in Lansing and Kalamazoo, Michigan. He discussed his career with the editors of *What Can I Do Now? Business and Finance*.

**Q.  How long have you worked in the field? Why did you decide to become a financial planner?**

**A.**  I became a financial planner on July 15, 1973. My family was in the petroleum business. When I got out of college I went to work for a large petroleum company wholesaling petroleum products. In 1973, after the first oil crisis, I found myself out of a job. So I looked around at all of the places we had lived and all of the jobs I had seen and decided to go where the money was and become a financial planner. I

wanted a career where I could control my own destiny and only I could fire myself.

**Q.  Please take us through a day in your work life. What are your typical responsibilities and hours?**

**A.**  7:00 A.M.: Download news highlights from the previous day and have my computer read them to me while I get ready for the day

9:00 A.M.: Check my calendar for upcoming appointments and organize staff to be prepared for appointments and projects

9:30 A.M.: Check email and do marketing on Facebook, LinkedIn, Twitter, and our Web site

10:00 A.M.: Prepare for the day's client meetings

---

number of financial planners work for banks, credit unions, corporations, mutual fund companies, insurance companies, accounting or law firms, colleges and universities, credit counseling organizations, and brokerage firms. In addition, many financial planners are self-employed.

Early in their careers, financial planners work for banks, mutual fund companies, or investment firms and usually receive extensive on-the-job training. The job will deal heavily with client-based and research activities. Financial planners may start their own business as they learn personal skills and build their client base. During the first few years, certified financial planners spend many hours analyzing

documents, meeting with other advisers, and networking to find new clients.

## WHERE CAN I GO FROM HERE?

Those who have not changed their career track in five years can expect to have established some solid, long-term relationships with clients. Measured success at this point will be the planners' service fees, which will be marked up considerably from when they started their careers.

Those who have worked in the industry for 10 years usually have many clients, a good track record, and a six-figure income. Experienced financial planners can also

Noon: Participate in a client appointment or a working lunch on upcoming projects

1:00 P.M.: Check email and work on any National Association of Personal Financial Advisors items; I am president of its Midwest Region this year

3:00 P.M.: Attend an appointment or work on marketing, upcoming projects, or do research

4:30 P.M.: Work on client billing, as well as marketing on Facebook, LinkedIn, Twitter, and our Web site

6:00 to 7:00 P.M.: I usually have an appointment with a client or work out at the gym.

Additionally, I am currently writing a book and try [to] find four hours here and there to be able to give it my undivided attention, usually on Friday afternoons.

Q. **What are the most important personal and professional qualities for financial planners?**

A. Financial planners must

- be self motivated
- be willing to work long hours
- have a thirst for knowledge
- not be willing to accept what someone tells them without checking out all the facts for themselves
- be willing to continuously learn new things
- be honest
- be very patient

Q. **What is the employment outlook for financial planners?**

A. There will always be a need for good, honest, hardworking financial planners and advisers. They may not always have the best starting salaries, but they will probably have some of the best salaries later on down the road, if the planner is good.

move into careers in investment banking, financial consulting, and financial analysis. Because people skills are also an integral part of being a financial planner, consulting, on both personal and corporate levels, is also an option. Many planners will find themselves attending business school, either to achieve a higher income or to switch to one of the aforementioned professions.

## WHAT ARE THE SALARY RANGES?

There are several methods of compensation for financial planners. Fee-only means that compensation is earned entirely from fees from consultation, plan develop-ment, or investment management. These fees may be charged on an hourly or project basis depending on clients' needs or on a percentage of assets under management. Commission-only compensation is received from the sale of financial products that clients agree to purchase to implement financial planning recommendations. There is no charge for advice or preparation of the financial plan. Fee-offset means that compensation received in the form of commission from the sale of financial products is offset against fees charged for the planning process. Combination fee/commission is a fee charged for consultation, advice, and financial plan preparation on an hourly, project, or percentage basis. Planners might also receive commissions from recommended products targeted to achieve goals and objectives. Some planners work on a salary basis for financial services institutions such as banks, credit unions, and other related organizations.

The median annual gross income of certified financial planners was $195,394 in 2008, according to the *2008 Survey of Trends in the Financial Planning Industry,* which was conducted by the College for Financial Planning. These incomes were earned from financial plan writing, product sales, consulting, and related activities.

The U.S. Department of Labor reports that financial planners earned a median annual salary of $69,050 in 2008. The most experienced financial planners with the highest level of education earned more than $166,400, while the least-experienced financial planners earned less than $34,390.

Firms might also provide beginning financial planners with a steady income by paying a draw, which is a minimum salary based on the commission and fees the planner can be expected to earn.

Some financial planners receive vacation days, sick days, and health insurance, but that depends on whether they work for financial institutions or on their own.

## WHAT IS THE JOB OUTLOOK?

Employment for financial planners is expected to increase much faster than the average for all occupations through 2016, according to the U.S. Department of Labor. While recent economic setbacks to the U.S. economy have dampened growth to some extent, opportunities should still continue to be good. Employment is expected to grow in the future for a number of reasons. As the economy rebounds, more funds should be available for investment, as personal income and inherited wealth grow. Demographics will also play a role; as increasing numbers of baby boomers turn 50, demand will grow for retirement-related investments. Most people, in general, are likely to turn to financial planners for assistance with retirement planning. Individual saving and investing for retirement are expected to become more important, as many companies reduce pension benefits and switch from defined-benefit retirement plans to defined-contribution plans, which shift the investment responsibility from the company to the individual. Furthermore, a growing number of individual investors are expected to seek advice from financial planners regarding the increasing complexity and array of investment alternatives for assistance with estate planning.

"This industry used to be listed as the best job to have in America," says Carl Amos Johnson. "I think the recent financial meltdown has shown that it certainly is not the easiest job if it is done well. The future is very bright for this career, but the individuals who choose it must be incredibly bright and versatile themselves. The Center for Retirement Research at Boston College states that by 2025, nearly one in five Americans will be age 65 or over compared to one in eight today. The number of folks needing financial planning and investment advice is going to grow rapidly."

The field of financial planning is highly competitive. Many beginners are forced to leave the field because they are unable to build a sufficient clientele. Once established, however, planners have a strong attachment to their occupation because of high earning potential and considerable investment in training. Job opportunities should be best for mature individuals with successful work experience and industry certifications.

# Human Resources Workers

## SUMMARY

**Definition**
Human resources workers formulate policy and organize and conduct programs relating to all phases of personnel activity.

**Alternative Job Titles**
Personnel specialists

**Salary Range**
$27,980 to $55,710 to $163,220+

**Educational Requirements**
Bachelor's degree

**Certification or Licensing**
Recommended

**Employment Outlook**
Faster than the average

**High School Subjects**
Business
Psychology

**Personal Interests**
Business
Business management

"I've always enjoyed the human capital side of business," says Paul Rowson, managing director of the WorldatWork Washington, D.C., Office and Conference Center, who also has 31 years combined experience in general management, business development, and human resources. "Being good at attracting, motivating, and developing people always seemed to me to be the difference between success and failure as a business. What could be more exciting than to be entrusted with a position to lead and influence *global* best practices in managing human capital?"

## WHAT DOES A HUMAN RESOURCES WORKER DO?

*Human resources workers* are the liaison between the management of an organization and its employees. They see that management makes effective use of employees' skills, while at the same time improving working conditions for employees and helping them find fulfillment in their jobs. Most positions in this field involve heavy contact with people, at both management and nonmanagement levels.

Human resources workers are experts in employer-employee relations. They interview job applicants and select or recommend those who seem best suited to the company's needs. Their choices for hiring and advancement must follow the guidelines for equal employment opportunity and affirmative action established by the federal government. Human resources workers also plan and maintain programs for wages and salaries, employee benefits, and training and career development.

*Personnel managers* and *employment managers* are concerned with the overall functioning of the personnel department and may be involved with hiring, employee orientation, record keeping, insurance reports, wage surveys, budgets, grievances, and analyzing statistical data and reports. *Industrial relations directors* formulate the policies to be carried out by the various department managers.

*Government personnel managers* oversee the human resources (HR) departments of entire towns or cities. They may supervise dozens of human resources managers who are responsible for handling the HR needs of hundreds to tens of thousands of workers.

Of all the personnel specialists, the one who first meets new employees is often the *recruiter.* Companies depend on *personnel recruiters* to find the best employees available. To do this, recruiters develop sources through contacts within the community. In some cases, they travel extensively to other cities or to college campuses to meet with college career services directors, attend campus job fairs, and conduct preliminary interviews with potential candidates.

*Employment interviewers* interview applicants to fill job vacancies, evaluate their qualifications, and recommend hiring the most promising candidates. They sometimes administer tests, check references and backgrounds, and arrange for indoctrination and training. They must also be familiar and current with guidelines for equal employment opportunity (EEO) and affirmative action.

In very large organizations, the complex and sensitive area of EEO is handled by specialists who may be called *EEO representatives, affirmative-action coordinators,* or *job-development specialists.* These specialists develop employment opportunities and on-the-job training programs for minority or disadvantaged applicants; devise systems or set up representative committees through which grievances can be investigated and resolved as they come up; and monitor corporate practices to prevent possible EEO violations. Preparing and submitting EEO statistical reports is also an important part of their work.

*Job analysts* are also called *compensation analysts* or *position classifiers.* They study all of the jobs within an organization to determine job and worker requirements. Through observation and interviews with employees, they gather and analyze detailed information about job duties and the training and skills required. They write summaries describing each job, its specifications, and the possible route to advancement. Job analysts classify new positions as they are introduced and review existing jobs periodically. These job descriptions, or position classifications, form a structure for hiring, training, evaluating, and promoting employees, as well as for establishing an equitable pay system.

*Occupational analysts* conduct technical research on job relationships, functions, and content; worker characteristics; and occupational trends. The results of their studies enable business, industry, and government to utilize the general workforce more effectively.

Developing and administering the pay system is the primary responsibility of the *compensation manager.* With the assistance of other specialists on the staff, compensation managers establish a wage scale designed to attract, retain, and motivate employees. A realistic and fair compensation program takes into consideration company policies, government regulations concerning minimum wages and overtime pay, rates currently being paid by similar firms and industries, and agreements with labor unions. The compensation manager is familiar with all these factors and uses them to determine the compensation package.

*Training specialists* prepare and conduct a wide variety of education and training activities for both new and existing employees. Training specialists may work under the direction of an *education and training manager.* Training programs may cover such special areas as apprenticeship programs, sales techniques, health and safety practices, and retraining displaced workers. The methods chosen by training specialists for maximum effectiveness may include individual training, group instruction, lectures, demonstrations, meetings, or workshops, using such teaching aids as handbooks, demonstration models, multimedia programs, and reference works. These specialists also confer with management and supervisors to determine the needs for new training programs or revision of existing ones, maintain records of all training activities, and evaluate the success of the various programs and methods. *Training instructors* may work under the direction of an education and training manager. *Coordinators of auxiliary person-*

*nel* specialize in training nonprofessional nursing personnel in medical facilities.

Training specialists may help individuals establish career development goals and set up a timetable in which to strengthen job-related skills and learn new ones. Sometimes this involves outside study paid for by the company or rotation to jobs in different departments of the organization. The extent of the training program and the responsibilities of the training specialists vary considerably, depending on the size of the firm and its organizational objectives.

Benefits programs for employees are handled by *benefits managers* or *employee-welfare managers.* The major part of such programs generally involves insurance and pension plans. Since the enactment of the Employee Retirement Income Security Act (ERISA), reporting requirements have become a primary responsibility for personnel departments in large companies. The retirement program for state and local government employees is handled by *retirement officers.* In addition to regular health insurance and pension coverage, employee benefit packages have often grown to include such things as dental insurance, accidental death and disability insurance, automobile insurance, homeowner's insurance, profit sharing and thrift/savings plans, and stock options. The expertise of *benefits analysts and administrators* is extremely important in designing and carrying out the complex programs. These specialists also develop and coordinate additional services related to employee welfare, such as car pools, child care, cafeterias and lunchrooms, newsletters, annual physical exams, recreation and physical fitness programs, and counseling. Personal and financial counseling for employees close to retirement age is growing especially important.

In some cases—especially in smaller companies—the personnel department is responsible for administering the occupational safety and health programs. The trend, however, is toward establishing a separate safety department under the direction of a *safety engineer, industrial hygienist,* or other safety and health professionals.

Personnel departments may have access to resources outside the organization. For example, *employer relations representatives* promote the use of public employment services and programs among local employers. *Employee-health maintenance program specialists* help set up local government-funded programs among area employers to provide assistance in treating employees with alcoholism or behavioral medical problems.

In companies where employees are covered by union contracts, *labor relations specialists* form the link between union and management. Prior to negotiation of a collective-bargaining agreement, *labor relations managers* counsel management on their negotiating position and provide background information on the provisions of the current contract and the significance of the proposed changes. They also provide reference materials and statistics pertaining to labor legislation, labor market conditions, prevailing union and management practices, wage and salary surveys, and employee benefit programs. This work requires that labor relations managers be familiar with

sources of economic and wage data and have an extensive knowledge of labor law and collective-bargaining trends. In the actual negotiation, the employer is usually represented by the director of labor relations or another top-level official, but the members of the company's labor relations staff play an important role throughout the negotiations.

Specialists in labor relations, or union-management relations, usually work for unionized organizations, helping company officials prepare for collective-bargaining sessions, participating in contract negotiations, and handling day-to-day labor relations matters. A large part of the work of labor relations specialists is analyzing and interpreting the contract for management and monitoring company practices to ensure their adherence to the terms. Of particular importance is the handling of grievance procedures. To investigate and settle grievances, these specialists arrange meetings between workers who raise a complaint, managers and supervisors, and a union representative. A grievance, for example, may concern seniority rights during a layoff. Labor relations disputes are sometimes investigated and resolved by *professional conciliators* or *mediators.* Labor relations work requires keeping up to date on developments in labor law, including arbitration decisions, and maintaining close contact with union officials.

*Government personnel specialists* do essentially the same work as their counterparts in business, except that they deal with public employees whose jobs are subject to civil service regulations. Much of government personnel work concentrates

> ## To Be a Successful Human Resources Worker, You Should...
>
> - have excellent communication skills
> - be highly organized
> - be fair-minded
> - be able to work as a member of a team
> - be highly ethical

on job analysis, because civil service jobs are strictly classified as to entry requirements, duties, and wages. In response to the growing importance of training and career development in the public sector, however, an entire industry of educational and training consultants has sprung up to provide similar services for public agencies. The increased union strength among government workers has resulted in a need for more highly trained labor relations specialists to handle negotiations, grievances, and arbitration cases on behalf of federal, state, and local agencies.

Human resources professionals work under pleasant conditions in modern offices. Human resources workers are seldom required to work more than 35 or 40 hours per week, although they may do so if they are developing a program or special project. The specific hours you work as a human resources worker may depend upon which company you work for.

Labor relations specialists often work longer hours, especially when contract agreements are being prepared and negotiated. The difficult aspects of the work may involve firing people, taking disciplinary actions, or handling employee disputes.

## WHAT IS IT LIKE TO BE A HUMAN RESOURCES WORKER?

Margaret Whelan is the president-elect of the International Public Management Association for Human Resources and the general manager of the Personnel Department for the City of Los Angeles. "I entered my career in human resources by accident," she says. "I was hired by the City of Los Angeles as a junior administrative assistant and was assigned to the Accounting Division in the Department of Recreation and Parks. The junior administrative assistant program was designed to hire recent college graduates and train them for administrative jobs. I worked in accounting for two months and when a vacancy occurred in the department's Personnel Division I jumped at the opportunity to work in the area of human resources, where I have worked ever since.

"The City of Los Angeles," she continues, "has 43 departments and approximately 50,000 employees. My main duties are to manage the day-to-day operation of the Personnel Department, which is the central personnel agency for the City of Los Angeles and includes employee selection (recruiting and testing), position classification, workers' compensation and safety, employee benefits, civil service appeals, employee training, equal employment opportunity, medical services, and general administration. My secondary duties include providing support services to the mayor and city council members."

Margaret says that one downside to her career in human resources is that "not all problems can be fixed and the result of that is that everyone loses, which I find disheartening. One of the things I like the most about human resources is every day is a new day and when you think you've seen it all you'll find that there is always a new wrinkle that makes it different. I love the challenge of figuring out how to fix a situation to the benefit of the individual or the agency."

## DO I HAVE WHAT IT TAKES TO BE A HUMAN RESOURCES WORKER?

To be a successful human resources worker, you must be able to communicate effectively and clearly both in speech and in writing and interact comfortably and easily with people of different levels of education and experience.

You will also need to be objective and fair-minded because you will often need to consider matters from both the employee's and the employer's point of view.

Human resources workers must be able to cooperate as part of a team; at the same time, they must be able to handle responsibility individually. It is important to be organized because you are often responsible for tracking many different things regarding many different people.

"The most important personal and professional qualities I've found to be important for people to be successful

### Good Advice

Margaret Whelan offers the following advice to high school students who are interested in careers in human resources:

What has benefited me the most in my career is my ability to write and analyze. In college I majored in history because I liked hearing the stories of other people and cultures, and I also liked to understand institutions such as government. I enjoy research, which I think makes me a better analyst. Pay attention in school, read as much as possible (particularly the classics), don't rely strictly on the Internet for research, and think things through before coming up with an opinion or an action plan. Don't be afraid to step outside of your comfort zone.

in the human resources field are to be morally ethical in all of one's dealings," says Paul Rowson. "Have personal courage. Be a good listener. Have emotional intelligence. Be inquisitive and act upon informed instinct and solid data. Never be satisfied with 'average.' Keep your sense of humor. And most of all, be known for being a developer of talent."

## HOW DO I BECOME A HUMAN RESOURCES WORKER?
### Education
#### High School

Since most human resources workers have a college degree, it is a good idea in high school to take college preparatory classes. A solid background in math, science, and English should be helpful in college-level work. You might especially focus on classes that will help you understand and communicate easily with people. English, speech, and psychology classes are all good choices. Business classes can help you understand the fundamental workings of the business world, which is also important. Finally, foreign language skills could prove very helpful, especially in areas where there are large numbers of people who speak a language other than English.

### Postsecondary Training

High school graduates may start out as personnel clerks and advance to a professional position through experience, but such situations are becoming rare. Most employers require human resources workers to have a college degree.

There is little agreement as to what type of undergraduate training is preferable for human resources work. Some employers favor college graduates who have majored in human resources, human resources administration, or industrial and labor relations, while others prefer individuals with a general business background. Another opinion is that human resources workers should have a well-rounded liberal arts education, with a degree in psychology, sociology, counseling, or education. A master's degree in business administration is also considered suitable preparation. Students interested in human resources work with a government agency may find it an asset to have a degree in personnel administration, political science, or public administration.

Individuals preparing for a career as a human resources professional will benefit from a wide range of courses. Classes might include business administration, public administration, psychology, sociology, political science, and statistics. For prospective labor relations specialists, valuable courses include labor law, collective bargaining, labor economics, labor history, and industrial psychology.

Work in labor relations may require graduate study in industrial or labor relations. While not required for entry-level jobs, a law degree is a must for those who conduct contract negotiations, and a combination of industrial relations courses and a law degree is especially desirable. For a career as a professional arbitrator, a degree in industrial and labor relations, law, or personnel management is required.

### Certification or Licensing

Many human resources professional associations offer certification programs. These programs usually consist of a series of classes and a test. For example, the International Foundation of Employee Benefits Plans offers the certified employee benefit specialist designation to candidates who complete a series of college-level courses and pass exams on employee benefits plans. Other organizations that offer certification include the International Public Management Association for Human Resources, American Society for Training and Development, the Society for Human Resource Management, and WorldatWork Society of Certified Professionals. Though voluntary, certification is highly recommended and can improve chances for advancement.

# Human Resources Worker Profile: Paul Rowson

Paul Rowson is the managing director of the WorldatWork Washington, D.C., Office and Conference Center. He discussed his career with the editors of *What Can I Do Now? Business and Finance*.

**Q. How did you train for this job?**

**A.** I received most of my management training on the job and from watching and observing great managers. The hospitality industry is a place where one can find themselves with incredible management responsibilities and decision-making authority at a very early stage of one's career. Although I had no formal college internship in human resources, I thought of each of my early job experiences as working internships. I got the chance to take on many different projects with a variety of managers. Each one of them prepared me for broader and bigger responsibilities.

**Q. What are your main and secondary job duties?**

**A.** My main duty in my current role is to provide leadership in our association's Washington, D.C., Office and Conference Center. This leadership is not only in the area of strategic direction, but also in fostering the relationships that the association needs to develop and maintain as the thought and practice leader for the total rewards profession. ["Total rewards" can be defined as all of the tools available to the employer that may be used to attract, motivate, and retain employees].

**Q. What are some of the pros and cons of your job?**

**A.** The pros of my job are that, in many respects the WorldatWork Washington, D.C., Office and Conference Center is a "start up" venture for WorldatWork. When we arrived here as a new team we had basic objectives, but the opportunity was ours to shape and define with no limits and very basic guidelines. We had the freedom to be both entrepreneurial and intrapreneurial too. I like being in uncharted waters with a very talented team of people. I also enjoy autonomy in making the day-to-day decisions necessary to achieve our goals in the Washington, D.C., office with the benefit of a very capable and experienced team to support me. The cons of the job are few, but ones that can't be overlooked. Our office is distant from the main office in Scottsdale, Arizona. That distance in miles and time zones poses [communication] challenges, [promotes] variety in office cultures, and limits day-to-day interaction with the larger Scottsdale staff. I have to pay attention to these factors and constantly find ways to minimize the gap.

**Q. What have been some of the most rewarding experiences in your career?**

**A.** I remember managing college relations and internships for one the most respected and admired hospitality companies in the world, helping a start-up human resources Web service provider grow from three to 180 company clients, and helping the employees of a Fortune 500 financial services giant weather the toughest moments in its economic and regulatory history. I've been blessed with many rewarding opportunities and experiences in my career. I can honestly say each one prepared me for the role I have today with my colleagues at WorldatWork, serving an entire community of practitioners in the total rewards profession.

## Internships and Volunteerships

Internships are an excellent way to learn more about the demands of a career in human resources while you are still in school. Schools requiring an internship usually will have relationships with area businesses that are willing to host interns. The Society for Human Resource Management offers a database of internship and career opportunities at its Web site (http://www.shrm.org).

"When I was in college," says Margaret Whelan, "I worked as a student professional worker in the Personnel Department and worked in the city's Recruitment Division. The training wasn't formal but the exposure was broad. I worked in this capacity during my sophomore and junior years. I was assigned to work on a program that was designed to hire high school students in city departments. This was my first opportunity to experience how positive it is to offer a person a job. I worked for some wonderful people who were role models and who I still think about to this day. I hope they would be proud of me."

Colleges and universities have placement counselors who can help graduates find employment. Also, large companies often send recruiters to campuses looking for promising job applicants. Otherwise, interested individuals may apply directly to local companies.

While still in high school, you may apply for entry-level jobs as personnel clerks and assistants. Private employment agencies and local offices of the state employment service are other possible sources for work. In addition, newspaper want ads often contain listings of many HR jobs.

Beginners in human resources work are trained on the job or in formal training programs, where they learn how to classify jobs, interview applicants, or administer employee benefits. Then they are assigned to specialized areas in the HR department. Some people enter the labor relations field after first gaining experience in general human resources work, but it is becoming more common for qualified individuals to enter that field directly.

## WHO WILL HIRE ME?

Close to 90 percent of human resources workers are employed in the private sector. Of those specialists who work in the private sector, 13 percent work in administrative and support services; 10 percent work in professional, scientific, and technical services; 9 percent in finance and insurance firms; 9 percent in health care; and 7 percent in manufacturing. The companies that are most likely to hire personnel specialists are the larger ones, which have more employees to manage.

## WHERE CAN I GO FROM HERE?

After trainees have mastered basic personnel tasks, they are assigned to specific areas in the department to gain specialized experience. In time, they may advance to supervisory positions or to manager of a major part of the human resources program, such as training, compensation, or EEO/affirmative action. Advancement may also be achieved by moving into a higher position in a smaller organization. A few experienced employees with exceptional ability ultimately become top executives with titles such as director of personnel, director of human resources, or director of labor relations. As in most fields, employees with advanced education and a proven track record are the most likely to advance in human resources positions.

## WHAT ARE THE SALARY RANGES?

Human resources workers earn salaries that vary widely depending on the nature of the business and the size and location of the firm, as well as on the individual's qualifications and experience.

According to a survey conducted by the National Association of Colleges and Employers, an entry-level human resources specialist with a bachelor's degree in human resources, including labor and industrial relations, earned $41,680 annually in 2007.

Median annual earnings of human resources, training, and labor relations specialists were $55,710 in 2008, according to the U.S. Department of Labor (DoL). Salaries ranged from less than $27,980 to more than $93,880. The DoL reports the following mean salaries for human resources professionals by industry: federal government, $76,460; employment services, $53,900; and business, professional, labor, political, and similar organizations, $48,920. Human resources managers earned salaries that ranged from less than $56,770 to $163,220 or more in 2008.

Benefits for human resources workers depend on the employer; however, they usually include such items as health insurance, retirement or 401(k) plans, and paid vacation days.

## WHAT IS THE JOB OUTLOOK?

Employment for human resources, training, and labor relations managers and specialists is expected to grow faster than the average for all careers through 2016, according to the DoL. The DoL predicts especially strong growth for training and development specialists and employment, recruitment, and placement specialists.

There will continue to be strong competition for jobs, as there will be an abundance of qualified applicants. Opportunities will be best in the private sector as businesses continue to increase their staffs as they begin to devote more resources to increasing employee productivity, retraining, safety, and benefits. Employment should also be strong with consulting firms that offer personnel and benefits and compensation services to businesses that cannot afford to have their own extensive staffs. As jobs change with new technology, more employers will need training specialists to teach new skills. Employment for human resources workers may be affected by the trend in corporate downsizing and restructuring. Applicants who are certified will have the best prospects for employment.

Paul Rowson says that there will also be good opportunities in the public sector, most notably the federal sector. "Of the 22,000 federal sector practitioners in cabinet-level departments and agencies, 64 percent are 45 years or older, and 22 percent are age 55 and older and eligible to retire today."

# Management Analysts and Consultants

## SUMMARY

**Definition**
Management analysts and consultants analyze business or operating procedures to devise the most efficient methods of accomplishing work. They gather and organize information about operating problems and procedures and prepare recommendations for implementing new systems or changes.

**Alternative Job Titles**
Business consultants

**Salary Range**
$41,910 to $73,570 to $250,000+

**Educational Requirements**
Bachelor's degree; advanced degrees required for top positions

**Certification or Licensing**
Voluntary

**Employment Outlook**
Much faster than the average

**High School Subjects**
Business
Computer science
Speech

**Personal Interests**
Business
Business management
Current events
Economics

"Consulting is a very viable, diversified, and interesting profession," says business consultant Bette Price. "Whether one works for a large firm, a small boutique firm, or as an independent really depends on the individual. But the opportunities one has in this profession to make a valuable impact and help companies to grow through objective and outside expertise [makes this] a career path worth exploring."

## WHAT DOES A MANAGEMENT ANALYST OR CONSULTANT DO?

*Management analysts* and *consultants* are called in to solve a diverse range of organizational problems. They come into a situation in which a client is unsure or inexpert and recommend actions or provide assessments. There are many different types of management analysts and consultants. In general, they all require knowledge of general management, operations, marketing, logistics, materials management and physical distribution, finance and accounting, human resources, electronic data processing and systems, and management science.

Management analysts and consultants may be called in when a major manufacturer must reorganize its corporate structure when acquiring a new division. For example, they assist when a company relocates to another state by coordinating the move, planning the new facility, and training new workers. They are often needed when a rapidly growing small company needs a better system of control over inventories and expenses.

The work of management analysts and consultants is quite flexible—it varies from job to job. In general, management analysts and consultants collect, review, and analyze data, make recommendations, and assist in the implementation of their proposals. Some projects require several consultants to work together, each specializing in a different area. Other jobs require the analysts to work independently.

Public and private organizations use management analysts for a variety of reasons. Some organizations lack the resources necessary to handle a project. Other organizations, before they pursue a particular course of action, will consult an analyst to determine what resources will be required or what problems will be encountered. Some companies seek outside advice on how to resolve organizational problems that have already been identified or to avoid troublesome problems that could arise.

Firms providing consulting practitioners range in size from solo practitioners to large international companies employing hundreds of people. The services are generally provided on a contract basis. A company will choose a consulting firm that specializes in the area that needs assistance, and then the two firms negotiate the conditions of the contract. Contract variables include the proposed cost of the project, staffing requirements, and the deadline.

After getting a contract, the analyst's first job is to determine the nature and extent of the project. He or she analyzes statistics, such as annual revenues, employment, or expenditures. He or she may also interview employees and observe the operations of the organization on a day-to-day basis.

The next step for the analyst is to use his or her knowledge of management systems to develop solutions. While preparing recommendations, he or she must take into account the general nature of the business, the relationship of the firm to others in its industry, the firm's internal organization, and the information gained through data collection and analysis.

Once they have decided on a course of action, management analysts and consultants usually write reports of their findings and recommendations and present them to the client. They often make formal oral presentations about their findings as well. Some projects require only reports; others require assistance in implementing the suggestions.

Management analysts and consultants generally divide their time between their own offices and the client's office or production facility. They can spend a great deal of time on the road.

Most management analysts and consultants work at least 40 hours per week plus overtime, depending on the project. The nature of consulting projects—working on location with a single client toward a specific goal—allows these professionals to totally immerse themselves in their work. They sometimes work 14- to 16-hour days, and six- or seven-day workweeks can be fairly common.

While self-employed, consultants may enjoy the luxury of setting their own hours and doing a great deal of their work at home; the trade-off is sacrificing the benefits provided by the large firms. Their livelihood depends on the additional responsibility of maintaining and expanding their clientele on their own.

Although those in this career usually avoid much of the potential tedium of working for one company all day, every day, they face many pressures resulting from deadlines and client expectations. Because the clients are generally paying generous fees, they want to see dramatic results, and the management analyst can feel the weight of this.

## WHAT IS IT LIKE TO BE A MANAGEMENT ANALYST OR CONSULTANT?

Bette Price has worked as a business consultant since 1982 when she founded The Price Group. "As a consultant who

> ### To Be a Successful Management Analyst or Consultant, You Should...
>
> - have good interpersonal and communication skills
> - have an analytical personality
> - be attentive to detail
> - be highly organized
> - have strong leadership skills
> - be a good listener
> - be highly ethical

deals with management and leadership issues," she explains, "my services cover a broad range, including team building, one-on-one executive coaching, the use of assessments to help develop leadership skills and to hire the right individuals into leadership roles, surveying employees to determine the appropriate management changes or training that may be required, and problem solving in a variety of areas. In this capacity I often serve as the CEO's confidant regarding decision making and in the role of a trusted advisor. Recently a colleague and I have completed extensive research on Generation Y (the Millennials), in particular those who are college educated and geared for future leadership roles. Thus, much of today's consulting evolves around helping organizations to leverage the talent of a new generation to ensure their company's future management and growth.

"Because each client has specific needs," Bette continues, "one of the things I love best about this career is that no two days are ever alike. One day I can be dealing with an executive team, using assessments to help them understand how to more effectively work with each other as a team and another day I can be working one-on-one with the CEO or the department head to resolve an issue or help implement some necessary change. My greatest responsibility is to be a good listener so that I truly hear what the client thinks the issues are, [and] then to be knowledgeable enough to discern the appropriate [resolution] and a strong enough communicator to ensure that everyone gets a congruent message on what changes will be made. When it's dealing with one individual from a development standpoint, my greatest responsibility is to be confidential, honest, and willing to ask the difficult questions that perhaps no one else has been willing to ask so that the individual can truly learn and move forward. Each day and each client bring about unique challenges that truly keep me on my toes and give me opportunities to make a positive difference. That's the only constant."

Bette says that one of the least favorite parts of her job is the fact that work can be very cyclical. "In an uncertain economy," she explains, "you can be working a lot one month and wonder where the work will come from the next. So, you can never rest on your laurels. But, that is offset by what I like most—the diverse issues that keep things interesting, the

knowledge that I have the ability to help and make a positive difference, the continual learning that I personally receive by always dealing with new and challenging issues, and the fact that I do have control of my own destiny. If I plan and schedule my work well, I am free to take vacations when I want, to combine business travel with visits to friends and family and work hard so I can play hard. It's a profession that I can continue to enjoy for as long as I'm willing to work and bring value to my clients, thus it is an ageless profession that keeps me young in my thinking and vital in my life."

Loraine Huchler is the founder and president of MarTech Systems Inc., an engineering consulting firm that "assesses and manages risk in water-related utility systems." Before launching her company 12 years ago, she worked for a large corporation for eight years as an internal consultant; she also worked for the U.S. Department of Defense for six years. "I had a keen interest in business and the competition in the marketplace," Loraine explains when asked why she pursued a career in this field. "My first job after college was for the Department of Defense, and I disliked the lack of competition. I spent several years working in civil service before finding a job as an internal consultant in a for-profit organization." One of Loraine's first responsibilities as an internal consultant was to manage a product line. "I was responsible for analyzing the cost to manufacture the product, reviewing sourcing of raw materials, conducting a competitive analysis for pricing and positioning in the marketplace, and tracking sales and profit margins," she explains. "I really enjoyed the sense of ownership and the clear goals for sales and margin targets. I was also responsible for launching a new product; it started with discussions with research and development, followed by designing a field test protocol, and testing the product at several sites. After a series of successful field tests, I had to develop marketing materials and internal product documentation followed by a presentation at the national sales meeting. Launching a new product results in a great sense of accomplishment!"

As the founder and president of a consulting firm, Loraine's days consist of managing her business as well as delivering services to her clients. "My target market is manufacturing," she explains, "and my area of specialization is operations, specifically utility operations. On days that I am delivering services, I will either be on-site at a plant such as a power plant or refinery, inspecting the water utility systems, collecting data or conducting discussions with plant managers, or I will be in the office, analyzing data and writing reports. On days that I am managing my business, I might be writing my quarterly column for a trade journal, reviewing expense reports for my colleagues who work for me, billing my clients, writing proposals, attending conferences, or updating my Web site. The majority of my business is repeat business from existing clients or referrals, so I spend very little time selling. As a business owner, my days are very long, but I have a lot of flexibility and set my own hours."

## Mean Annual Earnings for Management Analysts by Industry, 2008

Management, scientific, and technical consulting services: $96,420

Computer systems design and related services: $88,030

Management of companies and enterprises: $80,770

Federal executive branch: $80,140

State government: $56,480

Source: U.S. Department of Labor

Loraine says the most rewarding aspect of being a business consultant is the trust that her clients have in her abilities. "My clients share information with me that is critical to their competitive advantage and trust that I will protect the confidentiality of that information," she explains. "My clients rely on me for sound business counsel, and it is very rewarding when my advice makes a positive difference in their business. The most frustrating aspect of being a business consultant is a consequence of being a small organization; I spend a lot of time creating and sustaining relationships with my colleagues. These colleagues are a peer group who provide collegiality, information, and business insights that would be provided by coworkers in larger organizations."

## DO I HAVE WHAT IT TAKES TO BE A MANAGEMENT ANALYST OR CONSULTANT?

Management analysts and consultants are often responsible for recommending layoffs of staff, so it is important that they learn to deal with people diplomatically. Their job requires a great deal of tact, enlisting cooperation while exerting leadership, debating their points, and pointing out errors. Consultants must be quick thinkers, able to refute objections with finality. They also must be able to make excellent presentations.

A management analyst must also be unbiased and analytical, with a disposition toward the intellectual side of business and a natural curiosity about the way things work best. They should also have excellent communication skills. "To be an effective consultant," says Bette Price, "you must be incredibly skilled at listening as well as effectively communicating—both in your speaking and writing. Ethics has always been a critical trait, but today, even more so with all the uncertainty brought about by situations like Enron and the latest financial crisis. That's why being involved with an organization like the Institute of Management Consultants USA is so important, since they are the sole entity to certify consultants and award the certified management consultant designation—a major part of which regards to ethical behavior. Beyond that, consultants must be organized, well skilled in their areas of expertise, have analytical skills and, if they are an independent consultant, must be able to market [their skills]."

"Without a doubt," says Loraine Huchler, "the ability to communicate is the most important skill for a business consultant. Besides the obvious skills of writing and speaking, business consultants must be masters of organizing information and explaining issues to their clients. Other aspects of communication that are often overlooked includes aspects of 'etiquette:' clear responses to emails, with specific information and actions; meaningful phone messages; prompt follow-up and follow-through for commitments to provide information or respond back to clients; and striking the right 'balance' of contacting clients and prospects."

## HOW DO I BECOME A MANAGEMENT ANALYST OR CONSULTANT?

### Education

#### High School

In high school, take business, mathematics, and computer science classes. Management analysts and consultants must pass on their findings through written or oral presentations, so be sure to take English and speech classes, too.

#### Postsecondary Training

Employers generally prefer to hire management analysts and consultants with a master's degree in business or public administration, or at least a bachelor's degree and several years of appropriate work experience. Many college majors provide a suitable education for this occupation because of the diversity of problem areas addressed by management analysts and consultants. These include many areas in the computer and information sciences, engineering, business and management, education, communications, marketing and distribution, and architecture and environmental design.

When hired directly from school, management analysts and consultants often participate in formal company training programs. These programs may include instruction on policies and procedures, computer systems and software, and management practices and principles. Regard-

less of their background, most management analysts and consultants routinely attend conferences to keep abreast of current developments in the field.

## Certification or Licensing

The Institute of Management Consultants USA offers the certified management consultant designation to those consultants who meet minimum educational and experience criteria, and pass a rigorous examination process. All types of consultants (i.e., internal consultants, technical

## Rewarding Moments

Bette Price details some of her most rewarding experiences as a business consultant:

I have had many interesting and/or rewarding experiences through the years but perhaps one of the most interesting and rewarding was a few years ago when I was hired for a small assignment—to help the executive of a new unit of a Fortune 500 company prepare for his presentation to the board of directors for his plan on how to get a joint venture project off the ground and successful. The presentation was so successful that the joint board gave him a standing ovation when he was finished. He then asked how else I might help him to achieve his envisioned success. That ended up being a nearly yearlong project in which I developed an entire culture program that each and every employee participated in to ensure that there was consistency and congruency in how the organization functioned. I flew all over

the country to work with each location's employees. The executive and I remain close friends to this day.

There is one other experience that I feel very good about. I was recommended to a small entrepreneurial company to possibly help them with public relations. When I got there it was evident to me that the company was nowhere near ready to use public relations. As a matter of fact, it was my view that the entire company was not even positioned right in the marketplace for what they actually did, or could do going forward. As a result I worked with their marketing vice president and the president to totally reposition the company and, as a result, they were the first in their industry to receive a contract from one of the largest retailers in the nation to manage their entire waste stream. The company grew exponentially as one of the first in the nation to lead the way in handling environmental waste issues for major retailers and hotels. That was a very exciting and rewarding time.

consultants, strategy consultants, etc.) are eligible for certification; the requirement is that they must consult to management of organizations. Certification is voluntary, but provides an additional advantage to those who are interested in demonstrating their competency, experience, and ethics as measured against globally recognized professional standards. The certification is recognized in 46 countries, which is an advantage to those desiring to start an international consulting practice.

### Internships and Volunteerships

Internships are an excellent way to learn more about the demands of a career in business consulting while you are still in school. Schools requiring an internship usually will have a formal internship program set up with a variety of companies. Students aren't usually paid for their work, but receive credit hours for their participation. As an intern at a consulting firm, you might conduct research, edit report drafts, or help create presentations.

You can also explore the world of business and business consulting by contacting local consulting firms to see if they offer any volunteer opportunities. Your business teacher or counselor might be able to provide you with some names of local companies.

## WHO WILL HIRE ME?

There are approximately 678,000 management analysts and consultants in the United States, with slightly more than 25 percent of these workers self-employed. Federal, state, and local governments employ many of the others. The Depart-

ment of Defense employs the majority of those working for the federal government. The remainder work in the private sector for companies providing consulting services. Although management analysts and consultants are found throughout the country, the majority are concentrated in major metropolitan areas.

## WHERE CAN I GO FROM HERE?

Most government agencies offer entry-level analyst and consultant positions to people with bachelor's degrees and no work experience. Many entrants are also career changers who were formerly mid- and upper-level managers. With more than 25 percent of the practicing management consultants self-employed, career changing is a common route into the field.

Anyone with some degree of business expertise or an expert field can begin to work as an independent consultant. The number of one- and two-person consulting firms in this country is well over 100,000. Establishing a wide range of appropriate personal contacts is by far the most effective way to get started in this field. Consultants have to sell themselves and their expertise, a task far tougher than selling a tangible product the customer can see and handle. Many consultants get their first clients by advertising in newspapers, magazines, and trade or professional periodicals. After some time in the field, word-of-mouth advertising is often the primary method of attracting new clients.

A new consultant in a large firm may be referred to as an associate for the first

# Career Profile: Valerie Walling

Valerie Walling is a certified public accountant and the president of V Solutions Consulting, a financial consulting company in Littleton, Colorado. She discussed her career with the editors of *What Can I Do Now? Business and Finance*.

**Q. Can you tell us about V Solutions Consulting and your educational and professional background?**

**A.** My firm, V Solutions Consulting, advises organizations in internal controls and anti-fraud design, SOX 404, and corporate governance and provides virtual CFO services, interim management and business consulting, budgeting, business process improvement, policies and procedures documentation, financial reporting, and financial analysis. I work with many different industries and with government and nonprofit entities.

My college major was in accounting, and my high grades all through school gave me many opportunities in the strong job market at the time. I chose a top-level accounting firm that provided audit services to major corporations. After three years with that firm, which was a very good education in itself, I realized that the career path there was not my first choice because I was always reviewing other people's decisions and work while doing audits. I really wanted to be making decisions inside a company. So I found an accounting position inside a commercial real estate company that was growing rapidly. In a few years I had taken on a lot of responsibility and was managing a new real estate venture with properties across the country. Over time, I learned many different skills and added more as I worked with two more companies in financial and administrative management positions. I learned about managing people, creating meaningful reporting for top management and owners, and working with boards of directors and public company financial reporting requirements.

When I started my consulting practice, I worked in the areas I had developed expertise in my previous jobs. For example, I helped my former employer develop a searchable Policies and Procedure Manual for its 2,000-person sales force. I also helped some local companies with accounting and financial reporting needs. Then a new law, commonly referred to by its sponsors' names, "Sarbanes-Oxley," was passed in 2002. This law required public companies to meet several requirements to prove that they were taking steps to avoid errors and fraud in their financial reporting. I was hired to help a large utility and energy services company develop the tools and reporting to meet the requirements of the new law. I was part of a large team for the first project, but my next projects in this area were as an independent consultant for smaller public companies. Being solely responsible for the success of the projects and reporting to audit committees of boards of directors created another skill set that I was able to use for future client assignments.

**Q. What do you like least and most about being a business consultant?**

**A.** I enjoy being an independent consultant because of the stimulating variety

*(continued on next page)*

*(continued from previous page)*

of the work and learning something new every day. I can be an adviser to senior management of a company and learn all about that company's operations. I can often work from my home office at varying hours and am not required to be at the same place every day at the same time. The challenge is that an independent consultant does not have a company paying his or her salary and benefits, so must work hard contacting potential clients to ensure that there is future work in place. The business development part of the job continues at all times and you have to be willing to reach out to prospective clients regularly.

**Q. What is one of the most interesting or rewarding things that has happened to you while working in the field?**

**A.** I was once asked to evaluate maintenance and operations practices in the aircraft operations division of a client for whom I was providing internal audit compliance consulting. The client's audit committee asked me to assume this project because the division had been having problems that had not been fixed internally by the company. I had to learn very quickly about the requirements of aircraft maintenance and operations, something I had never worked with before. I was able to make some good recommendations to help solve their problems, and it was a very interesting part of the overall project.

Consulting is a very rewarding and challenging career. It is best for people who like to be challenged and find solutions to problems. It can be frustrating at times because the support system is not like that of a large company, but a consultant can be proud of having his or her own business. When you finish working on a project for a company and the managers are happy enough with your work that they recommend you to other companies, you can feel good about your achievement.

---

couple of years. The next progression is to senior associate, a title that indicates three to five years' experience and the ability to supervise others and do more complex and independent work. After about five years, the analyst who is progressing well may become an engagement manager with the responsibility to lead a consulting team on a particular client project. The best managers become senior engagement managers, leading several study teams or a very large project team. After about seven years, those who excel will be considered for appointment as junior partners or principals. Partnership involves responsibility for marketing the firm and leading client projects. Some may be promoted to senior partnership or director, but few people successfully run this full course. Management analysts and consultants with entrepreneurial ambition may open their own firms.

## WHAT ARE THE SALARY RANGES?

Salaries and hourly rates for management analysts and consultants vary widely, according to experience, specialization, education, and employer. In 2008, management analysts and consultants had median annual earnings of $73,570, according to the U.S. Department of Labor. Salaries ranged from less than $41,910 to $133,850 or more.

Many consultants can demand between $400 and $1,000 per day. Their fees are often well over $40 per hour. Self-employed management consultants receive no fringe benefits and generally have to maintain their own office (and pay their own health insurance), but their pay is usually much higher than salaried consultants. They can make more than $2,000 per day or $250,000 in one year from consulting just two days per week.

Typical benefits for salaried analysts and consultants include health and life insurance, retirement plans, vacation and sick leave, profit sharing, and bonuses for outstanding work. All travel expenses are generally reimbursed by the employer.

## WHAT IS THE JOB OUTLOOK?

Employment of management analysts and consultants is expected to grow much faster than the average for all occupations through 2016, according to the U.S. Department of Labor (DoL). Industry and government agencies are expected to rely more and more on the expertise of these professionals to improve and streamline the performance of their organizations.

Many job openings will result from the need to replace workers who transfer to other fields or leave the labor force.

"Consulting is the fastest growing industry in the economy," says Bette Price, "and all areas of consulting are expected to experience high growth. The top three reasons for this projected growth are: the aging of the baby boomers, mergers and acquisitions, and international demand for American expertise."

Competition for management consulting jobs will be strong. Employers can choose from a large pool of applicants who have a wide variety of educational backgrounds and experience. The challenging nature of this job, coupled with high salary potential, attracts many. Those with a graduate degree, experience and expertise in the industry, as well as a knack for public relations, will have the best employment prospects.

Trends that have increased the growth of employment in this field include advancements in information technology and e-commerce, the growth of international business, and fluctuations in the economy that have forced businesses to streamline and downsize.

The DoL predicts that opportunities will be best at very large consulting firms that have expertise in international business and in smaller firms that focus on providing consulting services in specific areas such as biotechnology, engineering, information technology, health care, marketing, and human resources.

# SECTION 3

Do It Yourself

So you're thinking about a career in business or finance—good choice! Not only are business and finance exciting, rewarding, and highly respected fields—they offer many varied opportunities for employment. Although many business and finance careers require a college education and/or on-the-job experience, there are many business- and finance-related activities for people who are your age. Read on for some suggestions.

## ❏ READ BOOKS AND PERIODICALS

Your school or local library is a great place to start to learn more about business and finance. There, you'll find books and periodicals about business- and finance-related topics, including what to do on your first day on the job; applying to business school; famous business professionals such as Steve Jobs, Jack Welch, and Meg Whitman; career options (such as CEO, accountant, and financial analyst); and almost any other topic imaginable. For a list of books and periodicals about business and finance, check out "Get Involved" in Section 4.

## ❏ SURF THE WEB

The Internet offers a wealth of information regarding opportunities in business or finance. You can do a quick Google search on these words, visit the Web sites of Fortune 500 companies, or even study lists of top business schools in the United States. To help get you started, we've prepared a list of what we think are some of the best business- and finance-related sites on the Web. Check out "Surf the Web" in Section 4 for a list of informative Web sites.

## ❏ TAKE HIGH SCHOOL CLASSES

A high school education will provide you with a strong foundation for a career in business or finance. Choose your classes carefully, and keep in mind that electives count as much as core classes. Math classes should be part of your yearly curriculum, from basic freshman math offerings to more advanced statistics and probability classes. Many high schools have a set curriculum for students interested in pursuing a business career, which involves classes such as basic accounting, finance, management, or economics. Since computers play a major role in business and finance, take classes to become familiar with important computer programs such as Excel, PowerPoint, and other programs used by business and finance professionals. Any classes that require written projects, such as English, language arts, or history, will also help you hone your communication skills. Classes such as communication or speech will also provide you with good practice in how to convey your thoughts and ideas to others.

From the start of your high school career, you should be in close contact with your counselors. Tell them about your career goals so they may guide you in the proper sequence of classes to take, as well as suggest extracurricular activities to join or particular scholarships to pursue.

## ❑ PARTICIPATE IN ACTIVITIES OFFERED BY BUSINESS CLUBS AND ORGANIZATIONS

A variety of clubs and organizations provide activities for students who are interested in exploring business and finance careers. One such club is the school-based Junior Achievement (JA) program. Founded in 1919 by a group of businessmen and industrialists, the program's mission is to provide education for workplace readiness, entrepreneurship, and financial knowledge to young people worldwide. Junior Achievement partners with area schools and local business leaders to provide classroom instruction, practical lessons, and experiments to better prepare students to succeed in whatever business path they choose.

Age-appropriate activities are provided by school grade. For example, in the middle school program JA Finance Park students learn about concepts such as banking, budgeting, credit vs. debt, exchange, and taxes through classroom lectures, role-playing, and site-based experiences. High school students in the JA Be Entrepreneurial program are encouraged to create their own business, whether it be selling a product, or

promoting a service. Students examine the potential market for their business, determine how to gain a competitive advantage over similar businesses, and learn to create a viable business plan. Sophisticated lessons taught in the Entrepreneurial program will not only help students learn the concepts of a successful business start-up, but point them in the right direction of becoming productive and contributing members of society. For more information on Junior Achievement Worldwide, visit http://www.ja.org.

Another youth business club for high school and middle school students is the Future Business Leaders of America (FBLA). The largest business association for students, this organization is composed of 215,000 members in the high school division and 15,000 members in the middle school division. Local chapters are located throughout the United States. The FBLA's goals include developing competent business leadership, assisting students in the establishment of career goals, and creating more interest in and understanding of the American business system. Members are invited to the annual FBLA conference, where they can participate in educational programs and curriculum to better prepare them for entrepreneurship or a career in business. The FBLA also offers various competitions, awards, and scholarships for members who demonstrate above average achievement within their chapter. In addition, Future Business Leaders of America partners with several noted charities and organizations to help raise money for causes such as research and advocacy for the health of premature babies. For more information on the FBLA, or to find a chapter near your home, visit http://www.fbla-pbl.org.

## ❑ MAKE THE MOST OF YOUR SUMMER VACATION

Another good way to learn more about business and finance is to participate in related summer programs at colleges and universities. Summer programs usually consist of classes, seminars, workshops, field trips, and hands-on activities that introduce you to opportunities in these fields. Participating in these programs will allow you to explore different aspects of business and finance, meet other young people who are interested in these fields, and interact with faculty members. Summer programs are covered in depth in "Get Involved" in Section 4; check out this section for further information.

## ❑ VOLUNTEER AS A FUND-RAISER

Are you passionate about a particular cause? Fighting cruelty to animals? Working to help cure a disease that has affected a family member or friend? Perhaps your community has recently experienced a natural disaster, and you want to help? Once you've identified your passion, find a group or foundation that works toward helping your cause. For example, there are many founda-

tions devoted to promoting respiratory health. One in particular is the Respiratory Health Association of Metropolitan Chicago, whose mission is promoting lung health and fighting lung disease through education and advocacy. Your work as a volunteer fund-raiser could include making phone calls to obtain corporate donations, mailing informational packets to interested individuals, or helping out during fund-raising events.

Keep in mind that fund-raising skills can be honed without participating in an event organized by a foundation. Why not start your own fund-raising event or project? Events such as a coat drive, bake sale, or car wash may seem small in scale, but you'll soon learn that when it comes to fund-raising, every penny counts! Perhaps your cause may not be as major as raising money to fight lung disease but closer to home, such as raising money for a school trip.

For example, a football team in Cheyenne, Wyoming, wanted to participate in a regional football tournament during the Thanksgiving holiday, but couldn't get enough players to commit due to high travel expenses. It was the idea of one football player to organize a car wash in order to raise funds. They found a local car dealer that was willing to donate space and water hookup, organized the varsity players to work various shifts (and wear their football jerseys), and advertised their event during the first few games of the season. The good news? The team lucked out with sunny weather and more dirty cars than they ever imagined. The bad news? They lost the tournament.

## ❏ PURSUE JOB-SHADOWING OPPORTUNITIES

Job shadowing a business or finance professional is a great way to learn more about these fields. Do your parents or relatives work in the business or financial arena? If so, you may want to take advantage of these important connections.

Check with your high school's guidance department for shadowing opportunities, as they often have lists of participating companies. Another option is contacting a business that interests you—make your request to the company's human resource department, which will then match you with an appropriate employee.

If you are lucky enough to obtain a job-shadowing opportunity, make sure not to just arrive promptly, but come prepared as well. Dress according to the office dress code (you can verify ahead of time whether the office prefers formal dress or business casual); have a list of questions written down, do some preliminary research on the company and its mission, and be ready for an action packed day!

What should you expect? If you are shadowing a management analyst, for example, you may sit in on a client assessment, perhaps visit the client's place of business, and may even be asked to perform some basic tasks such as preparing documents or conducting basic research. If you are shadowing a franchise owner of a restaurant, you may witness front-of-the-house operations such as taking orders and working the cash register or back-of-the house operations such as preparing inventory orders, recording daily sales records, scheduling work shifts, or managing employees.

When your shadowing experience is finished, don't forget to send your contact a thank-you note. He or she will be impressed by this gesture, and who knows, may keep you in mind if a job opening arises in the future.

## ❏ CONDUCT AN INFORMATION INTERVIEW

Talking with business and finance professionals is an excellent way to learn more about career options, work environments, and the skills you will need for career success. What is an information interview? It is a conversation between you and a business or finance professional (auditor, financial planner, management analyst, or franchise owner, etc.) about his or her career. You can conduct an information interview in person, on the telephone, or via email. Usually the person you want to interview chooses the format. Here are a few basic questions to ask during an information interview:

- How long have you worked in this field?
- What made you want to enter this career?

- How did you train for this field?
- What are your primary and secondary job duties?
- What are your typical work hours?
- What are the most important personal and professional skills for people in your career?
- What is the employment outlook for your profession?
- What advice would you give to someone who wants to enter the field?

Some basic rules to keep in mind during an information interview include dressing appropriately (if conducting the interview in person), being attentive and acting interested during the interview (even if the job doesn't sound as exciting as you thought it would be), respecting time limits established by the worker (if he or she says that they only can give you 20 minutes of their time, don't try to stretch this time limit), and, after you have completed the interview, sending a thank-you note to the individual for his or her time.

## ❑ IMMERSE YOURSELF IN A DIFFERENT CULTURE

As a cultural adviser to a business or international corporation, you need to be an expert in a particular country's language as well as its culture and customs and political and business practices. You can study a foreign language in high school, or even take advanced courses at your local community college. You may even want to join your school's international club, which educates students about world cultures, including music, dance, and food.

If you really want to immerse yourself in the customs and practices of other countries, you should consider traveling abroad. Many programs offer educational travel in conjunction with schools or various civic organizations. Global Teens offered by New York's YMCA is one such program. Its mission is to help New York City area teens accomplish their goal of global exploration and awareness. The program offers structured itineraries of travel to countries such as Peru, Chile, Brazil, China, Korea, and Thailand. Students are able to experience firsthand the differences in food, culture, customs, and arts through interaction with the people of their host country. They also participate in community service projects, which differ according to the needs of their hosts. The NYC Global Teens project also plays host to other international teens for immersion in American culture. The YMCA Global Teens program hopes international travel not only provides teens with the experience of learning about different cultures, but also gives them a more educated standpoint in dealing with issues in their own "home village." For more information, contact The YMCA of Greater New York, http://www.ymcanyc.org/index.php?id=930.

Another respected program is the International Youth Camp and Exchange Program, sponsored by the Lions Club. For the last 30 years, hundreds of high school students have traveled to different countries as exchange students. They stay with a Lions host family, attend the local school, and learn about the country's culture and customs through daily activities. Travel and housing arrangements are made through local Lions chapters; expenses are paid through a combination of district funding, chapter sponsorship, and private means. The program's mission is to foster international understanding among different people of the world. For more information, or to download a youth camp and exchange application, contact Lions Club International at http://www.lions clubs.org or http://www.lionsclubs.org/ EN/our-work/youth-programs/youth-camp-and-exchange.

## ❏ RUN FOR STUDENT GOVERNMENT

Can running for student office help you in a possible career in the business or financial industries? Absolutely, considering any elected position requires many of the same skills possessed by managers, cultural advisers, public relations specialists, and event planners already working in their respective fields.

Let's say you want to run for student council president. A positive outcome won't materialize on election day without strategic planning, a solid understanding of what the student body needs and wants from their class representative, frugal campaign spending, and top-notch public relations.

By serving in an elected position you'll have the ability to negotiate with school administrators, teachers, and students regarding a variety of issues, including better cafeteria food, philanthropic projects, and extracurricular activities.

Don't think you need to run for office in order to garner important business skills. After all, behind every good leader is an even greater adviser. As a campaign worker, you can learn the ropes of public relations—yes, even as you hand out campaign buttons or hang posters touting your candidate!

## ❏ SERVE AS THE TREASURER OF A CLUB

It's never too early to begin learning about the work of accountants and auditors. You can certainly hone skills needed to do these jobs by volunteering to be a treasurer for a school club. If you serve as the treasurer of your high school's international club, for example, your responsibilities would include keeping a running account of expenses and earnings. Fund-raising totals, contributions, or corporate sponsorships would be noted against all expenditures incurred from activities, educational supplies, equipment, or travel expenses. You would be responsible for presenting this information to all members at club meetings, to club sponsors, or even school administrators. Requests for special purchases or monetary reimbursements would come before the governing board of the club, but all transactions would be carried out by you, since as treasurer you would be holding club funds, or the very least, its checkbook.

Don't limit yourself to high school clubs; there may be opportunities to volunteer your services to organizations or social groups in your community.

## ❏ START A BUSINESS

The *Wall Street Journal* recently featured a story about teenage millionaires whose fortunes came from starting their own businesses. Perhaps your personal fortune is waiting to be made! Do you have a particular talent or service others may be interested in?

If you are an accomplished musician, you may want to consider marketing this talent. Target families with young children who may be interested in taking piano lessons or violin lessons. Your start-up costs and equipment are minimal. Dig up your old lesson books, scale sheets, and metronome. If your students do not have a piano at home, you may recommend that they rent a simple keyboard or violin from a local music store (or rent these instruments yourself and add the cost to your instructional fee). Create flyers advertising your price per half-hour lesson, available times, and your past music experience. Be professional by arriving at your student's home promptly and with a detailed lesson plan.

If your talents lean toward a particular sport, why not advertise private coaching lessons in pitching, hitting, or even goal tending. One recent high school student found his niche by advertising hour-long training lessons to hone skills needed to be a star soccer goalie.

He advertised his business to the local town soccer club, and now is inundated with boys and girls eager to learn this skill. The student put together a set of drills, exercises, and stretches and applies them at every lesson. His start-up costs were minimal—soccer balls and facemasks. He often schedules lessons at the local park where a permanent soccer goal is already set up.

Even before he was a teenager, Robert was in charge of putting up outdoor Christmas lights at his home, which eventually became more elaborate as he grew older and more experienced. When neighbors complimented him on his work, he got the idea of creating Robert's Lighting Services. Now in his sixth year of business, Robert is in charge of lighting many houses in his neighborhood, as well as in other nearby subdivisions. His services include hanging holiday lights on trees, bushes, and rooftops. Other services available include concept design, takedown (one of his most popular services), and storage. Robert found it helpful to have a list of prices available to give customers, such as price per tree or shrub depending on the type of lighting used, price per foot to outline a roof versus ground work, as well as the standard price for takedown and storage. His start-up costs included the purchase of a 20-foot ladder, extension cords, timers, and extra light strands and bulbs. Robert carefully kept notes on any other purchases he made per customer, and added them to the final invoice along with a thank you tin of cookies. Robert is in such demand that many customers begin seeking out his services right after Halloween each year.

Don't let your age deter you from starting your own business. In fact, it may work in your favor. It certainly did in Robert's case. Sure, there were many professional agencies offering lighting services during the holiday season, but many customers chose to patronize a business operated by a neighborhood boy because they admired his sense of entrepreneurship. With a lot of hard work and a little luck, you could be the next Robert and develop the skills and experience necessary to find success in the worlds of business and finance.

# SECTION 4

## What Can I Do Right Now?

# Get Involved: A Directory of Camps, Programs, Competitions, and Other Opportunities

Now that you've read about some of the different careers available in business and finance, you might be anxious to experience these fields yourself, to find out what they're really like. Or perhaps you already feel certain that a career in business or finance is for you and want to get started right away. Whichever is the case, this section is for you! There are plenty of things you can do right now to learn about business and finance careers while gaining valuable experience. Just as important, you'll get to meet new friends and see new places, too.

The programs listed are run by organizations and institutions committed to business and finance and to recruiting young talent into the profession. Many are colleges or universities offering introductory or regular classes, or special workshops, in these areas. Others are professional organizations trying to put the experience and dedication of their members to work for you. The types of opportunities available are listed right after the name of the program or organization, so you can skim through to find the listings that interest you most. Take time to read over the listings and see how each compares to your situation: how committed you are to a business- or finance-related field, how much of your money and free time you're willing to devote to these fields, and how the program will help you after high school. These listings are divided into categories, with the type of program printed right after its name or the name of the sponsoring organization.

## ❏ THE CATEGORIES

### Camps

When you see an activity that is classified as a camp, don't automatically start packing your tent and mosquito repellent. Where academic study is involved, the term *camp* often simply means a residential program including both educational and recreational activities. It's sometimes hard to differentiate between such camps and other study programs, but if the sponsoring organization calls it a camp, so do we! Visit the following Web site for an extended list of camps: http://www.kidscamps.com.

### College Courses/Summer Study

These terms are linked because most college courses offered to students your age must take place in the summer, when you are out of school. Many summer study programs are sponsored by colleges and universities that want to attract future students and give them a head start in higher education. Summer study of almost any type is a good idea because it keeps your mind and your study skills sharp over the long vacation. Summer study at a college offers any number of additional benefits, including giving you the tools to make a well-informed decision about your future academic career.

## Competitions

Competitions are fairly self-explanatory, but you should know that there are only a few in this book because competitions on a regional or national level are relatively rare. What this means, however, is that if you are interested in entering a competition, you shouldn't have much trouble finding one yourself. Your school counselor or a teacher can help you start searching in your area.

## Conferences

Conferences for high school students are usually difficult to track down because most are for professionals in the field who gather to share new information and ideas with each other. Don't be discouraged, though. A number of professional organizations with student branches or membership options for those who are simply interested in the field offer conferences. Some student branches even run their own conferences. This is an option worth pursuing because conferences focus on some of the most current information available and also give you the chance to meet professionals who can answer your questions and even offer advice.

## Employment and Internship Opportunities

As you may already know from experience, employment opportunities for teenagers can be very limited—especially for jobs that require a bachelor's or graduate degree or those that can require a lot of on-the-job experience. While you won't be able to work as a CEO of a Fortune 500 company, you can get a large amount of experience working as an officer in a school club or as president or vice-president of your class. You may even be able to start your own small business (groundskeeping, music lessons, computer repair, etc.) that will give you an introduction to the world of business. Another option is to work part time at an after-school job to observe business professionals at work. The key is to take advantage of every opportunity you can to hone your business skills.

Basically, an internship combines the responsibilities of a job (strict schedules, pressing duties, and usually written evaluations by your supervisor) with the uncertainties of a volunteer position (no wages [or only very seldom], no fringe benefits, no guarantee of future employment). That may not sound very enticing, but completing an internship is a great way to prove your maturity, your commitment to a career, and your knowledge and skills to colleges, potential employers, and yourself. Some internships here are just formalized volunteer positions; others offer unique responsibilities and opportunities. Choose the kind that works best for you!

## Field Experience

This is something of a catchall category for activities that don't exactly fit the other descriptions. But anything called a field experience in this book is always a good opportunity to get out and explore the work of business and finance professionals.

## Membership

When an organization (such as Business Professionals of America) is in this category, it simply means that you are welcome to pay your dues and become a card-carrying member. Formally joining any organization brings the benefits of meeting others who share your interests, finding opportunities to get involved, and keeping up with current events. Depending on how active you are, the contacts you make and the experiences you gain may help when the time comes to apply to colleges or look for a job.

In some organizations, you pay a special student rate and receive benefits similar to regular members. Many organizations, however, are now starting student branches with their own benefits and publications. There are also some organizations, such as Future Business Leaders of America, that are geared specifically toward students. As in any field, make sure you understand exactly what the benefits of membership are before you join.

Finally, don't let membership dues discourage you from contacting these organizations. Some local organizations charge dues as low as $10 because they know that students are perpetually short of funds. When the annual dues are higher, think of the money as an investment in your future and then consider if it is too much to pay.

## Seminars

Like conferences, seminars are often classes or informative gatherings for those already working in the field, and are generally sponsored by professional organizations. This means that there aren't all that many seminars for young people. But also like conferences, they are often open to affiliated members. Check with various organizations to see what kind of seminars they offer and if there is some way you can attend.

## ❑ PROGRAM DESCRIPTIONS

Once you've started to look at the individual listings themselves, you'll find that they contain a lot of information. Naturally, there is a general description of each program, but wherever possible we also have included the following details.

### Application Information

Each listing notes how far in advance you'll need to apply for the program or position, but the simple rule is to apply as far in advance as possible. This ensures that you won't miss out on a great opportunity simply because other people got there ahead of you. It also means that you will get a timely decision on your application, so if you are not accepted you'll still have some time to apply elsewhere. As for the elements that make up your application—essays, recommendations, etc.—we've tried to tell you what's involved, but be sure to contact the program about specific requirements before you submit anything.

## Background Information

This includes such information as the date the program or organization was established, the name of the organization that is sponsoring it financially, and the faculty and staff who will be there for you. This can help you and your family gauge the quality and reliability of the program.

## Classes and Activities

Classes and activities change from year to year, depending on popularity, availability of instructors, and many other factors. Nevertheless, colleges and universities quite consistently offer the same or similar classes, even in their summer sessions. Courses like "Business 101" and "Finance 101," for example, are simply indispensable. So you can look through the listings and see which programs offer foundational courses like these and which offer courses on more variable topics. As for activities, we note when you have access to recreational facilities on campus, and it's usually a given that special social and cultural activities will be arranged for most programs.

## Contact Information

Wherever possible, we have given the title of the person whom you should contact instead of the name because people change jobs so frequently. If no title is given and you are telephoning an organization, simply tell the person who answers the phone the name of the program that interests you and he or she will forward your call. If you are writing, include the line "Attention: Summer Study Program" (or whatever is appropriate after "Attention") somewhere on the envelope. This will help to ensure that your letter goes to the person in charge of that program.

## Credit

Where academic programs are concerned, we sometimes note that high school or college credit is available to those who have completed them. This means that the program can count toward your high school diploma or a future college degree just like a regular course. Obviously, this can be very useful, but it's important to note that rules about accepting such credit vary from school to school. Before you commit to a program offering high school credit, check with your guidance counselor to see if it is acceptable to your school. As for programs offering college credit, check with your chosen college (if you have one) to see if they will accept it.

## Eligibility and Qualifications

The main eligibility requirement to be concerned about is age or grade in school. A term frequently used in relation to grade level is *rising*, as in "rising senior": someone who will be a senior when the next school year begins. This is especially important where summer programs are concerned. A number of university-based programs make admissions decisions partly in consideration of GPA, class rank, and standardized test scores. This is mentioned in the listings, but you must contact the program for specific numbers. If you are worried that your GPA or your ACT/SAT scores, for example, aren't good enough, don't let them stop you from applying to programs that consider such things in the admissions process. Often, a fine essay or even an example of your dedication and eagerness can compensate for statistical weaknesses.

## Facilities

We tell you where you'll be living, studying, eating, and having fun during these programs, but there isn't enough room to go into all the details. Some of those details can be important: what is and isn't accessible for people with disabilities, whether the site of a summer program has air-conditioning, and how modern the facilities and computer equipment are. You can expect most program brochures and application materials to address these concerns, but if you still have questions about the facilities, just call the program's administration and ask.

## Financial Details

While a few of the programs listed here are fully underwritten by collegiate and corporate sponsors, most of them rely on you for at least some of their funding. The 2009 prices and fees are given here, but you should bear in mind that costs rise slightly almost every year. You and your parents must take costs into consideration when choosing a program. We always try to note where financial aid is available, but most programs will do their best to ensure that a shortage of funds does not prevent you from taking part.

## Residential vs. Commuter Options

Simply put, some programs prefer that participating students live with other participants and staff members, others do not, and still others leave the decision entirely to the students themselves. As a rule, residential programs are suitable for local residents and young people who live out of town or even out of state. They generally provide a better overview of college life than programs in which you're only on campus for a few hours a day, and they're a way to test how well you cope with living away from home. Commuter programs may be viable only if you live near the program site or if you can stay with relatives who do. Bear in mind that, for residential programs especially, the travel between your home and the location of the activity is almost always your responsibility and can significantly increase the cost of participation.

## ❏ FINALLY . . .

Ultimately, there are three important things to bear in mind concerning all of the programs listed in this section. The first is that things change. Staff members come and go, funding is added or withdrawn, supply and demand determine which programs continue and which terminate. Dates, times, and costs vary widely because of a number of factors. Because of this, the information we give you, although as current and detailed as possible, is just not enough on which to base your final decision. If you are interested in a program, you simply must contact the organization concerned to get the latest and most complete information available, or visit its Web site. This has the added benefit of putting you in touch with someone who can deal with your individual questions and problems.

A second important point to keep in mind when considering these programs is that the people who run them provided the information printed here. The editors of this book haven't attended the programs and don't endorse them; we simply give you the information with which to begin your own research. And after all, we can't pass judgment because you're the only one who can decide which programs are right for you.

The final thing to bear in mind is that the programs listed here are just the tip of the iceberg. No book can possibly cover all of the opportunities that are available to you—partly because they are so numerous and are constantly coming and going, and partly because some are waiting to be discovered. For instance, you may be very interested in taking a college course but don't see the college that interests you in the listings. Call its admissions office! Even if the college doesn't have a special program for high school students, it might be able to make some kind of arrangements for you to visit or sit in on a class. Use the ideas behind these listings and take the initiative to turn them into opportunities.

## ❏ THE PROGRAMS
### American Collegiate Adventures at American University
#### College Courses/Summer Study

American Collegiate Adventures (ACA) offers high school students the chance to experience and prepare for college during their summer vacation. Adventures, which last four weeks, are based at American University in Washington, D.C. During the week, participants take college-level courses (for enrichment or college credit) that are taught by university faculty and visit other college campuses and recreation sites on weekends. Recent enrichment courses include Financial Markets; Public Speaking/Debating; Advertising, Marketing, and Popular Culture; and SAT and ACT Prep. There were no college-credit courses recently offered that focused on business and finance. Students live in comfortable en suite accommodations, just down the hall from an ACA resident staff member. Tuition (which includes room and board) for the program is approximately $6,195. Contact American Collegiate Adventures for current course listings and application procedures.

### American Collegiate Adventures
1811 West North Avenue, Suite 201
Chicago, IL 60622-1488

800-509-7867
info@acasummer.com
http://www.acasummer.com

## American Collegiate Adventures at the University of Wisconsin
### College Courses/Summer Study/ Employment and Internship Opportunities

American Collegiate Adventures (ACA) offers high school students the chance to experience and prepare for college during their summer vacation. Adventures are based at the University of Wisconsin in Madison; programs last for two, three, four, or six weeks. On weekdays, participants take college-level courses that are taught by university faculty. On weekends, they visit other regional colleges and recreation sites. All students live in comfortable en suite accommodations, just down the hall from an ACA resident staff member. Recent enrichment courses include Financial Markets; Public Speaking/Debating; Advertising, Marketing, and Popular Culture; Foreign Language; and SAT and ACT Prep. Students in the six-week program can also participate in internships. Recent internships were offered in advertising, business, government, law, photography, and sports broadcasting.

Tuition (which includes room and board) for the two-week program is approximately $2,895; the three-week program, $4,395; the four-week program, $5,595; and the six-week program, $6,995. Contact American Collegiate Adventures for current course listings and application procedures.

### American Collegiate Adventures
1811 West North Avenue, Suite 201
Chicago, IL 60622-1488
800-509-7867
info@acasummer.com
http://www.acasummer.com

## American Institute of Certified Public Accountants (AICPA)
### Conferences

Some state chapters of the AICPA offer conferences that allow high school students to explore career options in the field. Contact the AICPA or state chapters for more information.

### American Institute of Certified Public Accountants
1211 Avenue of the Americas
New York, NY 10036-8775
212-596-6200
http://www.aicpa.org

## Business Professionals of America
### Competitions/Conferences/Employment and Internship Opportunities/ Field Experience/Membership

Business Professionals of America (BPA) is a membership organization for middle school, high school, and college students who plan to or who are currently pursuing careers in business management, office administration, information technology, and other related fields. Members can take advantage of the Workplace Skills Assessment Program, which provides them the opportunity to demonstrate workplace skills learned through business education curricula, and the National Leadership Conference, at which students participate in educational workshops and leadership programs, listen to speakers, elect student officers, put their business acumen to the test in a competitive-events program, and, if interested, work as interns to help the conference run smoothly. Members can also participate in a two-day National Leadership Academy. Contact BPA for more information.

### Business Professionals of America

5454 Cleveland Avenue
Columbus, OH 43231-4021
800-334-2007
http://www.bpa.org

## College and Careers Program at the Rochester Institute of Technology

### College Courses/Summer Study

The Rochester Institute of Technology (RIT) offers its College and Careers Program for rising high school seniors who want to experience college life and explore career options in business and management and other areas. The following classes were recently offered in the Business and Management category: Accounting: The Mysteries of Financial Reporting; Finance: The Impact of the Global Economic Crisis; Economics Comes Alive in Your Daily Life; Hospitality & Service Management: Sustainable and Green Resorts Leading the Way; International Business: Issues in the New Global Economy; Management: Why are Creativity and Innovation

Essential in Business?; and Marketing: Will Your Idea Sell. The program, in existence since 1990, allows you to spend a Friday and Saturday on campus, living in the dorms and attending up to four sessions in the career areas of your choice. In each session, participants work with RIT students and faculty to gain hands-on experience in the topic area. The program is held twice each summer, usually once in mid-July and again in early August. The registration deadline is one week before the start of the program, but space is limited and students are accepted on a first-come, first-served basis. For further information about the program and specific sessions on offer, contact the RIT admissions office.

### College and Careers Program

Rochester Institute of Technology
    Office of Undergraduate
    Admissions
60 Lomb Memorial Drive
Rochester, NY 14623-5604
585-475-6631
http://ambassador.rit.edu/careers/
    sessions.php

## Collegiate Scholars Program at Arizona State University

### College Courses/Summer Study/ Employment and Internship Opportunities

The Collegiate Scholars Program allows high school students to earn college credit during summer academic sessions. Recent classes include Math for Business, Statistics, Economic Principles,

Accounting, Introduction to Agribusiness, Creativity in Entrepreneurship, Microeconomics, Macroeconomics, and Public Speaking. Students get the opportunity to explore careers and interact with college professors, as well as receive access to internships, mentoring programs, and research opportunities. Online classes are also available. Arizona high school seniors may apply, and they are evaluated for admission based on their "high school GPA and/or class rank, test scores, high school schedules, and involvement in other programs offering college credit." Contact the Collegiate Scholars executive coordinator for information on program costs and other details.

### Collegiate Scholars Program

Arizona State University
Attn: Executive Coordinator
480-965-2621
mark.duplissis@asu.edu
http://promise.asu.edu/csp

## Early Experience Program at the University of Denver

### College Courses/Summer Study

The University of Denver invites academically gifted high school students in grades 10-12 to apply for its Early Experience Program, which involves participating in university-level classes during the school year and especially during the summer. This is a commuter-only program. Interested students must submit a completed application (with essay), official high school transcript, standardized test results (PACT/ACT/PSAT/SAT), a letter of recommendation from a counselor or teacher, and have a minimum GPA of 3.0. Tuition is approximately $1,850 per four-credit class. Financial aid is available. Contact the Early Experience Program coordinator for more information.

### University of Denver

Center for Innovative and Talented
  Youth
Early Experience Program
Attn: Coordinator
1981 South University Boulevard
Denver, CO 80208-0001
303-871-3408
city@du.edu
http://www.du.edu/city/programs/
  year-round-programs/early-
  experience-program

## Exploration Summer Programs: Senior Program at Yale University

### College Courses/Summer Study

Exploration Summer Programs (ESP) has been offering academic summer enrichment programs to students for more than three decades. Rising high school sophomores, juniors, and seniors can participate in ESP's Senior Program at Yale University. Two three-week residential and day sessions are available. Participants can choose from more than 80 courses. Recent courses include Can You Hear Me Now?-Advertising + Marketing; Show Me the Money-Investment Methods; Speak Easy!-Public Speaking; Price, Profit, + Providing–Economics; Explo Apprentice-Introduction To Business Management; Make Your Point–Debate; and Guitars +

Gold Bars-Music Business + Marketing. All courses and seminars are ungraded and not-for-credit. In addition to academics, students participate in extracurricular activities such as tours, sports, concerts, weekend recreational trips, college trips, and discussions of current events and other issues. Students who stay on campus reside in residence halls in suites that house from two to nine students. Basic tuition for the Residential Senior Program is approximately $4,555 for one session and $8,390 for two sessions. Day session tuition ranges from approximately $2,100 for one session to $3,820 for two sessions. A limited number of need-based partial and full scholarships are available. Programs are also available for students in grades four through nine. Contact ESP for more information.

### Exploration Summer Programs
932 Washington Street
PO Box 368
Norwood, MA 02062-3412
781-762-7400
http://www.explo.org

## Explore-A-College at Earlham College
### College Courses/Summer Study
Rising high school freshmen, sophomores, and juniors can participate in Explore-A-College, a two-week college experience program that offers 10 classes. Students take one class for college credit and learn how to develop their time management, research, and discussion skills. One recent class of interest to readers of this book was Economics of Personal Finance. Students learned about the "economics of wealth accumulation, home ownership, and retirement planning...and the theoretical foundations of personal finance." Classes are typically held in late June; the application deadline is June 1. Students stay in residence halls on campus. Tuition is $1,600 (which includes room and board). Very limited financial aid is available. Contact the program director for more information.

### Earlham College
Explore-A-College
Attn: Program Director
801 National Road West
Richmond, IN 47374-4095
800-327-5426
http://www.earlham.edu/~eac

## Future Business Leaders of America
### Competitions/Conferences/Membership
Future Business Leaders of America (FBLA), the leading organization for high school students preparing for careers in business, is the largest student business organization in the world, with a quarter of a million members. It offers National Leadership Conferences in which student members participate in workshops and seminars, as well as competitions in the areas of technology, public speaking, business, finance, and management. Members also receive *Tomorrow's Business Leader*, which is published four times annually. Contact

Future Business Leaders of America for more information.

## Future Business Leaders of America

1912 Association Drive
Reston, VA 20191-1591
800-325-2946
membership@fbla.org
http://www.fbla-pbl.org

## Future Educators Association
### Conferences/Membership

The Future Educators Association is committed to helping students learn about careers in education. Currently it operates under the umbrella of Phi Delta Kappa (PDK) International, a fraternal organization with chapters throughout the United States and other countries. Middle and high school students who want to become educators can join a chapter at their school. Member benefits include access to scholarships and a state-of-the-art social networking Web site, the chance to attend the organization's annual conference, and opportunities for hands-on career exploration opportunities.

If you don't have a chapter at your school, than start one. All you need is one committed adult leader (a teacher or counselor) and at least one interested student (you, and we're sure you have a friend or two who might want to become a teacher).

## Future Educators Association

c/o Phi Delta Kappa International
408 North Union Street
Bloomington, IN 47405-3800
800-766-1156
fea@pdkintl.org
http://www.futureeducators.org

## High School Honors Program/ Summer Challenge Program/ Summer Preview at Boston University
### College Courses/Summer Study

Boston University offers three summer educational opportunities for high school students. Rising high school seniors can participate in the High School Honors Program, which offers six-week, for-credit undergraduate study at the university. Students take two for-credit classes (up to eight credits) alongside regular Boston College students, live in dorms on campus, and participate in extracurricular activities and tours of local attractions. Classes are available in more than 50 subject areas, including accounting, business for non-majors, communications, foreign languages, management, marketing, and public relations. The program typically begins in early July. Tuition for the program is approximately $4,120, with registration/program/application fees ($550) and room and board options ($1,897 to $2,055) extra. Students who demonstrate financial need may be eligible for financial aid.

Rising high school sophomores, juniors, and seniors in the university's Summer Challenge Program learn about college life and take college classes in a noncredit setting. The program is offered in three sessions. Students choose two seminars (which feature lectures, group and individual work, project-based assignments, and field trips) from a total of about 15 program options. Past seminars include Business: From the Ground Up; Creative Writing; and Mass Communications (which covered advertising, public relations, journalism, film, and television). In the Business: From the Ground Up seminar, students learned about fundamental business principles and how to create a business plan. Students live in dorms on campus and participate in extracurricular activities and tours of local attractions. The cost of the program is approximately $3,070 (which includes tuition, a room charge, meals, and sponsored activities).

Rising high school freshman and sophomores can participate in the one-week Summer Preview Program. This noncredit, commuter program introduces students to college life and a particular area of study. Recent seminars include Graphic Design, Learning the Art of Writing, Film Studies, and Medicine and Society. The cost of the program is $1,100 (which includes tuition, textbooks, lunch, and activities). No financial aid is available.

### Boston University High School Programs

755 Commonwealth Avenue,
  Room 105
Boston, MA 02215-1401
617-353-1378
buhssumr@bu.edu
http://www.bu.edu/summer/
  high-school-programs

## High School Summer College at Stanford University
### College Courses/Summer Study

Students who have completed their junior or senior year of high school can apply to Stanford University's High School Summer College. The program will also accept applications from "accomplished and mature" sophomores. This competitive program welcomes students from around the world who are ready to explore a challenging university environment and prepare for their college careers. Participants commute or live on campus and attend a selection of regular undergraduate classes from mid-June to mid-August. Course offerings vary from year to year, but recent courses include Accounting for Managers and Entrepreneurs; Introduction to Decision Making in Organizations; Business Strategy and Public Policy Decision Making; Introductory Economics; Introduction to Statistical Methods: Precalculus; Data Mining and Analysis; and foreign languages. As you would expect from an institution like Stanford, the course work is demanding and the grading stringent, but university credit is awarded upon successful completion of your courses. When not in class, you can enjoy the many activities on campus and you also participate in College Admission 101, which is designed to help you through the difficult process of choosing and successfully applying to colleges. The cost of the High School Summer College ranges from $6,697 to $9,733 depending on the number of course units taken, and includes room and board as well as tuition and program fees. Financial aid is available. For application information and current course offerings, contact the staff of the Stanford Summer Session; materials are usually available in late January, and rolling admissions are then open until mid-May.

### Summer Session Office

Stanford University
482 Galvez Street
Stanford, CA 94305-6079
650-723-3109
summersession@stanford.edu
http://summersession.stanford.edu/
highschool/overview.asp

## High School Summer Scholars Program at Washington University in St. Louis

**College Courses/Summer Study**

Rising sophomores and juniors can earn up to seven units of college credit by participating in the High School Summer Scholars Program. Two five-week sessions are available. More than 60 college courses are offered. Recent courses include Business Ethics, Introduction to Political Economy: Microeconomics, Introduction to Political Economy: Macroeconomics, Introduction to Statistics, and several foreign languages. Students spend 16–20 hours each week in class; during the rest of the time, they do homework, participate in planned social activities, and explore the campus and the St. Louis area. Applicants must have a B+ average and have a combined SAT score of at least 1800, a combined PSAT score of 180, or an ACT or PLAN

composite score of at least 25. Tuition for the program is about $5,935, which includes the classes, housing in a campus residence hall, three meals a day, and access to student health services. Financial aid is available. The average award is $2,300, and 80 percent of students receive financial aid. Contact the program director for more information, including details on application deadlines.

### Washington University in St. Louis

High School Summer Scholars Program
Attn: Program Director
One Brookings Drive
Campus Box 1145, January Hall, Room 100
St. Louis, MO 63130-4862
866-209-0691
mhussung@artsci.wustl.edu
http://ucollege.wustl.edu/programs/
highschool

## Independent Means Inc.

**Camps/College Courses/Summer Study**

Independent Means is an organization that educates children and teens about finance and money management. It offers two camps for young people ages 14 to 18 who are interested in learning more about business: Camp $tart-Up and Summer$tock. The camps, which offer concurrent sessions for boys and girls, are held at Scripps University in Claremont, California.

Camp $tart-Up, an eight-day overnight camp, teaches teens about entrepreneurism. Campers work in teams to "create a company, business plan, and PowerPoint presentation." Summer$tock, a seven-day overnight camp, teaches campers the basics of personal finance and investing. As a member of an investment team, campers "select stocks, manage risk, and build a balanced portfolio that will help them reach their financial dreams." In addition to time in the classroom, campers participate in extracurricular activities such as sports, games, and field trips.

Tuition for Camp $tart-Up is $2,000, while Summer$tock costs $1,750. Students who participate in both camps pay a discounted rate of $3,500. Additionally, those who apply early receive a 5 percent discount on tuition. Contact Independent Means Inc. for more information.

### Independent Means Inc.

Summer Programs
126 East Haley, #A16
Santa Barbara, CA 93101-2384
805-965-0475
mlittle@independentmeans.com
http://www.independentmeans.
  com/imi

## Intern Exchange International
### Employment and Internship Opportunities

High school students ages 16 to 18 (including graduating seniors) who are interested in gaining real-life experience in business, finance, and other fields can participate in a month-long summer internship in the United Kingdom. Internships are also available in hotel management, public relations/marketing/advertising, not-for-profit, retail sales, journalism, information technology, publishing, and other fields. Additionally, there are four hands-on Media & Design workshops for those between the ages of 15 to 18, including Print & Broadcast Journalism, Fashion & Design, Photography, and Video Production/Acting for the Camera. In the Business/Finance workshop, participants explore careers in these fields by working at an international bank and learning about letters of credit, banking fraud, internal auditing, and secured paper. They also work at a stock brokerage firm and learn about topics such as buying, selling, leveraging, marketing, and arbitrage. The cost of either program is approximately $7,335 plus airfare; this fee includes tuition, housing (students live in residence halls at the University of London), breakfast and dinner daily, housekeeping service, linens and towels, special dinner events, weekend trips and excursions, group activities including scheduled theatre, and a Tube Pass. Contact Intern Exchange International for more information.

### Intern Exchange International, Ltd.

2606 Bridgewood Circle
Boca Raton, FL 33434-4118
561-477-2434
info@internexchange.com
http://www.internexchange.com

## Internship Connection
### Employment and Internship Opportunities

Internship Connection provides summer or "gap year" internships to high school and college students in Boston and New York City. Internships are available in business, finance, advertising, public relations, restaurant management, and nearly 30 other fields. As part of the program, participants learn how to create a resume, participate in a job interview, and develop communication and personal skills that are key to success in the work world. They also get the chance to make valuable contacts during their internships that may help them land a job once they complete college. The program fee for interns in New York is $2,500. Those who attend the program in Boston pay $2,000. Contact Internship Connection for more information.

### Internship Connection
17 Countryside Road
Newton, MA 02459-2915
617-796-9283
carole@internshipconnection.com
http://www.internshipconnection.
  com

## Junior Achievement
### Competitions/Field Experience/Membership

Junior Achievement's mission is to provide education for workplace readiness, workplace ethics, entrepreneurship, and financial knowledge to young people worldwide. It offers membership (available through local chapters) and programs for students in kindergarten through high school. Some of the competitions offered by Junior Achievement include Global Business Challenge, Business Ethics Essay Competition, Careers with a Purpose Essay Competition, Global Student Company of the Year Competition, Responsible Business Competition, and the Responsible Business Competition. Job-shadowing opportunities are also available. Visit the Junior Achievement Web site for information on a chapter near you.

### Junior Achievement
One Education Way
Colorado Springs, CO 80906-4477
719-540-8000
newmedia@ja.org
http://www.ja.org

## Junior Scholars Program at Miami University—Oxford
### College Courses/Summer Study

Academically talented high school seniors can earn six to eight semester hours of college credit and learn about university life by participating in the Junior Scholars Program at Miami University—Oxford. Students may choose from more than 40 courses, including Introduction to Business; Business Computing; Introduction to Public Expression and Critical Inquiry; Principles of Microeconomics; Principles of Macroeconomics; Statistics, Principles of Marketing; and various foreign languages. In addition to academics, scholars participate in social events, recreational activities, and cocurricular seminars. Program participants live in an air-conditioned residence hall. Fees range from approximately $2,348 to $3,526 depending on the number of credit hours taken and applicant's place of residence (Ohio residents receive a program discount). There is an additional fee of approximately $200 for books. The application deadline is typically in mid-May. Visit the program's Web site for additional eligibility requirements and further details.

### Miami University—Oxford

Junior Scholars Program
202 Bachelor Hall
Oxford, OH 45056-3414
513-529-5825
juniorscholars@muohio.edu
http://www.units.muohio.edu/
   jrscholars

## Learning for Life Exploring Program

### Field Experience

Learning for Life's Exploring Program is a career exploration program that allows young people to work closely with community organizations to learn life skills and explore careers. Opportunities are available in Arts & Humanities, Aviation, Business, Communications, Engineering, Fire Service, Health, Law Enforcement, Law & Government, Science, Skilled Trades, and Social Services. Each program has five areas of emphasis: Career Opportunities, Service Learning, Leadership Experience, Life Skills, and Character Education. As a participant in the Business program, for example, you will learn about a variety of topics, including accounting, business computer information systems, business economics, business policy, international business, law and taxation, marketing, and product development.

To be eligible to participate in this program, you must have completed the eighth grade and be 14 years old *or* be 15 years of age but have not reached your 21st birthday. This program is open to both males and females.

To find a Learning for Life office in your area (there are more than 300 throughout the United States), contact the Learning for Life Exploring Program.

### Learning for Life Exploring Program

1325 West Walnut Hill Lane
PO Box 152079
Irving, TX 75015-2079
972-580-2433
http://www.learningforlife.org/
   exploring

## The Oxford Tradition at Oxford University

### College Courses/Summer Study

The Oxford Tradition is a special opportunity for high school students in grades 10 through 12. Participants in The Oxford Tradition spend the month of July studying two topics of their choice at two of the colleges that make up Oxford University, England. An international business class is offered, which you may select as your "major" and study six mornings a week. In this class, you learn about the world of international business through classroom instruction, workshops, and field trips to Oxford's Saïd Business School and local markets and businesses. Major projects during this course "include real-life case studies, consulting projects, a real-time investment game, and the design of a theoretical start-up venture." In selecting a "minor" to be studied three afternoons a week, you might consider speech and debate, creative writing, or psychology. Most faculty members have degrees from Oxford, and many also have degrees or teaching experience from such institutions as Harvard, Cambridge, and Yale. In addition to course work, all students take part in excursions around Oxford and its environs, enjoy lectures and discussions with many notable guest speakers, and gain insight into British culture past and present. They may also have an opportunity to travel to Paris, France.

Since so many of Oxford's facilities date back several centuries, participants may find that the past is very much part of the present: historical buildings are just one of the things sure to make your accommodations memorable. But living areas are, of course, tidy, suitably furnished, and very secure. Oxford's own porters and The Oxford Tradition's staff members are available 24 hours a day. Breakfast and dinner are served at the college dining hall, while you may take your lunch at any of the numerous restaurants and tea shops around town. The total cost for tuition, room and board, all group excursions, and transport to and from one of London's major airports is roughly $6,995. Addi-

tional expenses include airfare, lunches, and personal needs. Application must be made well in advance—only students who apply by mid-January are guaranteed their choice of majors and minors. For an application form and more details about the classes and speakers, contact The Oxford Tradition.

### The Oxford Tradition
OxBridge Academic Programs
601 Cathedral Parkway, Suite 7R
New York, NY 10025-2186
800-828-8349
http://www.oxbridgeprograms.com/
    oxford_tradition

## Pre-College Programs at the University of California—Santa Barbara
### College Courses/Summer Study
The University of California—Santa Barbara offers three programs for high school students who are interested in business and finance: Early Start, Academic & Enrichment, and Enrichment. In the Early Start Program, which lasts six-weeks, students take two college-level courses to help them explore career options and prepare for college study. Students interested in business and finance can take Principle of Micro-Economics, Statistics with Economics & Business Applications, and several foreign languages. Applicants must have completed the 10th, 11th, or 12th grades and have a GPA of at least 3.3 to be eligible for the program.

Students in the six-week Academic & Enrichment Program take one for-credit course and one noncredit, skills-based enrichment course. Applicants must have completed the 10th, 11th, or 12th grades and have a GPA of at least 3.15 to be eligible for the program. A typical 1+1 pairing for students interested in business might consist of Understanding the Stock Market and Business (noncredit) and Principles of Economics-Macro or Statistics with Economics & Business Applications (credit).

Students in the Enrichment Program take one or more noncredit courses that meet two to four times a week for approximately one and one-half to two hours. Recent courses include Understanding the Stock Market and Business; Yes But Will it Sell?-Advertising in America; and SAT or ACT Prep. Applicants must have completed the 10th, 11th, or 12th grades and have a GPA of at least 2.75 to be eligible for the program.

Students in the programs live in Santa Cruz Residence Hall, which is located near the Pacific Ocean. The rooms feature high-speed Internet access. Other amenities in the residence halls and on-campus include a recreation center, a pool table, video games, a multi-station computer center, and laundry room. The cost for either program is approximately $6,770 (which includes tuition, housing, three daily meals, and extracurricular activities). A nonrefundable application fee of $95 is also required.

### University of California—Santa Barbara
c/o Summer Discovery
1326 Old Northern Boulevard
Roslyn, NY 11576-2244

805-893-2377
http://www.summer.ucsb.edu/precollegeprograms.html

## Secondary School Program at Harvard University
### College Courses/Summer Study

High school students who have completed their sophomore, junior, or senior years may apply to Harvard's Secondary School Program. The program is held for six weeks each summer, and participants earn college credit. Students who live on campus take either two four-credit courses or one eight-credit course for college credit. Commuting students may take two concurrent four-credit courses or one eight-credit course. Recent courses include Principles of Economics, Principles of Economics: Microeconomics, Principles of Economics: Macroeconomics, Quantitative Methods in Economics and Business, Introduction to Managerial Finance, Financial Accounting, Managerial Accounting, Financial Strategy and Behavioral Finance, and several foreign languages. In addition to academics, students can participate in extracurricular activities such as intramural sports, a trivia bowl, a talent show, and dances. Tuition for the program ranges from $2,475 (per four-unit course) to $4,950 (per eight-unit course). A nonrefundable registration fee ($50), health insurance ($165), and room and board ($4,250) are extra. Contact the program for more information.

In addition to the aforementioned on-site offerings, Harvard also offers selected online classes to students who can't attend classes on campus.

## Secondary School Program

Harvard University
51 Brattle Street
Cambridge, MA 02138-3722
617-495-3192
ssp@dcemail.harvard.edu
http://www.summer.harvard.
   edu/2009/programs/ssp

## SkillsUSA

### Competitions

SkillsUSA offers "local, state, and national competitions in which students demonstrate occupational and leadership skills." Students who participate in its SkillsUSA Championships can compete in categories such as Advertising Design, Chapter Business Procedure, Community Service, Customer Service, Entrepreneurship, Extemporaneous Speaking, and Job Interview. SkillsUSA works directly with high schools and colleges, so ask your counselor or teacher if it is an option for you. Visit the SkillsUSA Web site for more information.

### SkillsUSA

14001 SkillsUSA Way
Leesburg, VA 20176-5494
703-777-8810
http://www.skillsusa.org

## Summer Academy for High School Students at Manhattanville College

### College Courses/Summer Study

Rising high school juniors and seniors can participate in the Summer Academy for High School Students. Participants take college-level courses for credit. Two month-long sessions are available. Recent courses include Principles of Economics, Fundamentals of Successful Research, and Fundamentals of Management. Students stay in residence halls on campus. Contact the Office of Summer School for information on tuition and application requirements.

### Manhattanville College

Attn: Summer School Program
   Director
2900 Purchase Street
Purchase, NY 10577-2131
914-323-2200
http://www.mville.edu/
   AcademicsandResearch/
   SummerSchool

## Summer @ Brown at Brown University

### College Courses/Summer Study

High school students in the Pre-College Courses Program at Brown can take one or more interesting college-level courses. Classes, which last anywhere from one to four weeks, are held Monday through Friday. More than 200 classes are available—some are available for credit. Students spend three hours a day in class, and the remaining time studying, interacting with professors and fellow students, and participating in cultural and social activities. A wealth of fascinating courses have been offered in recent years, including Introduction to Financial Markets, International Financial Markets and Investments, How a Nation's Economy Works: An Introduction to Macroeconomics, Work in the Global Economy, Financial Markets and Investments, Introduction to the Global Business Environment, and various foreign languages. There are also classes that will help students develop their communication or study skills or better prepare for the college admissions process, including Cracking the AP Code (one week), Putting Ideas Into Words (one week), Persuasive Communication (one week), Writing the Academic Essay (three weeks), and Writing the College Admissions Essay (one week). Program participants live in residence halls that are within walking distance of classes and other activities. Students who are interested in taking Pre-College Courses must have intellectual curiosity, be emotionally mature, and have strong academic records. The following tuition rates are charged for Pre-College Courses: one-week residential ($2,153), one-week commuter ($1,652); two-week residential ($3,265), two-week commuter ($2,255); three-week residential ($4,702), three-week commuter ($3,200); four-week residential ($5,454), four-week commuter ($3,449). Housing and meals are included in the residential tuition. A limited amount of financial aid is available.

Rising high school seniors can take a variety of for-credit classes in the Summer Session Credit Program, including Principles of Economics, Financial Accounting, and Persuasive Communication. Each class lasts seven weeks. Commuter and residential options are available; students who choose the residential option must take two courses. The cost for one course for commuter students is about $3,200 and $5,990 for two classes. Tuition for residential students is about $9,200.

Contact the Office of Summer & Continuing Studies for more information on these programs.

### Office of Summer & Continuing Studies

Brown University
42 Charlesfield Street, Box T
Providence, RI 02912-9063
401-863-7900
http://brown.edu/scs/pre-college/pre-college-courses.php

## Summer @ Georgetown University for High School Students
### College Courses/Summer Study

Academically gifted high school students can earn up to 12 college credits by participating in Georgetown University's Summer College. Rising sophomores, juniors, and seniors may apply. More than 100 courses are available, including Accounting, Expository Writing, Fundamentals of Finance, Fundamentals of Business, Introduction to Business, Principles of Macroeconomics, Principles of Microeconomics, Public Speaking, Statistics With Exploratory Data Analysis, and foreign languages (Arabic, Chinese, French, German, Italian, Japanese, Persian, Spanish).

Fundamentals of Business-Leadership in a Global Economy, a five-week, for-credit workshop, is also available. Students learn about accounting, finance, marketing, business law, management, communications, and organizational planning and behavior via classroom lectures and visits to area corporations.

Tuition for both programs is $1,018 per credit hour. Other costs include a pre-college fee ($398 per session), room ($782), and a meal plan ($864). Financial aid is available for "exceptional" students who can demonstrate financial need.

Students who live on campus stay in air-conditioned residence halls. Access to laundry facilities is provided. In their off-hours, students can attend dances, movie nights, ice cream socials, and other activities, as well as explore the campus and the Washington, D.C., area. Contact the university for more information.

### Summer Programs for High School Students
Georgetown University
Box 571006
Washington, DC 20057-1006
202-687-8700
scsspecialprograms@georgetown.
  edu
http://www12.georgetown.edu/scs/
  degrees-and-programs/summer-
  and-special-programs.cfm

## Summer College for High School Students at Syracuse University
### College Courses/Summer Study
Students who have completed their sophomore, junior, or senior year of high school are eligible to apply to the Summer College for High School Students at Syracuse University, which runs for six weeks from early July to mid-August.

Commuter and residential options are available. The program has several aims: to introduce students to the many possible majors and study areas within their interest area; to help them match their aptitudes with possible careers; and to prepare them for college, both academically and socially. Students attend classes, listen to lectures, and take field trips to destinations that are related to their specific area of interest. All students are required to take two for-credit courses during the program, and they receive college credit if they successfully complete the courses. Students interested in business and finance can take the following classes: Economic Ideas and Issues, Business Calculus, and various foreign languages.

Admission is competitive and is based on recommendations, test scores, and transcripts. The total cost of the residential program is about $6,995; the commuter option costs about $4,995. Some scholarships are available. The application deadline is in mid-May, or mid-April for those seeking financial aid. For further information, contact the Summer College.

A two-week enrichment program in Management is also available. As a program participant, you will "explore the fields of business and management with the experts, learn how your strengths and interests fit into the management picture, analyze an industry and present your findings to the class, and polish the specific skills that support your natural leadership" via readings, classroom instruction, and seminars by guest speakers. Tuition for the program is $1,845 for residential students and $1,178 for commuter students. Contact the Summer College for more information.

### Syracuse University
Summer College for High School
  Students
700 University Avenue
Syracuse, NY 13244-2530
315-443-4498
sumcoll@syr.edu
http://summercollege.syr.edu

## Summerfuel at the University of California—Berkeley
### College Courses/Summer Study

High school students who are interested in experiencing college life and learning about one or more of their favorite subjects can participate in the month-long Summerfuel program at the University of California—Berkeley. College credit is awarded to students who complete the program. Some recent courses include Business & Entrepreneurship, SAT Preparation, Creative Writing, Marketing & Advertising, Public Speaking, Introduction to Economics, and Fundamentals of Finance. Classes are taught by university faculty. Noncredit mini-courses—such as Entrepreneurial Ventures, Community Service & Leadership, and International Affairs: Discussion & Debate—are also available. In addition to course work, students participate in sports and other recreational activities, as well as take trips to a San Francisco Giants game, Alcatraz Island, area beaches, Six Flags Marine World, area colleges, and other local attractions. The cost for the residential

program is $6,195. Participants live in a double room in one of the college's dorms and also have access to laundry machines, recreational facilities, computer labs, and the Foothill Dining Hall (participants receive three meals a day during the week and two a day on weekends). All rooms have telephone/Internet access. Summerfuel programs are operated by Academic Study Associates, an organization that has been offering residential and commuter pre-college summer programs for young people for more than 25 years.

### Academic Study Associates
ASA Programs
375 West Broadway, Suite 200
New York, NY 10012-4324
800-752-2250
summer@asaprograms.com
http://www.asaprograms.com/
  summerfuel

## Summerfuel at the University of Massachusetts—Amherst
### College Courses/Summer Study

High school students who are interested in experiencing college life and learning about one or more of their favorite subjects can participate in the month-long Summerfuel program at the University of Massachusetts—Amherst. College credit is awarded to students who complete the program. Some recent courses include Business & Entrepreneurship, Fundamentals of Finance, Marketing & Advertising, Introduction to Pre-Calculus, and Public Speaking. Noncredit mini-courses are also available. Recent noncredit mini-courses include Entrepreneurial

Ventures, Community Service & Leadership, College Admissions Workshop, and Creative Writing. University faculty teach all of the classes. In addition to course work, students participate in sports and other recreational activities, as well as take trips to a Boston Red Sox game, area beaches, Six Flags New England, and other local attractions. The cost for the residential program is $6,195. Participants live in air-conditioned, suite-style apartments. Summerfuel programs are operated by Academic Study Associates, an organization that has been offering residential and commuter pre-college summer programs for young people for more than 25 years.

**Academic Study Associates**
ASA Programs
375 West Broadway, Suite 200
New York, NY 10012-4324
800-752-2250
summer@asaprograms.com
http://www.asaprograms.com/
    summerfuel

## Summer College Programs for High School Students at Cornell University

### College Courses/Summer Study

Rising high school juniors and seniors and recent graduates can participate in Cornell University's Summer College, which offers three- and six-week classes for college credit. More than 20 courses are available. Recent courses of interest to readers of this book include Introduction to Business Management, Hotel Operations Management: Tactics for Profitability, Economics, Communication, and various foreign lan-

guages. Students who took Introduction to Business Management learned about the following topics: business organization, leadership, human resources, strategic management, marketing, finance, ethics, and the role of technology in business. They also met with guest speakers from a variety of business backgrounds and participated in discussions and team-building activities and an integrated case study on Nike. You must bear in mind that all Summer College classes are regular undergraduate courses condensed into a very short time span, so they are especially challenging and demanding. Program participants live in residence halls on campus and enjoy access to campus facilities. The cost for the program is $5,310 (which includes room and board). Applications are typically due in late April, although Cornell advises that you submit them well in advance of the deadline; those applying for financial aid must submit their applications by April 1. Further information and details about the application procedure are available from the Summer College office.

**Cornell University Summer College for High School Students**
B20 Day Hall
Ithaca, NY 14853-2801
607-255-6203
http://www.sce.cornell.edu/sc/
    programs

## Summer Institutes at Marist College

### College Courses/Summer Study

Rising high school juniors and seniors who are interested in business and other fields can participate in 13-day Pre-College Institutes. Rising sophomores and recent high school graduates can also apply but are only accepted on a space-available basis. Recent institutes include Business, Creative Writing, Criminal Justice, Environmental Science, Fashion, Game Design, and Sports Communication. In the Business Institute, participants will learn about basic business principles, information technology as it relates to business, ethical issues, the growing importance of entrepreneurial ventures, and globalization via classroom lectures, hands-on activities, and guest speakers. College credit is awarded to students who complete the programs. Students live in Marist residence halls and can use the college's library and recreational facilities. Tuition is $2,900 (which includes fees, housing, all meals, field trips, and course materials). The college suggests that participants bring a small amount of spending money for souvenirs and personal items. Contact the Office of Undergraduate Admission for information on application deadlines and other details.

### Marist College
Office of Undergraduate Admission
Attn: Summer Pre-College
3399 North Road
Poughkeepsie, NY 12601-1350
845-575-3226
http://www.marist.edu/summer
 institutes

## Summer Program for High School Students at Columbia University
**College Courses/Summer Study**

Rising ninth through 12th graders can participate in Columbia University's weeklong Summer Program for High School Students. More than 65 classes are available. Recent Freshman-Sophomore Division Courses include The Stock Market and Introduction to Creative Writing. Recent Junior-Senior Division Courses include Introduction to Business Finance and Economics; Creative Writing: Introductory and Advanced Workshops; and Communicating with Consumers: The Basics of Marketing, Advertising, and Public Relations. A course on college preparation is also available. All courses are rigorous, but are unavailable for college credit. During the week, students take classes from 10:00 A.M. to 12:00 P.M.; break for lunch and activities from 12:00 to 2:30 P.M.; and return to class from 2:30 to 4:30 P.M. In the evenings and on weekends, residential students participate in a wide variety of extracurricular activities, including on-campus events (such as parties, a talent show, a scavenger hunt, an open mike night, and organized sports) and off-campus excursions in and around New York City (such as guided walking tours, films, and trips to museums, concerts, restaurants, beaches, and amusement parks). Participants also have access to university libraries, computer labs, a fitness center, a student activity center, and other facilities. Commuter students pay approximately $3,400 per session. Residential students pay $6,225, which includes housing and dining. All students pay an additional fee of $135 for activities and health coverage. The university also suggests that residential students bring an additional $700 in spending money.

Additionally, study abroad programs are available in Barcelona, Spain, and the Middle East. Contact the School of Continuing Education for more information.

### Columbia University
Summer Program for High School
  Students
School of Continuing Education
203 Lewisohn Hall
2970 Broadway, Mail Code 4119
New York, NY 10027-6902
212-854-9666
http://www.ce.columbia.edu/hs

## Summer Program for High School Students at New York University
**College Courses/Summer Study**

Rising high school juniors and seniors in the New York City-area can participate in the university's Summer Program for High School Students. During this commuter program, students take one or two courses for college credit (for up to eight credits) and get a feel for college life. (A noncredit writing workshop is also available.) Some of the classes that were recently offered include Economic Principles, A Short History of Wall Street, Intercultural Communication, and various foreign languages. Students are not allowed to live on campus, and must find living arrangements within commuting distance of the campus. Tuition varies by class credit amount and subject area. The application deadline is typically in mid-April. Financial aid is available. Contact the Office of Undergraduate Admissions for more information.

### Summer Program for High School Students
New York University
Office of Undergraduate
  Admissions
22 Washington Square North
New York, NY 10011-9191
212-998-4500
http://www.nyu.edu/summer/2009/
  highschool/program.html

## Summer Programs for Youth at Southern Methodist University
**College Courses/Summer Study**

Southern Methodist University (SMU) offers several opportunities for high school students.

Gifted and highly motivated high school students who have completed the 10th or 11th grades can participate in the College Experience Program. This five-week residential program allows students to experience college-level instruction and earn up to six college credits. Students take two courses (such as Business Ethics, Pre-Calculus Mathematics, and Introduction to Calculus for Business and Social Science) from the SMU summer school schedule. Applicants must submit an academic transcript, recommendations, an essay, and PSAT, SAT, or ACT scores. Tuition for the program is approximately $2,470. An additional $1,600 for room and board and a nonrefundable registration fee of $35 are also required.

Students ages five through 18 can participate in one- or two-week enrichment workshops via the Summer Youth Program. Program areas for upper-level students include Computer Animation;

Web Design, Photoshop, & Digital Photography; Gaming; Applied Science; Creative Arts; Test Preparation & College Planning; Reading and Literature Enhancement Skills; Writing Enhancement Skills; Skills for School Success; and Dyslexia Technology. Each class in this nonresidential program lasts five days and costs $199.

There are also several other programs for high school students, including Girls Talk Back: Making Yourself Heard; Summer Sports Camps; Engineering Camp for Girls; Academic-Skills Enhancement Workshops; and Visioneering (an engineering exploration program that is held each spring). Contact the university for more information.

### Southern Methodist University
College Experience Program
PO Box 750383
Dallas, TX 75275-0383
214-768-0123
gifted@smu.edu
http://www.smu.edu/continuing_
  education/youth

### Southern Methodist University
Summer Youth Program
5236 Tennyson Parkway
Plano, TX 75024-3526
214-768-5433
smu.youth.programs@smu.edu
http://smu.edu/education/youth

## Summer Scholars Institute at Pace University
**College Courses/Summer Study**

Rising high school juniors and seniors can participate in Pace University's Summer Scholars Institute, a two-week program that allows them to take college-level courses and get a taste of college life. Each major features two classes—one in the morning, and one in the afternoon. In the evenings, students participate in activities that help them learn how to write better college essays and applications, as well as explore the culture of New York City. One recent major of interest to readers of this book was Business Marketing, which featured the following classes: Interactive-Integrated Marketing for Success and Professional Selling for Success. The cost of the program is $1,000 for commuters (which includes one meal a day and social events) and $2,000 for residents (which includes room, two meals a day, and social events). Financial aid is available. Applications are typically due in mid-June.

### Pace University
Summer Scholars Institute
Attn: Program Coordinator
Pforzheimer Honors College
W207E Pace Plaza
New York, NY 10038
212-346-1192
summerscholar@pace.edu
http://www.pace.edu/page.
  cfm?doc_id=17156

## Summer Scholars Pre-College Programs at George Washington University
**College Courses/Summer Study**

Rising high school seniors can participate in Six-Week Courses, which include a mandatory Writing Seminar for Summer Scholars and an elective course. College credit is awarded for the completion of this program. Recent elective courses include Introduction to Business and Economic Statistics, Principles of Economics, Public Communications, and various foreign languages. Students live in air-conditioned residence halls that have mini-fridges, microwaves, and telephones. Wireless Internet is available. Students also have access to a community lounge, kitchen, library, athletic facilities, and laundry facilities. The resident rate for the program is about $6,100; the commuter rate is $4,400. A $40 application fee and $200 to $250 for textbooks and supplies are also required. Financial aid is available. The application deadline is typically in mid-April. Contact the university for more information.

### George Washington University
Summer Scholars Pre-College
  Programs
1922 F Street, NW, Suite 304
Washington, DC 20052-0042
202-994-6360
gwsummer@gwu.edu
http://www.summerscholars.gwu.
  edu

## Summer Scholars Program at the University of Notre Dame
### College Courses/Summer Study
The Summer Scholars Program consists of nearly 15 two-week classes for rising high school juniors and seniors. Recent classes include Investments and Entrepreneurship, Policy Debate & Public Speaking, and Psychology. Students in the Investments and Entrepreneurship Program will learn about how businesses function by tracking stocks, listening to

speakers, taking field trips, and listening to lectures that cover topics such as business ethics, investing in stocks, business law, real estate, and communications and public speaking. They also work with other students to develop a business plan and present the plan in a simulated business-presentation environment. The application deadline for the program is typically in early March. Tuition for this mandatory residential program is $2,500 (which includes room/board and meals) plus a $45 application fee. A limited amount of financial aid is available. Contact the Office of Pre-College Programs for more information.

### University of Notre Dame
Office of Pre-College Programs
202 Brownson Hall
Notre Dame, IN 46556-5601
574-631-0990
precoll@nd.edu
http://precollege.nd.edu/
  summer-scholars

## Summer Seminars at the University of Southern California
### College Courses/Summer Study
Rising high school sophomores, juniors, and seniors who are interested in business and other subjects can get a taste of college life by participating in four-week Summer Seminars at the University of Southern California. Commuter and residential options are available. Readers of this book might be interested in taking Exploring Entrepreneurship, which "blends business theory and the practice of being an entrepreneur." Students create their own companies and learn the

traits of successful companies by taking field trips to emerging companies in the Los Angeles area. A typical schedule involves lectures from 9:00 A.M. to 12:00 P.M., a break for lunch, a workshop from 1:30 to 4:30 P.M., a study session from 4:00 to 6:00 P.M., dinner, and free time in the evening. In addition to classes, workshops, and studying, students participate in a variety of recreational activities (dancing, karaoke, a movie night) and field trips (the Hollywood Walk of Fame, a youth symphony concert, Disneyland, Knott's Berry Farm, the J. Paul Getty Museum, the Santa Monica Pier, a Dodgers baseball game, or a visit to the beach).

Participants who choose the residential option stay in dormitories on campus that have a common hallway with bathroom and showers. Each room has analog phone ports, Ethernet ports, a Microfridge (a half-sized refrigerator with attached microwave), and cable TV hookup. Students must bring their own telephones, televisions, cables for Internet hookup, linens, and toiletry items. The cost of attendance for residential students is about $6,105 (and includes room and board and lab, program, and health center fees). The cost of attendance for commuter students is about $4,300 (and includes a meal plan and lab, program, and health center fees). Financial aid is available. The application deadline is typically in late March.

### University of Southern California
Continuing Education and Summer Programs

3415 South Figueroa Street, Suite 107
Los Angeles, CA 90089-0874
213-740-5679
summer@usc.edu
http://cesp.usc.edu

## Summer Studies at the University of Richmond
### College Courses/Summer Study

The University of Richmond offers several exploration programs for high school students, including the Summer Scholars Program. The Summer Scholars Program seeks to provide high school students a "realistic, first-hand experience of college including the challenges and rewards that come with it, all while experiencing 'life on campus.'" Rising juniors and seniors are eligible to participate in this three-week, for-credit residential program. Approximately five courses are offered each summer. One recent course of interest is Microeconomics via Classroom Experiments, where students learned the pros and cons of market economies. Participants "learned the theories, simulated the economic models, discussed the ideas, and practiced the concepts with problems sets and computer exercises, and simulated these theories in classroom experiments." Applicants must have a competitive grade point average and enjoy intellectual stimulation and academic challenges. Program participants stay in air-conditioned residence halls and have access to study lounges, vending machines, and laundry facilities. The cost of the program is $4,200 (which includes tuition, textbooks and classroom supplies, residence hall lodging, a meal plan, and extracurricular activities). Financial assistance is available. Students also can use on-campus facilities such as the library, computer labs, and a sports center. The application deadline is typically in early May. Contact the director of summer programs for more information.

### University of Richmond
School of Continuing Studies
Director of Summer Programs
28 Westhampton Way
Richmond, VA 23173-0001
804-289-8133
scs@richmond.edu
http://summer.richmond.edu/
scholars

## Summer Study at Pennsylvania State University

### College Courses/Summer Study

Students who have completed the ninth, 10th, and 11th grades can apply to participate in the university's Summer Enrichment Program. The program offers three-and-a-half week and two-week options and recently featured classes in the following subject areas: Advertising, Algebra, Business & Marketing, Calculus, Community Service Workshop, Creative Writing, Debate, KAPLAN SAT or ACT Prep Course, Pre-Calculus, Psychology, Study Skills, TOEFL Prep by Kaplan, and Web Page Design. In the Business & Marketing category, a class called You're Fired: Business and Marketing was recently offered. Participants learned about "the interaction between buyer and seller, the role of the consumer, and successful ways to act and react in professional situations." They also learned how to develop a busi-

ness plan (that included marketing strategies and plans) via hands-on activities.

There is also a six-and-a-half-week for-credit program that features more than 75 college credit courses and more than 25 noncredit enrichment classes. Rising high school juniors and seniors and recent graduates may apply. Recent for-credit courses include Introductory Macroeconomic Analysis and Policy, Basic Writing Skills, Information People and Technology, and Introduction to Creative Writing. Noncredit course areas include advertising, business and marketing, creative writing, digital photography, and journalism/communications.

Tuition for the Summer Enrichment Program is approximately $6,995 for the six-and-a-half-week program; $4,495 for the three-and-a-half-week program; and $2,495 for the two-week program. Limited financial aid is available. Contact the Summer Study Program for more information.

### Summer Study Program
The Pennsylvania State University
900 Walt Whitman Road
Melville, NY 11747-2293
800-666-2556
info@summerstudy.com
http://www.summerstudy.com/
pennstate

## Summer Term/Young Scholars Program at the University of Maryland

### College Courses/Summer Study

Rising high school juniors and seniors with a GPA of at least 3.0 may take one or more classes for credit in the University of Maryland's Summer Term program. Two six-week sessions and four three-week sessions are available. College credit is awarded to students who satisfactorily complete coursework. Recent classes include Business and Management; Accounting and Information Assurance; Finance; Logistics, Business, and Public Policy; Marketing; Management and Organization; Economics; and various foreign languages. Participants live in residence halls at the University of Maryland and take their meals on campus or in selected College Park restaurants. A commuter option is also available. Contact the Office of Extended Studies for information on current tuition costs and application deadlines.

Students in the Young Scholars Program spend three weeks in July exploring various fields and taking a college-level course. College credit is awarded to those who satisfactorily complete the class. Past courses include Discovering New Ventures-Foundations of Entrepreneurship; Introduction to Technology Marketing and Product Development; and Speak Up! People, Publics, and You. Those who sign up for Discovering New Ventures-Foundations of Entrepreneurship "learn the basic business, strategy, and leadership skills needed to launch new ventures; how to assess the feasibility of a start-up venture, as well as how to apply best practices for planning, launching, and managing new companies." They take field trips to start-up companies to see how business theories and concepts are actually put into practice. Program participants commute or live in the residence halls at the University of Maryland and take their meals on

campus or in selected College Park restaurants. To apply, you must be a rising high school junior or senior and submit an application form, an essay, two letters of recommendation, a current transcript, and an application and enrollment fee of $205 by mid-May. Admissions decisions are based primarily on the recommendations, the applicant's academic record (they must have a GPA of 3.0 or higher), and overall academic ability. Residential tuition for the program is about $2,935; tuition for commuters is approximately $1,815. For further details and an application form, contact the Office of Extended Studies.

### Office of Extended Studies
University of Maryland
0132 Main Administration Building
College Park, MD 20742-5000
301-405-7762
http://www.summer.umd.edu

## Summer University at Johns Hopkins University
### College Courses/Summer Study

Rising high school juniors and seniors and recent graduates can participate in the Summer University program. Participants live on Hopkins' Homewood campus for five weeks beginning in early July. Classes leading to college credit are available in more than 30 areas. Past courses include Introduction to Business, Statistical Analysis, Principles of Marketing, Introduction to Calculus, Elements of Macroeconomics, Elements of Microeconomics, Economic Development, Oral Presentations, Technical Communication, and foreign language (Arabic,

French, German, and Spanish) courses. Students who live in the greater Baltimore area have the option of commuting. Applicants must submit an application form, essay, transcript, two recommendations, and a nonrefundable application fee (rates vary by date of submission). Tuition for residential students is $6,300 (for two courses, room and board, and up to six credits). Commuter students pay $630 per credit hour (books, supplies, meals, and special activities are not included in this price). Applicants must have at least a 3.0 GPA (on a 4.0 scale). Contact the Office of Summer Programs for more information.

**Johns Hopkins University**
Pre-College Program
Office of Summer Programs
3400 North Charles Street
Shaffer Hall, Suite 203
Baltimore, MD 21218-2685
800-548-0548
summer@jhu.edu
http://www.jhu.edu/~sumprog

## Summer Youth Explorations at Michigan Technological University
**College Courses/Summer Study**

Michigan Technological University (MTU) offers the Summer Youth Explorations program for students in grades six through 12. Participants attend one of five weeklong sessions, choosing either to commute or to live on campus. Students undertake an Exploration in one of many career fields through laboratory work, field trips, and discussions with MTU faculty and other professionals. Some recent Explorations include Entrepreneurship: Start a Business While in High School; Computer Graphics and Design; Create Your Future! What Do You Want to Be? How Do You Do It?; and Learning to Lead: A Leadership Introduction for Everyone. The cost of the Summer Youth Program is $650 for the residential option, $395 for commuters. Applications are accepted up to one week before the Exploration begins.

**Summer Youth Explorations**
Michigan Technological University
Youth Programs Office, Alumni
  House
1400 Townsend Drive
Houghton, MI 49931-1295
906-487-2219
http://youthprograms.mtu.edu/syp

# Read a Book

When it comes to finding out about business and finance, don't overlook a book. (You're reading one now, after all.) What follows is a short, annotated list of books and periodicals related to business and finance. The books cover topics such as choosing a career, applying to business school, international business careers, and much more. Don't be afraid to check out the professional journals, either. The technical stuff may be way above your head right now, but if you take the time to become familiar with one or two, you're bound to pick up some of what is important to business and finance professionals, not to mention begin to feel like a part of their world, which is what you're interested in, right?

We've tried to include recent materials as well as old favorites. Always check for the most recent editions, and, if you find an author you like, ask your librarian to help you find more. Keep reading good books!

## ❏ BOOKS

Alba, Jason. *Vault Career Guide to Accounting.* 3d ed. New York: Vault Inc., 2008. This guide provides an overview of the accounting industry and identifies the areas that provide the most job opportunities. The author covers the major accounting firms and other employers in the field.

Amos Jr., James H. *The Complete Idiot's Guide to Franchising.* New York: Alpha, 2005. Franchise opportunities, risks, and rewards are covered in this easy-to-read *Idiot* guide written by the former CEO of Mail Boxes, Etc. The book details how franchises operate, how aspiring franchisers obtain financing, and more.

Baker, Jennifer. *Vault Guide to Education Careers.* New York: Vault Inc., 2009. This book provides the scoop on the different careers available in the field of education including those in teaching, administration, and counseling.

Blanchard, Ken, Don Hutson, and Ethan Willis. *The One Minute Entrepreneur: The Secret to Creating and Sustaining a Successful Business.* New York: Doubleday Business, 2008. Mixing anecdotes and the stories behind some of America's most successful companies and straight up facts and figures on becoming an entrepreneur, this book provides an entertaining and informative read to anyone interested in succeeding in business. Authors focus on four keys to success: ensuring sales exceed expenses, the importance of collecting on bills, always striving for customer satisfaction, and caring for your employees.

Bodine, Paul. *Great Application Essays for Business School.* New York: McGraw-Hill, 2005. With today's competitive race to get into the best business schools, applicants need more than good grades and test scores. Schools look to application essays to get a true sense of the applicants' views and their ability to communicate thoughts effectively. This book covers guidelines on successful essay structure, common mistakes to avoid, and more than 20 writing samples of the most frequently asked essay questions.

Bouknight, Omari, and Scott Shrum. *Your MBA Game Plan: Proven Strategies for Getting into the Top Business Schools.* Rev. ed. Franklin Lakes, N.J.: Career Press, 2007. The MBA has become one of the most sought after degrees as the job market has become leaner and meaner. This resource written by school admission experts covers everything involved in getting into the business school of your choosing, from the GMAT to application essays and recommendation letters, to acing the admission interviews.

Cahn, Steven M., and Catharine R. Stimpson. *From Student to Scholar: A Candid Guide to Becoming a Professor.* New York: Columbia University Press, 2008. This volume may be slender (only 112 pages in length), but it is packed with insightful information on what to expect during the journey from student to educator. You'll read about writing your dissertation, conducting the job search, interviewing, excelling on the job, and getting published and gaining tenure. A priceless read for any future scholar.

Camenson, Blythe. *Careers for Self-Starters & Other Entrepreneurial Types.* 2d ed. New York: McGraw-Hill, 2004. This series of books focuses on different personality types and the careers that best suit their common interests and strengths. This edition examines the skills of the self-starter and the hot job markets that look for those talents, such as freelancing writing, franchise ownership, and public speaking.

Canfield, Jack, Mark Victor Hansen, Dahlynn McKowen, and Tom Hill. *Chicken Soup for the Entrepreneur's Soul: Advice and Inspiration on Fulfilling Dreams.* Santa Barbara, Calif.: Chicken Soup for the Soul, 2006. Stories from famous entrepreneurs such as Tom Chappell, founder of Tom's of Maine; the original Pampered Chef, Doris Christopher; and others will inspire and educate readers on opportunities for the entrepreneurial spirit. With its mix of personal vignettes and advice, this book is an easy and entertaining read.

Christie, Sally. *Vault Guide to International Careers.* New York: Vault Inc., 2004. An estimated 90 million people work outside their home country. This guide details the international job opportunities in teaching, corporate business, and foreign service. Includes a section on the countries with the most job openings and covers both the risks and the rewards of working abroad.

Cooperman, Susan H. *Professional Office Procedures.* 5th ed. Upper Saddle River, N.J.: Prentice Hall, 2008. The author covers practical tips on applying book smarts to the real world workforce with inspiring personal stories from the trenches. This edition includes a whole new section on technology, including using the Internet and software applications to work smarter, not harder.

Crittendon, Robert. *The New Manager's Starter Kit: Essential Tools for Doing the Job Right.* New York: AMACOM Books, 2007. Written by a former Fortune 500 executive, this guide covers business basics in a straightforward and easy-to-read manner. Includes tips on interviewing prospective employees effectively and fairly, how to manage and balance customer and employee expectations, and more.

D'Alessandro, David. *Career Warfare: 10 Rules for Building a Successful Personal Brand on the Business Battlefield.* New York: McGraw-Hill, 2008. The author uses a no-nonsense style to address the "war" of building a brand and protecting it. The book includes stories from the field and helpful advice from experts who have proven their ability to get ahead in business.

DeCenzo, David A., and Stephen P. Robbins. *Fundamentals of Human Resource Management.* 9th ed. Hoboken, N.J.: Wiley, 2006. This book covers the basics of human resource management as well as details many topics in the news today, such as employee drug testing, minimum wage, work benefits, and stock options.

Edelfelt, Roy, and Alan Reiman. *Careers in Education.* 4th ed. New York: McGraw-Hill, 2003. If you think you might like to enter the educational profession, this book has all the information you need to make an informed career choice, including salary information for different jobs, first-person reports from teachers and others, degree and/or certification requirements, and future prospects for job growth in specific careers in education.

Editors of VGM. *Resumes for Education Careers.* 3d ed. New York: McGraw-Hill, 2004. The competition for jobs in every field is intense these days, and using the methods contained in this book can help those interested in careers in education to break through the logjam of applicants. Advice on maximizing one's chances of landing an interview is backed up by dozens of sample résumés and cover letters.

Gaylord, Gloria, and Glenda Ried. *Careers in Accounting.* 4th ed. New York: McGraw-Hill, 2006. The field of accounting offers many different job opportunities in diverse markets, from number crunching for a corporate client, to writing tax policy in government, to overseeing the budget for a nonprofit. Each of these jobs requires different skill sets and personalities. This book covers these wide-ranging areas of accounting and recommends education and entry methods for each job market. Also includes a section on what to expect in entry-level positions for first-time job seekers in accounting.

Goldberg, Jan. *Great Jobs for Accounting Majors.* 2d ed. New York: McGraw-Hill, 2005. This book covers work opportunities and job-seeking tips for recent graduates. Also includes a section on personal stories from the workplace to give a sense of what the industry is really like to work in and lists resources for more information and research.

Halloran, Ed. *Careers in International Business.* 2d ed. New York: McGraw-Hill, 2003. Jobs in international business are exciting and appealing, so job seekers face stiff competition for positions. This guide covers need-to-know information such as how to find jobs in the international marketplace and how to conduct yourself in this varied business setting, being mindful and respectful of cultural differences and sensitivities.

Isiadinso, Chioma. *The Best Business Schools' Admissions Secrets: A Former Harvard Business School Admissions Board Member Reveals the Insider Keys to Getting In.* Naperville, Ill.: Sourcebooks Inc., 2008. Just as a company needs to brand itself to stand out among its competition, so too do MBA applicants to outshine and outsmart other prospective students. In this guide, the author shares her secrets to branding oneself, from the essays to the interviews, to land an application in the "yes" pile.

Jones, Nancy Langdon. *So You Want to Be a Financial Planner: Your Guide to a New Career.* 4th ed. Sunnyvale, Calif.: AdvisorPress, 2007. This is a thorough guidebook for anyone interested in becoming a financial planner. Written by a financial expert, this book contains information on how to find the best schools and obtain licensure and other credentials, as well as reviews related products such as hardware, software, and Web sites. Also helpful is the section detailing how to start-up a financial planning business (commission based or fee-only) and tips on how to attract clients. A must read for any future financial professional.

Lambert, Stephen. *Great Jobs for Business Majors.* 3d ed. New York: McGraw-Hill, 2008. You've just graduated from college with a degree in business—now what? This book will provide the answers. It is filled with industry profiles that will be of interest to business school graduates—from retail to health care, sales to nonprofit work, including some careers that may surprise you, and will help readers find the perfect job that best suits their personality, strengths, and career and life goals. The book also gives step-by-step suggestions on how to prepare and survive a job search. Tips include how to craft a winning résumé, how to write cover letters, and interview dos and don'ts. Also helpful is a resource section that lists professional associations, journals and publications, and Web sites devoted to a variety of industries.

Lesonsky, Rieva. *Start Your Own Business.* 4th ed. Newburgh, N.Y.: Entrepreneur Press, 2007. Learn what it takes to start your own business, especially during the crucial first three years. Written by the editorial director of *Entrepreneur Magazine*—as well as other magazine insiders—this book provides information on how to build a brand, time management, trademarks and copyrights, and other start-up advice. The technology section goes in depth on topics from online marketing to using technology to boost productivity. Various vendors are also listed in the book offering services such as equipment manufacturing, business development, and small business loans.

McGraw-Hill. *Resumes for Business Management Careers.* 3d ed. New York: McGraw-Hill, 2006. This book features more than 100 sample résumés, covering different occupations and industries. It also has a worksheet section that helps readers gather information about their education, experience, and career goals that can be used when creating their own résumé. Sample cover letters are also included to help readers write a winning letter of introduction, one that will catch the attention of any recruiter or human resource manager. This résumé guide will prove helpful for new college grads, or older workers embarking on a career change or re-entering the job market.

Montauk, Richard. *How To Get Into the Top MBA Programs.* 4th ed. Upper Saddle River, N.J.: Prentice Hall, 2007. Are you thinking about applying to business school? If so—hold on—at least until you've read this book, which identifies the important steps in navigating the application process, from finding the right program, to marketing yourself, to surviving school once you've been accepted. Each chapter is devoted to a step in the application process.

Napolitano, John P. *The Complete Idiot's Guide to Success as a Personal Financial Planner.* New York: Alpha, 2007. As with all books in the *Idiot* series, this guide presents information, in this case, on careers in financial planning, in an easy to understand, yet thorough, format. The book has four sections—your future in financial planning, earning a living in this industry, being your own boss, and expanding your business.

Princeton Review. *Best 296 Business Schools, 2009 Edition.* New York: Princeton Review, 2008. Since today's competitive climate makes it even more important to make the most of your education dollars, it makes sense to find the program that best suits your needs. Princeton Review tallied its list of the best business and law schools via an exhaustive survey of students from across the nation. The categories given are vast. The toughest schools to gain entrance to? Yale University's Law School and Stanford University's Business School. Most family-friendly campus? Brigham Young University. Most Welcoming of Older Students? City University of New York—Queens.

Princeton Review. *Cracking the GMAT with DVD, 2009 Edition.* New York: Princeton Review, 2008. This book will help readers ace the GMAT by learning to think like the test writers, take advantage of computer algorithms from which most of the GMAT is based, and identify any "traps" within the test. The accompanying DVD is a virtual classroom that offers practice exams, more than 250 practice questions, study guides, and helpful information on composing essays.

Seid, Michael, and Dave Thomas. *Franchising For Dummies.* 2d ed. Hoboken, N.J.: For Dummies, 2006. This book provides information on owning a franchise. You'll learn the power of brand franchising, how to operate a franchise business, and methods of attracting customers. Myths about franchises are debunked, including the variety of businesses available as a franchise— there is certainly more out there

than just fast food chains! Don't miss the section containing the 10 most important questions to ask yourself before committing to a franchise.

Shoup, Kate. *What Can You Do With a Major in Business: Real People. Real Jobs. Real Rewards.* Hoboken, N.J.: Wiley, 2005. This book provides an overview of the various options that are available to those with a degree in business. It features profiles of real life graduates, detailing their job search and their experiences in their new career. Some careers covered include marketing field manager, import broker, and public relations specialist.

Stair, Lila B., and Leslie Stair. *Careers in Business.* 5th ed. New York: McGraw-Hill, 2005. You know you want a career in business—but what exactly does that mean? Read this book to learn more about finding that perfect niche in such a vast field. It will help you to identify your unique skills and career goals to zone in on the specialty that suits you best.

Stephenson, James. *Ultimate Home-based Business Handbook: How to Start, Run and Grow Your Own Profitable Business.* Newburgh, N.Y.: Entrepreneur Press, 2004. Many of today's successful companies started out as home-based businesses, often operating from the kitchen or spare room. The author, a noted consultant for home-based businesses, tells the secrets of how. This guide will help readers "start smart"—identifying the best business ideas, navigating the needed paperwork and legalese, implementing basic marketing and sales operational systems, and organizing their workspace. The book also includes hundreds of resources, many of which are online, to help aspiring business owners every step of the way.

Stephenson, James. *Ultimate Start-Up Directory.* 2d ed. Newburgh, N.Y.: Entrepreneur Press, 2007. Whether you are mulling over starting a tree house kit business or offering cooking classes, you'll get a step-by-step guide on how to market your ideas, advertise your business, and even secure paying customers. More than 1,350 business ideas from 30 different industries are presented with a company overview, potential customer base, any franchising costs, as well as income and profit levels.

Strayer, Susan. *Vault Guide to Human Resources Careers.* New York: Vault Inc., 2005. Human resources (HR) is more than the administrative department of a company; today HR is seen as a major player in helping organizations run smoother and encourage employees to work harder and grow in their careers. This book describes how the HR department fits into an organization's framework, various career paths available within the field, the type of education and training needed for this career, as well as different functions of the HR professional. There is also an informative section on salaries and professional development.

Stroman, James, Kevin Wilson, and Jennifer Wauson. *Administrative Assistant's and Secretary's Handbook.* 3d ed. New York: AMACOM Books, 2008. Administrative assistants do more than just answer phones; they are an integral part of any corporation or other business. This book details the various skills and responsibilities of administrative assistants—ranging from coordinating meetings, making travel arrangement, conducting research, writing presentations, and acting as a department's organizational backbone. Among the topics discussed are computer skills, time and stress management, customer service, and event planning.

Sumichrast, Michael, and Martin Sumichrast. *Opportunities in Financial Careers.* New York: McGraw-Hill, 2004. This book provides information on more than 100 careers available within the financial industry. It will help readers determine if this career choice is right for them, as well as the education and training needed to succeed. Especially helpful is the section detailing the various branches of finance ranging from banks, savings and loans, securities and commodities, and the mortgage industry, including employment opportunities and earning potential for each one.

Weltman, Barbara. *The Complete Idiot's Guide to Starting a Home-Based Business.* 3d ed. New York: Alpha, 2007. Desperate to escape the corporate rat race? Interested in earning more money? Want to shorten your work commute to the distance it takes to walk from your kitchen or bedroom to your home office? If you've answered yes to any of these questions, then this book should be next on your reading list. Presented in a humorous yet informative style, this book provides a step-by-step guide to making your home-based business a dream come true. Topics include information on the different types of home businesses, tax considerations, and how to implement a successful marketing campaign. The guide also includes a comprehensive listing of the best home-based business ideas and their specific requirements.

Wetfeet. *Careers in Human Resources.* San Francisco: WetFeet, 2008. This book identifies the current hot industries for human resource professionals. Information on job specialties, education and training requirements, salaries, and career development is featured. There is also a section on how to successfully interview for coveted human resources positions.

Whitaker, Todd. *What Great Teachers Do Differently: Fourteen Things That Matter Most.* Larchmont, N.Y.: Eye on Education, 2003. This book contains plenty of practical thinking and ideas from current and former teachers on how to improve as an educator, from the general (working on one's listening and leadership skills) to the specific (addressing disruptive behavior in class, motivating underperforming students, preparing for standardized tests).

Wickham, Philip A., and Louise Wickham. *Management Consulting: Delivering an Effective Project.* 3d ed. Upper Saddle River, N.J.: Prentice Hall, 2008. Are you a student currently working toward a degree in management or business? If so, this book will be a useful resource. Opportunities in a wide range of industries are covered including art, engineering, media, and computers. There are also sections that provide information on cross-cultural consulting, contracting, and developing team leadership. The authors of this book have decades of experience consulting both in the corporate world and academia, making this book an informative resource.

## ❏ PERIODICALS

*Academe.* Published bimonthly by the American Association of University Professors (1133 19th Street, NW, Suite 200, Washington, DC 20036-3655, 202-737-5900), this magazine features education-related news, book reviews, and articles on local and international topics in higher education. Visit http://www.aaup. org/AAUP/pubsres/academe/default. htm to read past issues.

*American Educator.* Published quarterly, the professional journal of the American Federation of Teachers (555 New Jersey Avenue, NW, Washington, DC 20001-2029, amered@aft.org) contains articles for teachers and other education professionals. Recent issues can be viewed at http://www.aft.org/pubs-reports/american_educator.

*American Teacher.* Published eight times a year by the American Federation of Teachers (555 New Jersey Avenue, NW, Washington, DC 20001-2029), this newspaper is geared toward teachers in grades K through 12. It includes suggestions for classroom activities, profiles of noteworthy professionals, and the latest labor and legislative news related to education. Visit http://www.aft.org/pubs-reports/american_teacher to read sample issues.

*BusinessWeek.* Published weekly by The McGraw-Hill Companies Inc. (PO Box 8418, Red Oak, IA 51591-1418, 800-635-1200, http://www.businessweek.com), this magazine publishes the latest business news as well as features on investing, technology, innovation in the business world, management profiles, and articles for owners of small businesses. It also publishes annual rankings of United States colleges' undergraduate business and MBA programs.

*CFA Magazine.* This magazine is published bimonthly by the CFA Institute (560 Ray C. Hunt Drive, Charlottesville, VA 22903-2981, 800-247-8132, http://www.cfapubs.org/loi/cfm), a global, not-for-profit association of investment professionals. Recent issues of this magazine have not so surprisingly detailed the weakened economy and its impact on investing, including the erosion of public confidence in financial analysts. However, the mission of the CFA Institute, to promote ethical standards among its members and provide them with the latest news and educational opportunities, remains unchanged.

*Chief Executive.* Published eight times a year by Butler Publishing Inc. (110 Summit Avenue, Montvale, NJ 07645-1775, http://www.chiefexecutive.net), this is the only magazine written strictly for chief executive officers (CEOs) and their peers, providing ideas, strategies, and tactics for top executive leaders who are seeking to build more effective organizations. It includes profiles of noteworthy CEOs, describing the corporate challenges as well as the personal pressures they face, and stories of businesses they have turned around.

*The Chronicle of Higher Education.* Published 49 times a year by *The Chronicle of Higher Education* (1255 23rd Street, NW, 7th Floor, Washington, DC 20037-1125, 202-466-1000, http://chronicle.com), this newspaper bills itself as "The No. 1 source of news, information, and jobs for college and university faculty members and administrators." An online version, updated every day, is also available and includes access to job listings, discussion forums, résumé assistance, and salary information.

*CIO.* Published biweekly by CXO Media (492 Old Connecticut Path, PO Box 9208, Framingham, MA 01701-9208, 508-872-0080), this magazine for those in charge of companies' information technology (IT) budgets provides case studies and articles detailing the role of IT in achieving business goals as well as the latest on available technology and suggestions for implementing it successfully. Print and online editions are available, with sample articles posted at http://www.cio.com.

*Financial Analysts Journal.* Published bimonthly by the CFA Institute (560 Ray C. Hunt Drive, Charlottesville, VA 22903-2981, 800-247-8132), this publication contains articles of interest to investment professionals on topics including surviving in a down economy, the role of investment professionals in causing the economic downturn, the debate over increased government regulation of investment companies, and the danger of "information overload" in investing. Regular features include columns on investment tactics and ethics issues. Past articles are available online at http://www.cfapubs.org/loi/faj.

*Forbes.* Published biweekly by Forbes Magazine (60 Fifth Avenue, New York, NY 10011-8868, 800-295-0893, http://www.forbes.com), this business publication offers coverage of business news, new technology, entrepreneurs, and personal finance, and it is best known for its annual list of the richest Americans (known as the Forbes 400) and its list of billionaires.

*Fortune.* Published 25 times a year by Time Inc. (800-621-8000, http://www.fortune.com/customerservice, http://money.cnn.com/magazines/fortune), this global business magazine provides articles on investing, management, and business technology but is best known for its regular publishing of researched and ranked lists, including the Best Companies to Work For and the top 500 U.S. closely held and public corporations as ranked by their gross revenue, known as the Fortune 500.

*The Franchisee Voice.* This is published quarterly by the American Association of Franchisees & Dealers (PO Box 81887, San Diego, CA 92138-1887, 619-209-3775). People who own their own franchise (for example, a 7-11 store or a McDonald's restaurant) invest their own money in hopes of making a good living being their own boss while still receiving support and guidance from the franchisor organization. This magazine offers advice to franchisees on negotiating a good deal when investing in a business, tips on protecting one's rights should the relationship with the franchisor end, and nuts-and-bolts information about running a business. Visit http://www.aafd.org/franchisevoice.php to browse past articles.

*Franchising World.* Published monthly by the International Franchise Association (1501 K Street, NW, Suite 350, Washington, DC 20005-1412, 202-628-8000). Designed to encourage high ethical standards and promote success in the franchising community, this magazine keeps tabs on the overall state of the world of franchising, including reports on changes to or new government legislation affecting franchising, articles on international marketing opportunities, and news on upcoming industry events. Print and online editions are offered; a number of recent issues are available to read at http://www.franchise.org/Franchise-Industry-Fran-World.aspx.

*HR Magazine.* Published monthly by the Society for Human Resource Management (1800 Duke Street, Alexandria, VA 22314-3494, 800-283-7476), this publication bills itself as the most widely read and respected human resources (HR) publication in the world, offering news and features for human resources professionals at all career levels on topics such as employment law, recruiting, diversity, and technology, and profiles of companies that have successfully faced unique HR-related challenges. Some past issues are available online at http://www.shrm.org/Publications/hrmagazine.

*Inc.* Published 10 times a year by Mansueto Ventures LLC (Seven World Trade Center, New York, NY 10007-2195, 800-234-0999, http://www.inc.com), this publication is targeted toward entrepreneurs and small businesses, offering advice on all aspects of starting and succeeding with a new business as well as profiles of entrepreneurial success stories. It also publishes an annual list of the 500 fastest-growing private companies in the United States, known as the Inc. 500.

*Internal Auditor.* Published bimonthly by The Institute of Internal Auditors (247 Maitland Avenue, Altamonte Springs, FL 32701-4201, 407-937-1100, http://www.theiia.org/intauditor), this magazine is written for professionals who want to keep pace with all aspects of the field of internal auditing. Articles are geared toward all experience levels, from guidance for beginning auditors on introductory-level audit topics to reports on significant cases of corporate fraud and techniques for fraud deterrence and control. Consistent coverage of new technology provides information and resources about how best to integrate software and other technology to enhance an organization as well as examples of auditor-developed applications that address specific audit and administrative needs.

*Journal of Accountancy.* Published monthly by The American Institute of Certified Public Accountants (1211 Avenue of the Americas, New York, NY 10036-8701, 888-777-7077). Accounting is a field that requires a great deal of continuing education, especially given the frequency of changes in tax laws and generally accepted accounting principles. This journal helps keep CPAs and other accounting professionals up to date on the latest news and developments in the field, from the impact of legislative developments on the company bottom line to tips on getting the most out of accounting software such as Microsoft Excel. Read the latest issue online at http://www.aicpa. org/Magazines+and+Newsletters.

*Journal of Financial Planning.* Published monthly by the Financial Planning Association (1600 K Street, NW, Suite 201, Washington, DC 20006-2821, 800-322-4237), this journal is written to keep members of the financial planning profession informed on investment strategies and news relating to government regulation of the industry, but its coverage of personal finance issues (such as retirement savings and the effect of money conflicts on personal relationships) is useful for anyone interested in personal financial stability. You can browse articles online at http://www.fpanet.org.

*Journal of Teacher Education.* Published five times annually by SAGE Publications (800-818-7243, journals@sagepub.com, http://www. sagepub.com/journalsSubscribe. nav?prodId=Journal200961) for the American Association of Colleges for Teacher Education (1307 New York Avenue, NW, Suite 300, Washington, DC 20005-4721), this publication covers topics such as "accreditation,

assessment and evaluation, extended programs, teacher education faculty, and student teaching."

*Management Accounting Quarterly.* Published quarterly by Institute of Management Accountants (10 Paragon Drive, Montvale, NJ 07645-1718, 800-638-4427), this theory-heavy online journal offers an in-depth look at management accounting and financial management techniques for practitioners, academics, and other financial professionals. Recent articles have examined cost-accounting systems in Germany as opposed to in the United States, debated the merits of two proposed approaches to financial statement preparation, and described ways to quantify the costs to companies of reducing business risk. View the current issue online at http://www.imanet.org/publications. asp.

*Money.* Published monthly by Time Inc. (800-633-9970, http://www. money.com/customerservice, http:// money.cnn.com/magazines/moneymag), this magazine provides general business news and coverage of the financial markets as well as articles on a wide range of personal finance topics, from investing, saving, retirement and taxes to family finance issues such as credit, career and home improvement, and paying for college. *Money* is also well known for its annual list of America's Best Places to Live.

*NEA Today.* Published bimonthly by the National Education Association

(1201 16th Street, NW, Washington, DC 20036-3290, 202-833-4000), this resource explores the challenges of being an educator and provides tips and advice on prospering in the field. Visit http://www.nea.org/home/606.htm to read a sample issue.

*OfficePro.* Published nine times a year by the International Association for Administrative Professionals (PO Box 20404, Kansas City, MO 64195-0404, 816-891-6600), this magazine for career-minded office professionals features articles that are relevant to issues workers face in the office, including how to handle personality conflicts with coworkers; social-networking sites and their effect on businesses; standing up for yourself on the job; and tips for making one's office more environmentally friendly. One special edition per year features content aimed at office executives. Go to http://www.iaap-hq.org/publications to read sample articles.

*Public Personnel Management.* Published quarterly by the International Public Management Association for Human Resources (1617 Duke Street, Alexandria, VA 22314-3406, 703-549-7100, http://www.ipma-hr.org/content.cfm?pageid=87), this journal seeks to help human resources professionals at the federal, state, and local levels of government improve their job performance by reporting on trends, case studies, and the latest research on human resources issues and by providing them with information on resources and educational opportunities.

*Staffing Management.* Published quarterly by the Society for Human Resource Management (1800 Duke Street, Alexandria, VA 22314-3494, 800-283-7476), this magazine is aimed at human resources professionals and is filled with the latest techniques and trends in recruiting and hiring employees makes for interesting reading for job applicants as well, especially in an unsteady economy. Read about company testing practices, what to expect in interviews (both pre-employment and exit), how much emphasis companies place on an applicant's college major, the consequences of lying on an application or during an interview, and much more at http://www.shrm.org/Publications/StaffingManagementMagazine.

*Start Here.* Published by the American Institute of Certified Public Accountants (1211 Avenue of the Americas, New York, NY 10036-8701), this magazine is intended for high school or college students interested in a career in business and accounting, offering resources such as scholarship and internship listings, profiles of successful CPAs, and lists of available career opportunities. Go to http://www.startheregoplaces.com for more information.

*Strategic Finance.* Published monthly by Institute of Management Accountants (10 Paragon Drive, Montvale, NJ 07645-1718, 800-638-4427), this magazine covers trends in finance and accounting and offers career advice for accountants. Ethics and tax-specific issues are covered in columns every month, and recent issues have featured articles on conflicts between U.S. and international accounting standards as well as the importance of maintaining the security of customer financial information. Visit http://www.imanet.org/publications.asp to read sample articles.

*T+D.* Published monthly by the American Society for Training & Development (1640 King Street, Box 1443, Alexandria, VA 22313-1443, 703-683-8100), this magazine devoted to news and emerging technologies and trends in workplace training is geared toward business managers and those providing training, but those interested in a business career can also benefit from articles related to what qualities businesses are looking for in their attempt to locate and develop tomorrow's executives. Sample articles are available at http://www.astd.org/content/publications.

*Tomorrow's Teachers.* Published annually by the National Education Association (1201 16th Street, NW, Washington, DC 20036-3290, 202-833-4000), this resource for student members offers job-search strategies, advice on excelling during your first year on the job, and much more. Visit http://www.nea.org/home/606.htm to read a sample issue.

*The Wall Street Journal.* Published six times a week by Dow Jones & Company Inc. (One World Financial Center, 200 Liberty Street, New York, NY 10281-1003, 212-416-2000, http://www.wsj.com), this has been the world's leading business publication since 1889, covering U.S. and international business and financial news and issues and focusing more on what the news means than on what happened yesterday. Very simply, if you are interested in any type of business-related career, you should be reading the *Journal* every day. Reduced-rate subscriptions are often offered to undergraduate business students, and online as well as print subscriptions are available.

# Surf the Web

You must use the Internet to do research, to find out, to explore. The Internet is the closest you'll get to what's happening right now all over the world. This chapter gets you started with an annotated list of Web sites related to business and finance. Try a few. Follow the links. Maybe even venture as far as asking questions in a discussion room. The more you read about and interact with business professionals, the better prepared you'll be when you're old enough to participate as a professional.

One caveat: you probably already know that URLs change all the time. If a Web address listed below is out of date, try searching on the site's name or other keywords. If it's still out there, you'll probably find it. If it's not, maybe you'll find something better!

## ❑ THE SITES

### About.com: Business School
http://businessmajors.about.com

About.com tells you everything you always wanted to know "about" any given subject: in this case, business school. Major sections include Business School, Admissions Advice for Business Majors, Career Information and Advice for Business Professionals, and Resources for Future and Current Business Majors. There is also a business education blog and a free busi-

ness-oriented newsletter. This is a great site to visit to obtain a general overview of business education.

### Business Professionals of America
http://www.bpa.org

Business Professionals of America (BPA) is a membership organization for middle school, high school, and college students pursuing careers in business management, office administration, information technology, and other related fields. The BPA site has links to information on all the organization's activities, including the Workplace Skills Assessment Program, which provides students with the opportunity to demonstrate workplace skills learned through business education curricula, and the National Leadership Conference, at which students participate in educational workshops and leadership programs, listen to speakers, elect student officers, and put their business acumen to the test in a competitive-events program.

### Career Guide to Industries
http://www.bls.gov/oco/cg

Every two years, the U.S. Department of Labor publishes a guide to nearly 50 U.S. industries. Each industry article features the following sections: Significant Points, Nature of the Industry, Working

Conditions, Employment, Occupations in the Industry, Training and Advancement, Outlook, Earnings, and Sources of Additional Information. Many of the articles in the guide focus on business-related fields, including Advertising and Public Relations Services; Employment Services; Management, Scientific, and Technical Consulting Services; and Wholesale Trade. Visit the Career Guide to Industries Web site to access these useful articles.

### Career Voyages: Business Management and Administration
http://www.careervoyages.gov/business-main.cfm

Anyone considering a career in business or finance should check out this area of the Career Voyages site, a joint effort between the U.S. Departments of Labor and Education. The Web site features the following sections: General Management, Operations, Marketing and Sales, Finance and Accounting, Human Resources, Administrative Support, and Entrepreneurship. Each section contains an overview of the particular subindustry; a thorough list of education and training options; links to schools offering relevant training; a list of in-demand occupations for each subindustry; and other career information, including videos.

### Careers-in-Business.com
http://www.careers-in-business.com

This Web site provides a basic overview of opportunities in the business world. Sections include Accounting, Consulting, Finance, Marketing, and Non-Profit. Each section features an overview of the industry sector and career options, important skills and talents for career success, salaries for the field, top companies in the industry, and links to useful books and Web sites about business specialties.

### College Navigator
http://nces.ed.gov/collegenavigator

College Navigator is sponsored by the National Center for Education Statistics, an agency of the U.S. Department of Education. At the site, users can search for information on nearly 7,000 postsecondary institutions in the United States. Searches can be conducted by school name, state, programs/majors offered (including Business, Management, Marketing, and Related Support Services), level of award, institution type, tuition, housing availability, campus settings, percentage of applicants who are admitted, test scores, availability of varsity athletic teams, availability of extended learning opportunities, religious affiliation, and specialized mission. Additionally, users can export the results of their search into a spreadsheet, save the results of their session, and compare up to four colleges in one view. This is an excellent starting place to conduct research about colleges and universities.

### Franchise EXPO.com
http://www.franchiseexpo.com

If you hope to someday own and manage a franchise of your own, this is the Web site to browse. Its comprehensive list of franchises range from eateries, to entertainment establishments, to home-based franchises. Each franchise is conveniently grouped according to its theme—just click on a category to get further details. Information given for each franchise includes a history of the business, earning potential, franchise owner requirements, and testimonials from current franchise owners. Don't forget to check out the Resource section. You'll learn what it takes to run a franchise and even get advice on how to franchise your existing business.

### Finance FREAK.com
http://www.financefreak.com

According to this Web site, you shouldn't be a fool about money, but rather a freak about it. Specifically, a finance freak! Browse Finance FREAK.com to learn everything there is to know about money—how to make it, save it, invest it, and even owe it (paying it back quickly to avoid finance charges). The different categories about each action gives information basic enough for financial novices to understand, yet detailed enough to hold the attention of more savvy economic wizards. In the Banking, etc., section, for example, basic banking terms, such as *FDIC insured*, are explained and different lending and saving institutions are listed and presented to show which is best for different purposes. If you aspire to someday work as a financial planner, it may be wise to read the section, Be Smart & Rich. Here you will learn tips to make the most of your money and investments, spend wisely, and save like never before!

### Future Business Leaders of America
http://www.fbla-pbl.org

Future Business Leaders of America (FBLA), an organization for high school students preparing for careers in business, is the largest student business organization in the world, with a quarter of a million members. This site provides information on the organization's Business Achievement Awards and national leadership conferences, FBLA publications, and annual competitive events in the areas of technology, public speaking, business, finance, and management that offer valuable experience and cash prizes. Download a free FBLA Action Packet to find out more.

### GradSchools.com
http://www.gradschools.com

This site offers listings of graduate schools searchable by field of study (such as Business Programs or MBA Degree Specializations), format (campus, online, or both), and location (U.S. and international locations). From the home page, use the drop-down menu to choose the subject of your interest, such Business Administration, E-Commerce, or Finance. Listings include program info, degrees offered, school Web site, and email contact.

### Hoovers Online
http://www.hoovers.com

Hoover's Inc. provides "comprehensive insight and analysis about the companies, industries, and people that drive the economy." You can visit its Web site to learn more about companies in every industry—from Dell and Hallmark Cards, to Macmillan Publishers Limited and Peapod, to Thomson Reuters Corporation and Wal-Mart. Visitors can search by company name, geographic region, type or industry, and business lists (those companies that are named as the best in their industries). Each company entry includes contact information, a description of its products and/or services, financial information, recent job listings, and a wealth of other details. There is also a helpful section that provide information on industries such as Banking, Financial Services, and Retail. This is a good starting place to visit to learn about companies in your particular field, as well as business sectors.

### Junior Achievement
http://www.ja.org

Junior Achievement (JA) is dedicated to preparing young people for the real world by showing them how to generate and manage wealth, how to create jobs that make their communities more robust, and how to apply entrepreneurial thinking to the workplace. This site has links to available scholarships and JA activities at the elementary, middle and high school levels, and the Student Center tab has information on career assessment, planning your finances, choosing a college and finding ways to pay for tuition, and starting a business.

### *Occupational Outlook Handbook*
http://stats.bls.gov/search/ooh.htm

Every two years, the U.S. Department of Labor publishes a guide to career options in various U.S. industries. Hundreds of jobs are covered, including the following business- and finance-related careers: Accountants and Auditors, Administrative Services Managers; Financial Analysts and Personal Financial Advisors, Financial Managers, Management Analysts, Secretaries and Administrative Assistants, and

Top Executives. Each article contains the following sections: Significant Points; Nature of the Work; Training, Other Qualifications, and Advancement; Employment; Job Outlook; Earnings; Related Occupations; and Sources of Additional Information. This is a good site to visit to locate trustworthy information about business and finance careers.

### Start Here, Go Places in Business and Accounting
http://www.startheregoplaces.com

This site, sponsored by the American Institute of Certified Public Accountants, has a wealth of resources for high school or college students interested in a career in business and accounting. It can probably answer any possible question you have about the certified public accountant (CPA) profession, including course requirements, necessary skills, salary information, and career options upon receiving the CPA certification. There are also many activities you can participate in to explore your interest in these fields. Take a personality test to see if a career in accounting is for you, and if so, find out about different colleges' accounting programs and available scholarships, jobs, and internships, and try playing some of the online games to get a feel for how accounting relates to the real world!

### U.S. News & World Report: Best Business Schools
http://grad-schools.usnews.rankings andreviews.com/best-graduate-schools/ top-business-schools

Use this online guide to search for business schools by national ranking or name. Lists of best schools are provided for the following specialties: Accounting, Entrepreneurship, Executive MBA, Finance, Information System, International, Management, Marketing, Nonprofit, Part-time MBA, Production/Operations, and Supply Chain/Logistics. Free information is provided on tuition, enrollment, type (private or public), student/faculty ratio, and other categories, and a handy feature allows you to compare attributes of schools side-by-side to help narrow your choice. (Note: In order to read the full account information about each school, you must either buy the print publication or pay for the Premium Online Edition.)

### VentureLine MBA Glossary
http://www.ventureline.com/
glossary.asp

If you don't know the meaning of terms and phrases such as *hard assets*, *replacement value*, *bankruptcy*, and *disposal*, then a visit to this Web site should be in your future. The VentureLine MBA Glossary provides definitions for hundreds of accounting and financial terms that are used by industry professionals.

### Yahoo!: Business & Economy
http://dir.yahoo.com/Business_and_
Economy

It might seem odd to include the popular search engine Yahoo! among a list of business- and finance-oriented Web sites, but it won't seem so after you've visited it. If you're hungry for more after visiting the sites listed in this section, pull up a chair at Yahoo!'s feast. Yahoo! has done a tremendous amount of legwork for you. For example, if you're interested in business organizations, then scan through the nearly 11,200 sites currently included here. Finance and investment posts an impressive 1,296 sites, trade has 252 entries, marketing and advertising has 194 sites, and ethics and responsibility yields 74 links.

# Ask for Money

By the time most students get around to thinking about applying for scholarships, grants, and other financial aid, they have already extolled their personal, academic, and creative virtues to such lengths in essays and interviews for college applications that even their own grandmothers wouldn't recognize them. The thought of filling out yet another application fills students with dread. And why bother? Won't the same five or six kids who have been competing for academic honors for years walk away with all the really good scholarships?

The truth is that most of the scholarships available to high school and college students are being offered because an organization wants to promote interest in a particular field, encourage more students to become qualified to enter it, and finally, to help those students afford an education. Certainly, having a great grade point average is a valuable asset. More often than not, however, grade point averages aren't even mentioned; the focus is on the area of interest and what a student has done to distinguish himself or herself in that area. In fact, sometimes the only requirement is that the scholarship applicant must be studying in a particular area.

## ❑ GUIDELINES

When applying for scholarships there are a few simple guidelines that can help ease the process considerably.

### Plan Ahead

The absolute worst thing you can do is wait until the last minute. For one thing, obtaining recommendations or other supporting data in time to meet an application deadline is incredibly difficult. For another, no one does his or her best thinking or writing under the gun. So get off to a good start by reviewing scholarship applications as early as possible—months, even a year, in advance. If the current scholarship information isn't available, ask for a copy of last year's version. Once you have the scholarship information or application in hand, give it a thorough read. Try to determine how your experience or situation best fits into the scholarship, or if it even fits at all. Don't waste your time applying for a scholarship in business education, for example, if you dread talking in front of large groups of people.

If possible, research the award or scholarship, including past recipients and, where applicable, the person in whose name the scholarship is offered.

Often, scholarships are established to memorialize an individual who majored in business, finance, or a related field, for example, but in other cases, the scholarship is to memorialize the work of an individual. In those cases, try to get a feel for the spirit of the person's work. If you have any similar interests, experiences, or abilities, don't hesitate to mention these.

Talk to others who received the scholarship, or to students currently studying in the same area or field of interest in which the scholarship is offered, and try to gain insight into possible applications or work related to that field. When you're working on the essay asking why you want this scholarship, you'll have real answers: "I would benefit from receiving this scholarship because studying finance will help me become a better financial analyst."

Take your time writing the essays. Make sure that you answer the question or questions on the application; do not merely restate facts about yourself. Don't be afraid to get creative; try to imagine what you would think of if you had to sift through hundreds of applications. What would you want to know about the candidate? What would convince you that someone was deserving of the scholarship? Work through several drafts and have someone whose advice you respect—a parent, teacher, or counselor—review the essay for grammar and content.

Finally, if you know in advance which scholarships you want to apply for, there might still be time to stack the deck in your favor by getting an internship, volunteering, or working part time. Bottom line: The more you know about a scholarship and the sooner you learn it, the better.

## Follow Directions

Think of it this way: many of the organizations that offer scholarships devote 99.9 percent of their time to something other than the scholarship for which you are applying. Don't make a nuisance of yourself by pestering them for information. Simply follow the directions as they are presented to you. If the scholarship application specifies that you should write for further information, then write for it—don't call.

Pay close attention to whether you're applying for a grant, a loan, an award, a prize, or a scholarship. Often these words are used interchangeably, but just as often they have different meanings. A loan is financial aid that must be paid back. A grant is a type of financial aid that does not require repayment. An award or prize is usually given for something you have done: built a park or helped distribute meals to the elderly; or something you have created: a business plan, a musical composition, a design, an essay, a column, a film, a screenplay, or an invention. On the other hand, a scholarship is frequently a renewable sum of money that is given to a person to help defray the costs of college. Scholarships are given to candidates who meet the necessary criteria based on essays, eligibility, grades, or creative work, or sometimes all four. They do not have to be paid back.

Supply all the necessary documents, information, and fees, and make the deadlines. You won't win any scholarships by forgetting to include a recommendation from a teacher or failing to postmark the application by the deadline. Bottom line: Get it right the first time, on time.

## Apply Early

Once you have the application in hand, don't dawdle. If you've requested it far enough in advance, there shouldn't be any reason for you not to turn it in well in advance of the deadline. You never know, if it comes down to two candidates, your timeliness just might be the deciding factor. Bottom line: Don't wait, and don't hesitate.

## Be Yourself

Don't make promises you can't keep. There are plenty of hefty scholarships available, but if they all require you to study something that you don't enjoy, you'll be miserable in college. And the side effects from switching majors after you've accepted a scholarship could be even worse. Bottom line: Be yourself.

## Don't Limit Yourself

There are many sources for scholarships, beginning with your school counselor and ending with the Internet. All of the search engines have education categories. Start there and search by keywords, such as "financial aid," "scholarship," and "award." But don't be limited to the scholarships listed in these pages.

If you know of an organization related to or involved with the field of your choice, write a letter asking if they offer scholarships. If they don't offer scholarships, don't stop there. Write them another letter, or better yet, schedule a meeting with the executive director, education director, or someone in the public relations department and ask them if they would be willing to sponsor a scholarship for you. Of course, you'll need to prepare yourself well for such a meeting because you're selling a priceless commodity—yourself. Don't be shy, and be confident. Tell them all about yourself, what you want to study and why, and let them know what you would be willing to do in exchange—volunteer at their favorite charity, write up reports on your progress in school, or work part time on school breaks and full time during the summer. Explain why you're a wise investment. Bottom line: The sky's the limit.

## One More Thing

We have not listed financial aid that is provided by colleges and universities. Why? There are two reasons. First, because there are hundreds of schools that offer financial aid for students who are interested in studying business, finance, or a related major, and we couldn't possibly fit them all in this book. Second, listing just a few schools wouldn't be helpful to the vast majority of students who do not plan to attend these institutions. This means that it is up to you to check with the college that you want to attend for details on available financial aid. College financial aid officers will be happy to tell you what types of resources are available.

## ❏ THE LIST

### American Legion Auxiliary
8945 North Meridian Street
Indianapolis, IN 46260-5387
317-569-4500
alahq@legion-aux.org
http://www.legion-aux.org/scholar
ships/index.aspx

Various state auxiliaries of the American Legion, as well as its national organization, offer scholarships to help students prepare for a variety of careers. Most require that candidates be associated with the organization in some way, whether as a child, spouse, etc., of a military veteran. Interested students should contact the auxiliary for further information.

### Association on American Indian Affairs
Attn: Director of Scholarship
    Programs
966 Hungerford Drive, Suite 12-B
Rockville, MD 20850-1743
240-314-7155
lw.aaia@verizon.net
http://www.indian-affairs.org

Undergraduate and graduate Native American students who are pursuing a wide variety of college majors can apply for several different scholarships

of $1,500. All applicants must provide proof of Native American heritage. Visit the association's Web site for more information.

### Business Professionals of America
5454 Cleveland Avenue
Columbus, OH 43231-4021
800-334-2007
http://www.bpanet.org/students/
    Secondary/scholarshipS.aspx

Business Professionals of America, in partnership with several other organizations, offers approximately six scholarships to its high school-level members. Scholarships range from $500 to $1,500. Scholarships are also available for middle school and college students. Contact Business Professionals of America for more information.

### CollegeBoard: Scholarship Search
http://apps.collegeboard.com/
    cbsearch_ss/welcome.jsp

This testing service (PSAT, SAT, etc.) also offers a scholarship search engine at its Web site. It features scholarships worth nearly $3 billion. You can search by specific major (such as business) and a variety of other criteria.

### CollegeNET: MACH 25- Breaking the Tuition Barrier
http://www.collegenet.com/mach25/
    app

CollegeNET features 600,000 scholarships worth more than $1.6 billion. You can search by keyword (such as business) or by creating a personality profile of your interests.

### Executive Women International (EWI)

515 South 700 East, Suite 2A
Salt Lake City, UT 84102-2855
801-355-2800
ewi@ewiconnect.com
http://www.executivewomen.org/
  ScriptContent/community/comm_
  scholarship.cfm

EWI offers a scholarship program to high school juniors of both genders. Applicants, who must be members of local EWI chapters, compete at the chapter level, with winners moving on to competition at the national level. Scholarships of up to $10,000 are awarded. Each chapter conducts its own program and "develops its own criteria regarding deadlines, limiting areas, schools, and agencies they partner with." Visit the EWI Web site for a list of participating chapters. (Note: Scholarships are also available to adult students at "transitional points in their lives.")

### FastWeb

http://www1.fastweb.com

FastWeb is one of the best-known scholarship search engines around. It features 1.3 million scholarships worth more than $3 billion. To use this resource, you will need to register (free).

### Foundation for the Carolinas

Office of Scholarships
217 South Tryon Street
Charlotte, NC 28202-3201
704-973-4537
tcapers@fftc.org
http://www.fftc.org

The foundation administers more than 105 scholarship programs that offer awards to high school seniors and undergraduate and graduate students who plan to or who are currently pursuing study in a variety of disciplines—including business and accounting. (Note: Some scholarships require residency in North or South Carolina.) Visit the foundation's Web site for a list of awards.

### GuaranteedScholarships.com

http://www.guaranteed-scholarships.
  com

This Web site offers lists (by college) of scholarships, grants, and financial aid that "require no interview, essay, portfolio, audition, competition, or other secondary requirement."

### Hawaii Community Foundation

1164 Bishop Street, Suite 800
Honolulu, HI 96813-2817
888-731-3863
info@hcf-hawaii.org
http://www.hawaiicommunity
  foundation.org/scholar/scholar.php

The foundation offers scholarships for high school seniors and college students planning to or currently studying a variety of majors in college. There are several scholarships for college students interested in accounting, business, business administration, or finance. Applicants must be residents of Hawaii, demonstrate financial need, and attend a two- or four-year college. Visit the foundation's Web site for more information and to apply online.

### Hispanic College Fund (HCF)

1301 K Street, NW, Suite
  450-A West
Washington, DC 20005-3317
800-644-4223
hcf-info@hispanicfund.org
http://www.hispanicfund.org

The Hispanic College Fund, in collaboration with several major corporations, offers many scholarships for high school seniors and college students planning to or currently attending college. Applicants must live in the United States (including Puerto Rico) and have a GPA of at least 3.0 on a 4.0 scale. Contact the HCF for more information.

### Illinois Career Resource
###   Network

http://www.ilworkinfo.com/icrn.htm

Created by the Illinois Department of Employment Security, this useful site offers a scholarship search engine, as well as detailed information on careers (including business- and finance-related jobs such as accountants and auditors, financial analysts, financial managers, and secretaries). You can search for scholarships based on major (such as accounting, actuarial science, business-general, business management and administration, finance, etc.), and other criterion. This site is available to everyone, not just Illinois residents; you can get a password by simply visiting the site. The Illinois Career Resource Network is just one example of the type of sites

created by state departments of employment security (or departments of labor) to assist students with financial- and career-related issues. After checking out this site, visit your state's department of labor Web site to see what it offers.

### Imagine America Foundation

1101 Connecticut Avenue, NW,
  Suite 901
Washington, DC 20036-4303
202-336-6800
scholarships@imagine-america.org
http://www.imagine-america.org/
  scholarship/a-about-scholarship.asp

The Imagine America Foundation (formerly the Career College Foundation) is a nonprofit organization that helps students pay for college. It offers three $1,000 scholarships each year to high school students or recent graduates. Applicants must have a GPA of at least 2.5 on a 4.0 scale, have financial need, and demonstrate voluntary community service during their senior year. Scholarships can be used at more than 500 career colleges in the United States. These colleges offer a variety of fields of study, including accounting, accounting and finance, accounting technology/technician and bookkeeping, actuarial science, administrative assistant and secretarial science, banking and financial support services, business administration and management, business operations support and secretarial services, business statistics, business/commerce, business corporate/communications, business/managerial economics, business/office automation/technology/data entry, credit management, customer service management, customer service support/call center/teleservice operation, electronic commerce, entrepreneurial and small business operations, finance and financial management services, financial planning and services, franchising and franchise operations, human resources development, human resources management and services, international business/trade/conference, international finance, international marketing, investments and securities, labor and industrial relations, management science, marketing research, office management and supervision, receptionist, retailing and retail operations, small business administration/ management, and teacher education and professional development. Visit the foundation's Web site for more information.

### InVEST Scholarship Contest

127 South Peyton Street
Alexandria, VA 22314-2879
800-221-7917
invest@investprogram.org
http://www.iiaba.net/eprise/main/
   Invest/home/scholarships.html

InVEST is a school-to-work insurance program for high school and community college students who are studying insurance, risk management, business, or actuarial science. Two scholarships are available through the program: Classroom to Career Scholarship and the Higher Education Scholarship. High school students who intend to go directly from the classroom to a career in one of the aforementioned fields can apply for the Classroom to Career Scholarship. Those who are planning to or currently studying insurance, risk management,

business, or actuarial science can apply for the Higher Education Scholarship. Applicants for both scholarships must participate in an InVEST class. They must also submit a completed application; at least two different letters of recommendation from teachers, liaisons, mentors, or counselors; and a 500-word typed essay that details how they have benefited from participating in InVEST programs, their career goals and how they were influenced by InVEST, and details on academic honors they have received or extracurricular activities in which they have participated. They must also submit a copy of their academic transcript and a photograph of themselves. Contact InVEST for more information.

### Junior Achievement (JA)

One Education Way
Colorado Springs, CO 80906-4477
719-540-8000
scholarships@ja.org
http://www.ja.org/programs/
   programs_schol.shtml

Junior Achievement offers 15 national scholarships for graduating high school seniors who have completed a JA Company or JA Economics Program. Additional scholarships are offered by local JA chapters. Application requirements vary by scholarship. Contact JA for details.

### National Association of Negro Business and Professional Women's Clubs (NANBPWC)

1806 New Hampshire Avenue, NW
Washington, DC 20009-3206

202-483-4206
education@nanbpwc.org
http://www.nanbpwc.org

The NANBPWC offers the National Scholarship Program to African American graduating high school seniors. Applicants should have a 3.0 GPA on a 4.0 scale and must be referred by a NANBPWC club member. Applicants should submit a completed application, an official transcript of first-semester grades of senior year, two letters of recommendation, and a minimum 300-word essay addressing the topic, "Why is education important to me?" Visit the association's Web site to complete an application. The deadline is typically March 1. The NANBPWC also offers scholarships to high school students who are interested in pursuing careers in cosmetology, college students, and students age 35 and over.

### National Association of Secondary School Principals (NASSP)
c/o National Honor Society
1904 Association Drive
Reston, VA 20191-1537
703-860-0200
http://www.nhs.us

The NASSP has awarded the National Honor Society (NHS) Scholarships since 1946. It has provided more than $10 million in scholarships to NHS members. Students cannot apply directly, but are nominated through their school's NHS chapter. High school seniors who are members in good standing of their school chapter can be considered for nomination. State finalists receive $1,000 scholarships; state winners, $1,500 scholarships; regional winners, $2,500 scholarships; and the national winner, a $13,000 scholarship. Contact the NHS or your local high school NHS chapter for more information.

### National Conference of CPA Practitioners
Attn: Scholarship Committee
22 Jericho Turnpike, Suite 110
Mineola, NY 11501-2937
888-488-5400
lanak.ncCPAp@verizon.net
http://www.nccpap.org/Default.
aspx?tabid=56

The National Conference of CPA Practitioners partners with the American Institute of Certified Public Accountants to offer $1,000 scholarships to graduating high school seniors who are planning to pursue careers as certified public accountants. Applicants must have a GPA of at least 3.3 on a 4.0 scale, plan to attend college after graduation, and enroll as full-time students. Applicants must submit a completed application (available at the conference's Web site), academic transcripts, and a minimum 200-word essay that details why they want to become a certified public accountant. Contact the conference for more information.

### Phi Delta Kappa (PDK) Educational Foundation
408 North Union Street
Bloomington, IN 47405-3800
800-766-1156
http://www.pdkintl.org/awards/
index.htm

The PDK Educational Foundation offers Prospective Educator Scholarships to current high school seniors or college students who plan to or are currently studying education in college. To be eligible, applicants must meet one of the following criteria: be an undergraduate member of PDK who is enrolled in a college education program, or is a "high school senior intending to major in education who is a member of a Future Educators Association chapter in good standing, *or* is the child or grandchild of a Kappan in good standing; *or* has one of his/her reference letters written by a Kappan in good standing; *or* whose application is selected to represent the local PDK chapter." Contact the foundation for more information.

### Pi Lambda Theta
PO Box 6626
Bloomington, IN 47407-6626
800-487-3411
office@pilambda.org
http://www.pilambda.org/benefits/
   awards/ScholarshipsAwards.html

Pi Lambda Theta, the international honor society and professional association in education, offers more than 10 scholarships and awards for current undergraduate and graduate students who are pursuing education-related majors. Application deadlines and criteria vary by scholarship. Contact the society for more information.

### Sallie Mae
http://www.collegeanswer.com/
   paying/scholarship_search/pay_
   scholarship_search.jsp

Sallie Mae offers a scholarship database of more than 3 million awards worth more than $16 billion. You must register (free) to use the database.

### Scholarship America
One Scholarship Way
Saint Peter, MN 56082-0297
800-537-4180
http://www.scholarshipamerica.org

This organization works through its local Dollars for Scholars chapters throughout the United States. In 2008 it awarded more than $219 million in scholarships to students. Visit Scholarship America's Web site for more information.

### ScholarshipExperts.com
http://scholarshipexperts.com

ScholarshipExperts.com offers a free scholarship search engine, although you must register to access it. The database features 2.4 million scholarships worth more than $14 billion. The Web site also offers several of its own scholarships each year to students who are seeking funds for college. Scholarship themes and award amounts change annually. Visit ScholarshipExperts.com for details.

### Scholarships.com
http://www.scholarships.com

Scholarships.com offers a free college scholarship and grant search engine (although you must register to use it) and financial aid information. Its database of awards features 2.7 million listings worth more than $19 billion in aid.

### Society of Satellite
### Professionals International

55 Broad Street, 14th Floor
New York, NY 10004-2501
212-809-5199
http://www.sspi.org/
 ?page=Scholarships

The Society of Satellite Professionals International offers a scholarship program for high school seniors and college students who are committed to pursuing education and career opportunities in the satellite industry or a field making direct use of satellite technology. Past scholarship winners have pursued studies in broadcasting, business, distance learning, energy, government, imaging, meteorology, navigation, remote sensing, space law, and telecommunications. Scholarships range from $2,500 to $3,500. Applicants must demonstrate academic and leadership achievement, show potential for making a major contribution to the satellite communications industry, and be members of the society. Contact the society for more information.

### Sodexho Foundation

9801 Washingtonian Boulevard
Gaithersburg, MD 20878-5355
http://www.sodexofoundation.org/
 hunger_us/scholarships/scholar
 ships.asp

The Sodexho Foundation offers $5,000 STOP Hunger Scholarships to "recognize and reward students who have made a significant impact in the fight against hunger and its root causes in the United States." Applicants must be enrolled in an accredited education institution (kindergarten through graduate school) in the United States, have demonstrated volunteer service to nonfamily members that impacts hunger, and be citizens or permanent residents of the United States. Contact the foundation for more information.

### Teacher Education Assistance for College and Higher Education (TEACH) Grant Program

U.S. Department of Education
800-433-3243
http://www.federalstudentaid.ed.gov
http://studentaid.ed.gov/PORTALS
 WebApp/students/english/TEACH.jsp

The TEACH Grant Program provides grants of up to $4,000 a year to students who plan to teach in a public or private elementary or secondary school that serves low-income students. Applicants must agree to work as full-time teachers in a high-need field (bilingual education and English language acquisition, foreign language, mathematics, reading specialist, science, special education, and other identified teacher shortage areas). Grant recipients must teach for at least four academic years within eight calendar years of completing the program of study for which they received a grant. Grant awardees who fail to complete this obligation will have their grants converted to a Federal Direct Unsubsidized Stafford Loan and be charged interest from the date the grant was awarded.

Applicants for the TEACH Grant Program must be U.S. citizens, be enrolled as an undergraduate or graduate student in a postsecondary institution that has been selected to participate in the program, have a GPA of at least 3.25, and complete the Free Application for Federal Student

Aid. Contact the U.S. Department of Education for more information.

### United Negro College Fund (UNCF)

8260 Willow Oaks Corporate Drive
PO Box 10444
Fairfax, VA 22031-8044
800-331-2244
http://www.uncf.org/forstudents/
   scholarship.asp

Visitors to the UNCF Web site can search for information on thousands of scholarships and grants, many of which are administered by the UNCF. Its search engine allows you to search by major (such as accounting, advertising, banking, business, business administration, business education, business management, business sales, economics, entrepreneurship, finance, finance and banking, international business, management, management information science, marketing, marketing research, merchandise management, music business, office systems, public relations, retail, retail management, and sales and marketing), state, scholarship title, grade level, and achievement score. High school seniors and undergraduate and graduate students are eligible.

### U.S. Department of Education

Federal Student Aid
800-433-3243
http://www.federalstudentaid.ed.gov
http://studentaid.ed.gov/students/
   publications/student_guide/index.
   html

The U.S. government provides a wealth of financial aid in the form of grants, loans, and work-study programs. Each year it publishes *Funding Education Beyond High School*, a guide to these funds. Visit the Web sites listed above for detailed information on federal financial aid.

# Look to the Pros

The following professional organizations offer a variety of materials, including career information, lists of accredited schools, and salary surveys. Many also publish journals and newsletters with which you should become familiar. Some also have annual conferences that you might be able to attend.

When contacting professional organizations, keep in mind that they all exist primarily to serve their members, be it through continuing education, professional certification, political lobbying, or just "keeping up with the profession." While many are strongly interested in promoting their profession and passing information about it to the general public, these busy professional organizations do not exist solely to provide you with information. Whether you call or write, be courteous, brief, and to the point. Know what you need and ask for it. If the organization has a Web site, check it out first; what you're looking for may be available to download, or you may find a list of prices or instructions, such as sending a self-addressed stamped envelope with your request. Finally, be aware that organizations, like people, move. To save time when writing, first confirm the address, preferably with a quick phone call to the organization itself: "Hello, I'm calling to confirm your address. . . ."

## ❏ THE SOURCES

### Accreditation Council for Accountancy and Taxation

1010 North Fairfax Street
Alexandria, VA 22314-1574
888-289-7763
info@acatcredentials.org
http://www.acatcredentials.org

Contact the council for information on certification for business accountants, tax professionals, and retirement advisers.

### Advertising Educational Foundation

220 East 42nd Street, Suite 3300
New York, NY 10017-5806
212-986-8060
http://www.aef.com/index.html

Visit this organization's Web site for profiles of advertising workers and career information.

### Alpha Delta Kappa International

1615 West 92nd Street
Kansas City, MO 64114-3210
800-247-2311
headquarters@alphadeltakappa.org
http://www.alphadeltakappa.org

Alpha Delta Kappa is an "international honorary organization of women educators dedicated to educational excellence, altruism, and world understanding." It has more than 1,400 chapters in the United States. Membership, which is available by invitation only, is open to women educators and administrators who have been employed in the field for at least two years. Visit its Web site to read sample issues of *Alpha Delta KAPPAN Magazine*. (Note: Alpha Delta Kappa also offers an ancillary organization for male educators and administrators.)

### American Advertising Federation

1101 Vermont Avenue, NW,
   Suite 500
Washington, DC 20005-6306
800-999-2231
aaf@aaf.org
http://www.aaf.org

This organization represents more than 40,000 advertising professionals. Visit its Web site to learn more about internships, scholarships, and membership for college students.

### American Arbitration Association

1633 Broadway, 10th Floor
New York, NY 10019-6705
212-716-5800
http://www.adr.org

Contact the association for more information about dispute resolution in the workplace.

### American Association for Adult and Continuing Education

10111 Martin Luther King, Jr.
   Highway, Suite 200C
Bowie, MD 20720-4200
301-459-6261
office@aaace.org
http://www.aaace.org

The association's mission is "to provide leadership for the field of adult and continuing education by expanding opportunities for adult growth and development; unifying adult educators; fostering the development and dissemination of theory, research, information, and best practices; promoting identity and standards for the profession; and advocating relevant public policy and social change initiatives." Visit its Web site for information on publications and membership for college students.

### American Association of Colleges for Teacher Education

1307 New York Avenue, NW,
   Suite 300
Washington, DC 20005-4721
202-293-2450
aacte@aacte.org
http://www.aacte.org

This organization represents 800 PK–12 educator preparation programs in every U.S. state, the District of Columbia, Puerto Rico, the Virgin Islands, and Guam. Visit its Web site for job listings, a directory of member institutions, and information on the *Journal of Teacher Education*.

### American Association of Franchisees and Dealers (AAFD)

PO Box 81887
San Diego, CA 92138-1887
619-209-3775
Benefits@aafd.org
http://www.aafd.org

Visit the association's Web site for information about buying a franchise, a directory of AAFD-accredited franchisers, and a list of "8 Things to Look for in a Franchise."

### American Association of University Professors

1133 19th Street, NW, Suite 200
Washington, DC 20036-3655
202-737-5900
aaup@aaup.org
http://www.aaup.org

Contact the association for information about earnings and union membership for college professors.

### American Association of University Women (AAUW)

1111 16th Street, NW
Washington, DC 20036-4809
800-326-2289
connect@aauw.org
http://www.aauw.org

The association represents the professional interests of women in higher education. Visit its Web site for information on scholarships for college students and *AAUW Outlook.*

### American Board for Certification of Teacher Excellence

1225 19th Street, NW, Suite 400
Washington, DC 20036-2457
877-669-2228
http://www.abcte.org

This nonprofit organization "recruits, prepares, certifies and supports dedicated professionals to improve student achievement through quality teaching." Visit its Web site for information on certification and tips on finding a job.

### American Federation of Teachers (AFT)

555 New Jersey Avenue, NW
Washington, DC 20001-2029
202-879-4400
http://www.aft.org

The AFT is a professional membership organization for teachers at all levels. In addition to membership benefits, the federation offers information on important issues affecting educators, salary surveys, and useful periodicals.

### American Institute of Certified Public Accountants

1211 Avenue of the Americas
New York, NY 10036-8775
212-596-6200
http://www.aicpa.org

Visit the institute's Web site for publications, job listings, career resources, and information on the Uniform CPA Examination, educational training, scholarships for high school and college students, and membership for college students.

### American Institute of Professional Bookkeepers

6001 Montrose Road, Suite 500
Rockville, MD 20852-4873
800-622-0121
info@aipb.org
http://www.aipb.org

Visit the institute's Web site for information on certification and tips and advice for bookkeepers.

## American Management Association

1601 Broadway
New York, NY 10019-7434
877-566-9441
http://www.amanet.org

Visit the association's Web site for information about management trends, job listings, and membership for college students.

## American Marketing Association

311 South Wacker Drive,
 Suite 5800
Chicago, IL 60606-6629
800-262-1150
http://www.marketingpower.com

Visit the association's Web site for information on certification, job listings, and career resources.

## American Society for Training and Development

1640 King Street, Box 1443
Alexandria, VA 22313-1443
703-683-8100
http://www.astd.org

This is a professional membership organization for workplace learning professionals. Visit its Web site for information on certification, training programs, *Training+ Development* magazine, membership for college students, and job listings.

## Association for Career and Technical Education

1410 King Street
Alexandria, VA 22314-2749
800-826-9972

acte@acteonline.org
http://www.acteonline.org

The association's membership includes "career and technical educators, administrators, researchers, guidance counselors, and others involved in planning and conducting career and technical education programs at the secondary, post-secondary and adult levels." Visit its Web site for information on membership for college students and to read, What is Career and Technical Education?

## Association for Financial Professionals

4520 East West Highway,
 Suite 750
Bethesda, MD 20814-3574
301-907-2862
http://www.afponline.org

Contact the association for information on certification.

## Association of Executive and Administrative Professionals

900 South Washington Street,
 Suite G-13
Falls Church, VA 22046-4009
703-237-8616
headquarters@theaeap.com
http://www.theaeap.com/

Contact the association for information on seminars, conferences, and news on the industry.

## Association of Internal Management Consultants

824 Caribbean Court
Marco Island, FL 34145-3422
239-642-0580

info@aimc.org
http://www.aimc.org

Visit the association's Web site for job listings and general information about the field.

### Association of Management Consulting Firms
370 Lexington Avenue, Suite 2209
New York, NY 10017-6573
212-262-3055
info@amcf.org
http://www.amcf.org

Contact the association for information about the industry and scholarships for MBA students.

### Association of Professional Consultants
PO Box 51193
Irvine, CA 92619-1193
800-745-5050
apc@consultapc.org
http://www.consultapc.org

Contact the association for information on business consulting.

### Association of Professional Office Managers
PO Box 1926
Rockville, MD 20849-1926
240-654-9108
http://www.apomonline.org

Visit the association's Web site for information on publications and professional office management.

### Association to Advance Collegiate Schools of Business
777 South Harbour Island Boulevard, Suite 750

Tampa, FL 33602-5730
813-769-6500
http://www.aacsb.edu

Contact the association for information on accredited programs in business and accounting.

### BAI
115 South LaSalle Street, Suite 3300
Chicago, IL 60603-3801
info@bai.org
http://www.bai.org

Contact BAI for information on certification for bank auditors.

### Business Professionals of America
5454 Cleveland Avenue
Columbus, OH 43231-4021
800-334-2007
http://www.bpa.org

This is a "national co-curricular career and technical organization for high school, college, and middle school students preparing for careers in business and information technology." Visit its Web site for information on membership, programs, and scholarships for high school and college students.

### Certified Financial Planner Board of Standards
1425 K Street, NW, Suite 500
Washington, DC 20005-3686
800-487-1497
mail@CFPBoard.org
http://www.cfp.net

Visit the board's Web site to learn more about financial planning and to obtain a copy of the *Guide to CFP Certification*.

### CFA Institute

560 Ray C. Hunt Drive
Charlottesville, VA 22903-2981
800-247-8132
info@cfainstitute.org
http://www.cfainstitute.org

Visit the institute's Web site for information on certification for financial analysts.

### The Educational Foundation for Women in Accounting

136 South Keowee Street
Dayton, OH 45402-2241
937-424-3391
info@efwa.org
http://www.efwa.org

Contact the foundation for information on career opportunities for women in accounting and scholarships for college students.

### Federal Trade Commission (FTC)

600 Pennsylvania Avenue, NW
Washington, DC 20580-0001
202-326-2222
http://www.ftc.gov

The FTC is a government agency that was formed to protect the rights of the American consumer. Visit the FTC Web site for information on franchising, including the publication, *Buying a Franchise: A Consumer Guide*.

### Financial Planning Association

4100 East Mississippi Avenue,
  Suite 400
Denver, CO 80246-3053
800-322-4237
http://www.fpanet.org

Contact the association for information on financial planning, certification, the *Journal of Financial Planning*, and membership for college students.

### Institute for Certified Franchise Executives

1501 K Street, NW,
  Suite 350
Washington, DC 20005-1412
202-628-8000
http://www.franchise.org/
  certification.aspx

Contact the institute for information on certification.

### Institute of Certified Professional Managers

James Madison University
800 South Main Street, MSC 5504
Harrisonburg, VA 22807-0002
800-568-4120
http://www.icpm.biz

Contact the institute for information on certification.

### Institute of Internal Auditors

247 Maitland Avenue
Altamonte Springs, FL 32701-4201
407-937-1100
iia@theiia.org
http://www.theiia.org

Contact the institute for information on internal auditing, publications, career advice and job listings, membership for college students, and certification.

## Institute of Management Accountants

10 Paragon Drive
Montvale, NJ 07645-1718
800-638-4427
ima@imanet.org
http://www.imanet.org

Visit the institute's Web site for information on certification and scholarships and membership for college students.

## Institute of Management Consultants USA

2025 M Street, NW, Suite 800
Washington, DC 20036-3309
202-367-1134
office@imcusa.org
http://www.imcusa.org

Visit the institute's Web site for information on certification, details on membership for college students, and useful blogs and discussion groups.

## International Association of Administrative Professionals

PO Box 20404
Kansas City, MO 64195-0404
816-891-6600
http://www.iaap-hq.org

Contact the association for information on *OfficePro* newsletter, job listings, career advice, and membership for college students.

## International Association of Business Communicators

601 Montgomery Street, Suite 1900
San Francisco, CA 94111-2623
415-544-4700
http://www.iabc.com

Contact the association for information on membership for college students and accreditation (a type of certification) for public relations specialists and related workers.

## International Foundation of Employee Benefits Plans

PO Box 69
Brookfield, WI 53008-0069
888-334-3327
http://www.ifebp.org

Contact the foundation for information on certification for employee benefits specialists.

## International Franchise Association

1501 K Street, NW, Suite 350
Washington, DC 20005-1412
202-628-8000
ifa@franchise.org
http://www.franchise.org

Visit the association's Web site for comprehensive information regarding franchising.

## International Public Management Association for Human Resources

1617 Duke Street
Alexandria, VA 22314-3406
703-549-7100
http://www.ipma-hr.org

Contact the association for information on membership for college students, publications, and certification.

## ISACA

3701 Algonquin Road, Suite 1010
Rolling Meadows, IL 60008-3124

847-253-1545
http://www.isaca.org

Contact ISACA for information on certification (for auditors and information security professionals) and membership and scholarships for college students.

### Junior Achievement

One Education Way
Colorado Springs, CO 80906-4477
719-540-8000
newmedia@ja.org
http://www.ja.org

Junior Achievement's mission is to provide education for workplace readiness, entrepreneurship, and financial knowledge to young people worldwide. It offers programs for students in kindergarten through high school. Visit its Web site for information on programs and local chapters.

### Labor and Employment Relations Association

University of Illinois at Urbana-Champaign
121 Labor and Industrial Relations Building
504 East Armory Avenue
Champaign, IL 61820-6221
217-333-0072
LERAoffice@uiuc.edu
http://www.lera.uiuc.edu

Visit the association's Web site for information on labor relations, publications, and job listings.

### National Association of Personal Financial Advisors

3250 North Arlington Heights Road, Suite 109

Arlington Heights, IL 60004-1574
847-483-5400
info@napfa.org
http://www.napfa.org

This organization represents the professional interests of fee-only financial advisors. Visit its Web site for job listings and answers to frequently asked questions about the field.

### National Association of Women Business Owners

601 Pennsylvania Avenue, NW, South Building, Suite 900
Washington, DC 20004-2601
800-556-2926
national@nawbo.org
http://www.nawbo.org

Contact the association for information on membership for college students and resources for female business owners.

### National Business Education Association

1914 Association Drive
Reston, VA 20191-1596
703-860-8300
nbea@nbea.org
http://www.nbea.org

This is "the nation's largest professional organization devoted exclusively to serving individuals and groups engaged in instruction, administration, research, and dissemination of information for and about business." It offers membership for college students. Visit its Web site to learn more about membership benefits and publications such as *The International Review for Business Education*.

### National Center for Alternative Certification

4401A Connecticut Avenue, NW, Suite 212
Washington, DC 20008-2358
888-831-1338
info@pathwaystoteaching.com
http://www.teach-now.org

This organization was created with a discretionary grant from the U.S. Department of Education in 2003 to serve as a "one-stop, comprehensive clearinghouse for information about alternative routes to [teacher] certification in the United States." It helps those who already have a bachelor's degree become teachers without having to go back to college. Visit its Web site for answers to frequently asked questions about alternative certification routes, information on certification standards by state, statistics, and other resources.

### National Council for Accreditation of Teacher Education (NCATE)

2010 Massachusetts Avenue, NW, Suite 500
Washington, DC 20036-1023
202-466-7496
ncate@ncate.org
http://www.ncate.org

Visit the council's Web site to read the following resources: "What is the benefit of attending an NCATE-accredited college of education?," "I want to be a teacher, but cannot afford college tuition," and "How do I get a loan, grant, or scholarship to a college?"

### National Education Association

1201 16th Street, NW

Washington, DC 20036-3290
202-833-4000
http://www.nea.org

This is a membership organization for education professionals at all academic levels. Visit its Web site for information on membership for college students, scholarships for student members, and useful publications such as *Tomorrow's Teachers* and *Make It Happen: Be a Teacher*.

### National Management Association

2210 Arbor Boulevard
Dayton, OH 45439-1506
937-294-0421
nma@nma1.org
http://nma1.org

Contact the association for information on management careers.

### New York Society of Security Analysts (NYSSA)

1177 Avenue of the Americas, 2nd Floor
New York, NY 10036-2714
212-541-4530
membership@nyssa.org
http://www.nyssa.org

Visit the NYSSA Web site for information on membership for college students, a list of top employers of financial analysts, and scholarships for graduate students.

### Office and Professional Employees International Union

265 West 14th Street, 6th Floor
New York, NY 10011-7103

800-346-7348
http://www.opeiu.org

Contact this organization for information regarding union representation. Members work in a variety of industries, including banking and credit unions, higher education, hospitals, hotels, insurance, manufacturing, medical clinics, nursing homes, offices, shipping, social services, transportation, and utilities.

### Phi Delta Kappa (PDK) International

408 North Union Street
Bloomington, IN 47405-3800
800-766-1156
customerservice@pdkintl.org
http://www.pdkintl.org

PDK "strives to prepare the next generation of educators as well as to serve practicing teachers, administrators, college educators, and those concerned about public education." Visit its Web site for information on scholarships for high school seniors and college students, membership for college students, and useful publications. It also manages the Future Educators Association (http://www.futureeducators.org), a membership organization for middle school, high school, and college students who want to become educators.

### Public Relations Society of America

33 Maiden Lane, 11th Floor
New York, NY 10038-5150
212-460-1400
http://www.prsa.org

Visit the society's Web site for salary surveys, publications, a blog about public relations, an overview of accreditation (a type of certification), and information on membership and scholarships for college students.

### SIFE

The Jack Shewmaker SIFE World Headquarters
Robert W. Plaster Free Enterprise Center
Jack Kahl Entrepreneurship Center
1959 East Kerr Street
Springfield, MO 65803-4775
417-831-9505
sifehq@sife.org
http://www.sife.org

SIFE is an international nonprofit organization that seeks to "bring together the top leaders of today and tomorrow to create a better, more sustainable world through the positive power of business." It offers a variety of programs for college students. Visit its Web site for more information.

### Society for Human Resource Management

1800 Duke Street
Alexandria, VA 22314-3494
800-283-7476
http://www.shrm.org

Visit the society's Web site for information on college human resource management programs, certification, scholarships and membership for college students, and career resources.

### U.S. Securities and Exchange Commission

Office of Investor Education and Advocacy

100 F Street, NE
Washington, DC 20549-2000
202-942-8088
help@sec.gov
http://www.sec.gov

Visit the commission's Web site for information on laws and regulations pertaining to investors and the securities markets.

### U.S. Small Business Administration

409 Third Street, SW
Washington, DC 20416-0011
800-827-5722
answerdesk@sba.gov
http://www.sbaonline.sba.gov

This is an independent agency of the federal government that exists to "aid, counsel, assist, and protect the interests of small business concerns, to preserve free competitive enterprise, and to maintain and strengthen the overall economy of our nation." Visit its Web site for small business statistics, advice on starting a business, free online courses, and other relevant information.

### WorldatWork

14040 North Northsight Boulevard
Scottsdale, AZ 85260-3601
877-951-9191
http://www.worldatwork.org

WorldatWork is a "not-for-profit professional association dedicated to knowledge leadership in total rewards, compensation, benefits, and work-life." Visit its Web site for job listings, a glossary of industry terms, and information on certification, membership for college students, and *WorldatWork Journal.*

# Index

Entries and page numbers in **bold** indicate major treatment of a topic.

## A

About.com: Business School 195
accountants 15
**accountants and auditors** 15, **24–36**
    advancement 32, 34
    earnings 34–35
    educational requirements 28–31
    employers 31–32
    employment outlook 35–36
    high school requirements 28
    job, described 24–26
    personal requirements 28, 29
    postsecondary training 28–30
    starting out 31–32
    work environment 26–28
accounting clerks 18
account managers 14
Accreditation Council for Accountancy and Taxation 30, 211
administrative clerks 40
**administrative support workers 37–49**
    advancement 47
    earnings 47–48
    educational requirements 44–46
    employers 46–47
    employment outlook 46, 48–49
    high school requirements 44–45
    job, described 37–40
    personal requirements 41, 44
    postsecondary training 45
    starting out 46–47
    work environment 40–44
Advertising Educational Foundation 211
advertising managers 14
advertising workers 15
affirmative-action coordinators 117
agricultural economists 76
Allen, Jessica 94, 97, 99–102
Alpha Delta Kappa International 211–212
American Advertising Federation 212
American Arbitration Association 212
American Association for Adult and Continuing Education 212
American Association of Colleges for Teacher Education 212
American Association of Franchisees and Dealers (AAFD) 212–213
American Association of University Professors 213
American Association of University Women (AAUW) 213
American Board for Certification of Teacher Excellence 213
American Collegiate Adventures (ACA) at American University 155–156
American Collegiate Adventures (ACA) at the University of Wisconsin 156
American Federation of Teachers 213
American Institute of Certified Public Accountants (AICPA) 30, 31, 156, 213
American Institute of Professional Bookkeepers 213
American Legion Auxiliary 203
American Management Association 214

American Marketing Association 214
American Society for Training and
    Development 214
area managers 52
Association for Career and Technical
    Education 214
Association for Financial Professionals
    214
Association of Executive and
    Administrative Professionals 214
Association of Internal Management
    Consultants 214–215
Association of Management Consulting
    Firms 215
Association of Professional Consultants
    215
Association of Professional Office
    Managers 215
Association on American Indian Affairs
    203
Association to Advance Collegiate Schools
    of Business 215
assurance accountants 26
auditors 15. *See also* accountants and
    auditors

**B**

BAI 215
benefits analysts and administrators
    118–119
benefits managers 118
bilingual consultants 16
bill collectors 18
billing clerks 17–18
Birnecker, Robert 88
Birnecker, Sonat 87–91
Black, Todd 107–109
Bond, Rachel 33–34
bookkeeping clerks 18
budget accountants 25
budget analysts 96
business broadcasters 20

**business managers 50–62**
    advancement 60–61
    earnings 61
    educational requirements 58–60
    employers 60
    employment outlook 61–62
    high school requirements 58
    job, described 50–52, 56
    personal requirements 51, 57–58
    postsecondary training 58–59
    starting out 60
    work environment 57
Business Professionals of America
    156–157, 195, 203, 215
business reporters 20
business schools 59
**business teachers 20, 63–74**
    advancement 73
    earnings 66, 73–74
    educational requirements 68–70
    employers 70, 73
    employment outlook 74
    high school requirements 68
    job, described 64–65
    personal requirements 64, 67–68
    postsecondary training 68–69
    starting out 70, 73
    work environment 65–67
buyers 15

**C**

Career Guide to Industries 195–196
Careers-in-Business.com 196
Career Voyages: Business Management
    and Administration 196
certified financial planner (CFP)
    110–111
Certified Financial Planner Board of
    Standards 215–216
certified internal auditor 30
certified management accountant (CMA)
    30, 101–102

certified public accountants (CPAs) 30–32, 35
CFA Institute 216
chairmen 13
Chan, Catherine 98, 99, 103
chartered financial analyst (CFA) 101, 103, 104
chartered financial consultant (ChFC) 110
chief bank examiners 26
chief executive officers (CEOs) 13, 61
chief financial officers (CFOs) 13, 52
chief information officers 14
chief operating officers (COOs) 13
chief technology officers 52
cleaners 18
collection agents 18
collection correspondents 18
collection workers 18
College and Careers Program at the Rochester Institute of Technology 157
CollegeBoard: Scholarship Search 203
College Navigator 196
CollegeNET: Mach 25—Breaking the Tuition Barrier 203–204
Collegiate Scholars Program at Arizona State University 157–158
compensation analysts 117
compensation managers 118
computer database administrators 15
computer programmers 16
computer specialists 15
computer support specialists 18
consultants 86. See also management analysts and consultants
contract administrators 16
contract specialists 16
Cooperative Office Education (COE) 43
coordinators of auxiliary personnel 118
corporate accountants 24–25
cost accountants 25
cost estimators 16

credit analysts 96
cultural advisers 16
custodians 18
customer service representatives 18

**D**

Damlouji, Danielle 28
demographic economists 76
Deneault, Len 53–56
district managers 14, 52

**E**

Early Experience Program at the University of Denver 158
e-commerce 8
economics professors 76
**economists** 16, **75–84**
  advancement 82
  earnings 82–83
  educational requirements 81–82
  employers 82
  employment outlook 83–84
  high school requirements 81
  job, described 76–77
  personal requirements 76, 80–81
  postsecondary training 81
  starting out 82
  work environment 77–78, 80
The Educational Foundation for Women in Accounting 216
education and training manager 118
education secretaries 39–40
EEO representatives 117
employee-welfare managers 118
employer relations representatives 119
employment interviewers 117
employment managers 14, 117
**entrepreneurs 85–93**
  advancement 92–93
  best educational programs for 92
  earnings 93
  educational requirements 90–91

employers 91–92
employment outlook 93–94
high school requirements 90
job, described 85–87
personal requirements 87, 89–90
postsecondary training 90–91
self-assessment tools 89
starting out 91–92
top college programs for 92
work environment 87–89
environmental accountants 25
environmental economists 76
equal employment opportunity (EEO) 117
event planners 18
EWI. *See* Executive Women International (EWI)
executive recruiters 20
executive secretaries 19, 39
executive vice president 51–52
Executive Women International (EWI) 204
Exploration Summer Programs: Senior Program at Yale University 158–159
Explore-A-College at Earlham College 159
export managers 14
external auditors 24

**F**

facility managers 14
FastWeb 204
federal tax auditors 26
Federal Trade Commission (FTC) 216
Feight, Theodore 105, 111–113
file clerks 40
finance department 12
Finance FREAK.com 197
**financial analysts** 16, 25, **94–104**
  advancement 103–104
  earnings 99, 104
  educational requirements 100–102
  employers 102–103

employment outlook 104
high school requirements 100
job, described 94–97
personal requirements 96, 98–100
postsecondary training 100–101
starting out 102–103
work environment 97–98
financial economists 76
**financial planners** 16–17, 96, **105–115**
  advancement 112–113
  earnings 113–114
  educational requirements 110–111
  employers 111–112
  employment outlook 114–115
  high school requirements 110
  job, described 106–107
  personal requirements 106, 109–110
  postsecondary training 110
  starting out 111–112
  work environment 107–108
Financial Planning Association 216
Flesberg, Mary 63, 65–66, 68, 69
forensic accountants/auditors 25–26
Foundation for the Carolinas 204
Franchise EXPO.com 196–197
franchises 8, 87
Future Business Leaders of America (FBLA) 141–142, 159–160, 197
Future Educators Association 160

**G**

general accountants 25, 34
globalization 9
Global Teens program 144
government accountants 25
government economists 76
government personnel managers 117
government personnel specialists 119–120
GradSchools.com 197
graphic designers 18
GuaranteedScholarships.com 204

# H

Hawaii Community Foundation
204–205
High School Honors Program at Boston
University 160–161
High School Summer College at Stanford
University 161–162
High School Summer Scholars Program at
Washington University in St. Louis
162
Hispanic College Fund (HCF) 205
home-based businesses 9, 86, 93
Hoovers Online 197–198
Horton, Barb 48
House, Lisa 77–78, 81
Huchler, Loraine 130–132
human resources management 12–13
**human resources workers 116–126**
    advancement 124–125
    earnings 125
    educational requirements 121–122,
        124
    employers 124
    employment outlook 125–126
    high school requirements 121–122
    job, described 116–120
    personal requirements 120, 121
    postsecondary training 122
    starting out 124
    work environment 120–121
Hynek, Candice Flor 78, 80–83

# I

Illinois Career Resource Network 205
Imagine America Foundation 205–206
Independent Means Inc. 162–163
industrial accountants 24–25
industrial economists 76
industrial hygienists 119
industrial relations directors 14, 117
information architects 16
information clerks 38

information systems directors 14
initial public offerings (IPOs) 10, 12
Institute for Certified Franchise
Executives 91, 216
Institute of Certified Professional
Managers 216
Institute of Internal Auditors (IIA) 30–31,
216
Institute of Management Accountants
217
Institute of Management Consultants
USA 217
internal auditors 15, 25, 33–34
International Association of
Administrative Professionals (IAAP) 45,
217
International Association of Business
Communicators 217
International Foundation of Employee
Benefits Plans 217
International Franchise Association (IFA)
91, 217
International Public Management
Association for Human Resources 217
International Youth Camp and Exchange
Program 144–145
Internet 21
Internet consultants 16
Internet entrepreneurs 15, 52, 56
Internet executives 52
Internet store managers 15, 52, 56
Internet transaction specialists 16
Intern Exchange International 163
Internship Connection 164
investment analysts 16, 96
InVEST Scholarship Contest 206
ISACA 217–218

# J

janitors 18
job analysts 117
job-development specialists 117

job satisfaction, most important factors
  for  125
Johnson, Carl Amos  108, 109, 114–115
Johnson, Veronica  35–36
Junior Achievement (JA)  141, 164, 198,
  206, 218
Junior Scholars Program at Miami
  University—Oxford  164–165

**L**

Labor and Employment Relations
  Association  218
labor economists  76
labor relations managers  119
labor relations specialists  17, 119
labor union business agents  20
Largent, John  97–98, 100–102
Learning for Life Exploring Program  165
legal secretaries  19, 39
Lutz, Stephen  37, 42–45

**M**

Mackintosh, Stuart  77, 82–84
MacLeod, Barbara  100, 103
Malcolm Baldrige Quality Program  53–56
management accountants  24–25
**management analysts and consultants**
  **127–137**
    advancement  134, 136
    earnings  131, 136–137
    educational requirements  132–134
    employers  134
    employment outlook  137
    high school requirements  132
    job, described  127–129
    personal requirements  129, 132
    postsecondary training  132–133
    starting out  134
    work environment  129–131
management information systems
  directors  52
managerial/professional positions  13–17

manufacturers  9–10
marketing  12
marketing managers  14
marketing specialists  17
Matarazzo, Maria  71–72
mediators  119
medical secretaries  19–20, 39
merchandisers  10
mergers and acquisitions analysts  96
monetary economists  76
Morin, Dorothy  66–70
Mulling, Ben  27, 31, 50, 57–59

**N**

National Association for Business
  Economics (NABE)  83
National Association of Negro Business
  and Professional Women's Clubs
  (NANBPWC)  206–207
National Association of Personal Financial
  Advisors  218
National Association of Secondary School
  Principals (NASSP)  207
National Association of Women Business
  Owners  218
National Business Educational
  Association  218
National Center for Alternative
  Certification  219
National Conference of CPA Practitioners
  207
National Council for Accreditation of
  Teacher Education (NCATE)  219
National Education Association  219
National Management Association  219
New York Society of Security Analysts
  (NYSSA)  219
nonprofit organization directors  61

**O**

occupational analysts  117
*Occupational Outlook Handbook*  198

office administrators 15
Office and Professional Employees
  International Union 219–220
office clerks 18–19, 40
organizational economists 76
The Oxford Tradition at Oxford
  University 165–166

**P**

personal financial advisers 96
personal secretaries 39
personnel managers 14, 117
personnel recruiters 117
personnel specialists 17
Phi Delta Kappa (PDK) Educational
  Foundation 207–208
Phi Delta Kappa (PDK) International
  220
Pi Lambda Theta 208
plant managers 14
position classifiers 117
Pre-College Programs at the University of
  California—Santa Barbara 166–167
presidents 13
Price, Bette 127, 129–130, 132, 133, 137
private accountants 24–25
procurement services managers 17
production 12
professional conciliators 119
property accountants 25
public accountants 24
public relations managers 14
Public Relations Society of America
  220
public relations specialists 17
purchasing agents 17

**R**

Ramis, Todd 85, 90, 92
ratings analysts 96
Reaser, Lynn 75
receptionists 19, 38

recruiters 117
regional managers 14, 52
retail buyers 15
retirement officers 118
revenue agents 26
Rowson, Paul 116, 121, 123, 126

**S**

safety engineers 119
sales analysts 96
sales managers 14
Sallie Mae 208
Scholarship America 208
ScholarshipExperts.com 208
Scholarships.com 208
Secondary School Program at Harvard
  University 167–168
secretaries 19–20, 38–40
security analysts 16, 96
service providers 10
SIFE 220
Singleton, Tasheé 26–29, 32
SkillsUSA 168
small businesses 10, 17, 86–87
social secretaries 39
Society for Human Resource Management
  124, 220
Society of Satellite Professionals
  International 208–209
Sodexho Foundation 209
software developers 16
Start Here, Go Places in Business and
  Accounting 198
state tax auditors 26
statisticians 17
Stoff, Jennifer 41–43, 45
store managers 14
Summer Academy for High School
  Students at Manhattanville College
  168
Summer @ Brown at Brown University
  168–169

Summer Challenge Program at Boston University  160–161
Summer College for High School Students at Syracuse University  170–171
Summer College Programs for High School Students at Cornell University  172
Summerfuel at the University of California—Berkeley  171
Summerfuel at the University of Massachusetts—Amherst  171–172
Summer @ Georgetown University for High School Students  169–170
Summer Institutes at Marist College  172–173
Summer Preview at Boston University  160–161
Summer Program for High School Students at Columbia University  173–174
Summer Program for High School Students at New York University  174
Summer Programs for Youth at Southern Methodist University  174–175
Summer Scholars Institute at Pace University  175
Summer Scholars Pre-College Programs at George Washington University  175–176
Summer Scholars Program at the University of Notre Dame  176
Summer Seminars at the University of Southern California  176–177
Summer Studies at the University of Richmond  177–178
Summer Study at Pennsylvania State University  178
Summer Term at the University of Maryland  178–179
Summer University at Johns Hopkins University  179–180
Summer Youth Explorations at Michigan Technological University  180
Sumners, Glenn  24, 28, 36
support workers  17–20
Swonk, Diane  79–80
systems accountants  25

**T**

tax accountants  15, 26
tax analysts  96
tax auditors  26
Teacher Education Assistance for College and Higher Educational (TEACH) Grant Program  209–210
technical secretaries  39
technology  21
telecommuting  9
training instructors  118
training specialists  118
treasury analysts  96
typists  20

**U**

undergraduate business schools  59
Uniform CPA Examination  30
United Negro College Fund (UNCF)  210
U.S. Department of Education  210
U.S. News & World Report: Best Business Schools  198–199
U.S. Securities and Exchange Commission  220–221
U.S. Small Business Administration  221

**V**

VentureLine MBA Glossary  199

**W**

Walling, Valerie  135–136
Wall Street analysts  96
webmasters  20

Whelan, Margaret  120–121, 124
wholesale buyers  15
word processors  20
WorldatWork  221

**Y**

Yahoo!: Business & Economy  199
Young Scholars Program at the University
  of Maryland  178–179